Fallen Eagles

Fallen Eagles

Airmen Who Survived The Great War Only to Die in Peacetime

Norman Franks

Pen & Sword
AVIATION

First published in Great Britain in 2017 by
Pen & Sword Aviation
an imprint of
Pen & Sword Books Ltd
47 Church Street
Barnsley
South Yorkshire
S70 2AS

ISBN 978 1 47387 996 6

A CIP catalogue record for this book is available from the British Library

Typeset in Ehrhardt by
Mac Style Ltd, Bridlington, East Yorkshire
Printed and bound in the UK by CPI Group (UK) Ltd,
Croydon, CRO 4YY

Pen & Sword Books Ltd incorporates the imprints of Pen & Sword
Archaeology, Atlas, Aviation, Battleground, Discovery, Family History,
History, Maritime, Military, Naval, Politics, Railways, Select, Transport,
True Crime, Fiction, Frontline Books, Leo Cooper, Praetorian Press,
Seaforth Publishing and Wharncliffe.

For a complete list of Pen & Sword titles please contact
PEN & SWORD BOOKS LIMITED
47 Church Street, Barnsley, South Yorkshire, S70 2AS, England
E-mail: enquiries@pen-and-sword.co.uk
Website: www.pen-and-sword.co.uk

Contents

Photographs

I have collected aviation photographs for a long time, sharing them with fellow historians and enthusiasts. Covering the airmen recorded in this book, pictures have come from various friends and sources, including several schools some of these airmen attended. Sadly, many of the contributors are no longer with us, such as Hal Giblin, Frank Cheesman, Russ Manning, Bill Bailey, Ola Sater, Neal O'Connor, Mike O'Connor, Chaz Bowyer; Stuart Leslie, Pete Kilduff and Jeff Jefford. To all of them I am indebted. Thanks also goes to Peter Devitt of the RAF Museum, to Paul Baillie, researcher at the Public Archives at Kew, and also to a number of librarians who were happy to scour old records or newspaper archives on my behalf for background information.

Introduction

A few years ago when surfing the internet I came across a list of RAF officers who had died between the end of the First World War and the end of 1928. After no more than a casual glance, certain names began to stand out. Taking a more careful look, I was amazed at how many of these names I recognised.

Several of them I knew had died following the war, yet the more I looked, the more I discovered. What also staggered me was the number who had died during the final weeks of 1918 and in 1919, not far short of 300. While the number reduced for 1920 onwards, there were still many more than I would have guessed. Obviously quite a number of deaths were noted as being 'natural causes' which I assumed must have been deaths during the influenza pandemic, but over the early 1920s, there still seemed to be an inordinately large number of airmen dying.

I began to list what I shall refer to as the more interesting men who had died so soon after the end of hostilities, feeling a little sad that having survived the First Air War, they had died in a variety of ways during the early peace they had so gallantly fought for. I then rationalised the list by noting those airmen who had been decorated for their wartime actions and who had only died in aviation-related incidents. It was still a long list.

Initially I decided to write a series of articles about each lost, decorated airman, and some of these later appeared in *The Aeroplane* magazine, but a change of editor brought that to an end, so I decided to put together a book about some seventy men on my list who had continued flying, either in the RAF, other air forces, or in civilian flying situations, such as air races, aircraft testing, record breaking attempts, and so on. What I found was a myriad of interesting, if morbid, ways these former heroes had been lost. I also extended the period covered to, apart from one, the start of the Second World War. The total number of men covered stretched to over ninety.

The result here is, I hope, a fascinating variety of stories of airmen, still flying in the dawn of man's quest to fly, but whose luck finally ran out. Many of the names will be known to aviation enthusiasts and historians, but many others will read them as remarkable stories of how fate took a hand in their often short lives.

Norman Franks

Chapter One

1918–19

Captain S. T. Edwards DSC & Bar, 12 November 1918

I have shown the date here as 12 November, because that is the date Stearne Tighe Edwards was seriously injured in a crash, although he lingered in hospital for ten days before he passed away on the 22nd.

A Canadian from Franktown, Ontario, he was born on 13 February 1893 and grew up in Carleton Place, Ontario. His father was Edwin Dennis Edwards, married to Annie Caroline Edwards (née Tighe). Sadly Edwin Edwards died in 1912. Soon after completing his education at Carleton Place High School, and becoming a civil engineer, Stearne Edwards found a job in railway construction so by 1914 he was working in Port Nelson, Hudson Bay. With the declaration of war, it is said he walked the 200 miles to Toronto

Captain S. T. Edwards DSC & Bar.

in order to join the military, but one must assume, as a railway worker, he was able to get a ride some of the way, and hitched lifts by road.

Desirous of joining the Royal Naval Air Service, he discovered that they were only taking men who already held a pilot licence, and as the local Curtiss School was full, he found a place at the Wright Brothers School in Dayton, Ohio. Learning to fly at his own expense, he received the necessary licence, No. 350, dated 13 October 1915, issued by the Aero Club of America.

Finally allowed to join the RNAS, he soon found himself aboard ship headed for Britain, and once his training was completed, he was posted to No. 3 Wing in 1916, flying operationally until February 1917. On 9 March he went to No. 11 Squadron, then moved to 6 Naval in April, but when this unit was disbanded in July, moved to 9 Naval. In September he started to shoot down enemy aircraft, achieving five victories by the end of April, and was awarded the Distinguished Service Cross. *London Gazette,* 2 November 1917:

In recognition of his services on the following occasions:

On the 3rd September, 1917, with his flight he attacked a two-seater Aviatik. The enemy machine was observed to go down in a vertical nose dive, and the enemy observer was seen to collapse in his cockpit.

On the 21st September, 1917, he drove a two-seater machine down out of control, which crashed into the sea.

On the 23rd September, 1917, he attacked an Albatros Scout, which crashed into the sea.

On the same date he attacked three Albatros Scouts. One got on the tail of another officer's machine at very close range, shooting him up very badly. Flt. Cdr. Edwards attacked him from above, and the enemy machine turned on its back and went down in a vertical dive. He followed the enemy machine down to 8,000 feet, when its wings came off, and it fell to the ground.

Two more claims in October and another in February 1918 brought his score to eight, before 9 Naval became 209 Squadron RAF with the amalgamation of the RFC and RNAS on 1 April. By mid-May he had brought his score to sixteen for which he received a Bar to his DSC. *London Gazette* 21 June 1918:

For conspicuous bravery and most brilliant leadership of fighting patrols against enemy aircraft. On 2nd May 1918, while leading a patrol of four scouts, he encountered a hostile formation of eight enemy scouts and drove down one enemy machine completely out of control. Soon afterwards, he engaged another formation of six enemy scouts, driving one down to its destruction while his patrol accounted for another. He only broke off the fight owing to lack of ammunition. He has destroyed or driven down out of control many enemy machines since he was awarded the Distinguished Service Cross, and has at all times shown the greatest gallantry and a fine offensive spirit.

Clearly exhausted by his months of war flying and suffering near collapse, he was posted back to England and had a period in hospital to recuperate. Fully fit once more, he became a flying instructor at No. 2 Flying Training School at Marske. With the coming of peace, he was not alone in showing his exuberance by taking to the air. Therefore, on the day after the Armistice was signed, 12 November, he took off in a Sopwith Pup Scout (No. B4181) from the base of No. 38 Training Depot Squadron, Tadcaster, Yorkshire.

People on the ground saw him start spinning, or possibly going into a victory roll. Perhaps his exuberance led to a misjudgement, as it seems he left it too late to make a complete recovery, and dug a wing in. The Pup smashed into the ground. He was taken to a hospital in York with serious head injuries where he died on the 22nd. He was buried in Tadcaster Cemetery. He was 25 years old.

*   *   *

Captain D. V. Armstrong DFC, 14 November 1918

Even the less observant will notice that the date at the top is only three days following the Armistice, which occurred at 11 o'clock on the morning of Monday, 11 November 1918. There were celebrations, of course, but how much had occurred at the airfield of No. 151 Squadron that day, and for the next couple of days, is questionable. Bancourt, near Bapaume, saw 21-year old D'Urban Victor Armstrong take to the sky and head towards Bouvincourt, south-east of Péronne. It would be his last flight.

D'Urban Victor Armstrong was born on 26 July 1897 in Zululand, Natal, South Africa. He was the son of George and Ethel Armstrong, of 'Highwoods', 167 Springfield Drive, Durban. Educated at Hilton College, he joined the South African Defence Force when war came, and commissioned as a Second Lieutenant. Preferring to fight in

Captain D. V. Armstrong with his 151 Squadron CO, Major C. J. Quintin Brand MC.

the air rather than the ground, he applied to join the Royal Flying Corps in December 1915 and upon reaching England took flying lessons. He was awarded his Royal Aero Club Flying Certificate (No. 2461) on 12 February 1916.

After completing his formal training, he was sent to France where he was posted to No. 60 Squadron on 25 May. He served with this unit during the year, finally achieving his first air combat victory on 9 November, shooting down an Albatros DI Scout over Havrincourt, flying Nieuport Scout A211.

In 1917 he returned to England, or Home Establishment as it was referred to, for a rest. After some leave he was called upon for Home Defence duties and sent to No. 44 Home Defence Squadron, a unit that flew Sopwith Camels from Hainault

Farm on the north-west fringes of London. Here he came under the influence of Captain C. J. Q. Brand, better known as Quintin Brand, a future Air Vice-Marshal, and a fellow South African. In 1920, Brand and another South African, Pierre van Ryneveld, would both be knighted following their epic flight from England to the Cape of Good Hope.

Home Defence squadrons were trained to defend English towns and cities from both day and night raids by the Germans, which could come in the form of airships or large bomber aircraft such as Gotha or Staaken R.IV Giants. One of Armstrong's first recorded defence flights came on 12 August 1917: a force of thirteen Gothas were targeting Chatham docks but ended up bombing Southend. It was a daylight raid, and although some 139 defensive sorties were recorded, not very many aircraft made contact. Once in the air, of course, there was no radio contact to vector aircraft onto the raiders. Some pilots managed to intercept and some damage was inflicted on the German bombers. Armstrong was not amongst them, merely recording a sortie lasting from 17.33 to 18.47 hours.

Another daylight raid on the 22nd saw Armstrong again up in a Camel, this time between 10.19 and 11.25 hrs. A night raid by Gothas on 30 September and he was recording more night flying time. This was followed by another sortie on the night of 1/2 October, the target London. London was again the target on the night of 30 October/1 November, but again Armstrong found nothing to shoot at. It was all night raids now; 5/6 December, 18/19 December, 22/23 December. It had to be frustrating not to find anything, but in the dark night sky locating hostile aircraft was all but impossible.

However, Armstrong must have been doing something right, for at the end of the year he was made a flight commander with 78 (HD) Squadron at nearby Sutton's Farm (Hornchurch). In the first months of 1918 he made at least four night fighter interception patrols between January and May. On the last one, on the night of 19/20 May, in Camel C6713, he finally found a target. The raiders consisted of thirty-eight Gothas and three Giants, going for London. One Gotha was brought down by the crew of a Bristol Fighter, but it was thought that Armstrong had attacked it first. This, however, is now in doubt, but he did find a Gotha, at 23.55 pm, north-west of Orsett, flying at 12,000 feet. He spotted it below him but an alert German air gunner saw him too. Attacking and trying to avoid the gunner's fire, as he switched from a gun above the bomber to one firing below, Armstrong began to open fire, but his guns jammed after fifty rounds. Clearing the jam, he attacked again from point blank range, but apparently inflicted no damage. He finally had to break off at 00.15 am, having chased the bomber down to 9,000 feet.

During his off-duty periods he was fast becoming well known for his superb aerobatic flying, and several times gave wonderful exhibitions, but he was about to leave for France, having received a posting to No. 151 (Night Fighter) Squadron, commanded by Quintin Brand and based at Marquise and then Fontaine-sur-Maye. There were several night raids by German bombers on French targets or British positions, so a dedicated night fighter unit was much needed.

Within ten days Armstrong struck, shooting down a German LVG two-seater in the Estrée area. On 8 August he shot down another two-seater at night, this falling in flames in the same area. On the 24th, he shared the destruction of a Gotha of 15/BGIII, with fellow pilot Lieutenant F. C. Broome, its crew coming down near Arras to be taken prisoner. His final claim was a large Friedrichshafen GIII, this time its three-man crew perished. All four victories were made while flying Camel C6713, which he had named 'Doris'.

With an overall score of victories totalling five, not to mention his long period of service, he was awarded the Distinguished Flying Cross, the citation reading:

A brilliant pilot of exceptional skill. His success in night operations has been phenomenal; and the service he renders in training other pilots is of the greatest value, personally supervising their flying and demonstrating the only successful method of attack by night. On the night of 10-11th September, learning that an enemy aeroplane was over our front, he volunteered to go up. The weather

Armstrong's Sopwith Camel, in which he died.

conditions were such as to render flying almost impossible, the wind blowing about fifty miles an hour, his machine at times being practically out of control. The foregoing is only one of many instances of this officer's remarkable skill and resolution in night operations.

This appeared in the *London Gazette* of 3 December 1918, but by this date, Armstrong was dead.

The squadron had moved to Bancourt on 8 October. Over Bouvincourt he began to give one of his aerobatic displays, but on this occasion he crashed. Severely injured he was taken to No. 58 Casualty Clearing Station, but he did not recover. He was buried by this unit's padre and now lies in Tincourt New British Cemetery, east of Péronne. He was 21 years old.

* * *

Captain H. T. Fox-Russell MC, 18 November 1918

Henry Thornbury Fox-Russell was born in 1897, son of Physician and Surgeon Dr William and Mrs Ethel Maria Fox-Russell of 5 Victoria Terrace, Holyhead, Anglesey, coming originally from Ireland. There were to be seven children, six boys including twins, and one daughter. Henry completed his education at St Bee's, Cumberland between 1909 and 1910 and when war came he immediately volunteered. He was commissioned into the 1/6 (Carnarvon & Anglesey) Battalion of the Royal Welsh Fusiliers (TF). Too young for active duty he was moved to the 2/6 RWF, but shortly before the 1/6 sailed for Gallipoli he was moved back, so saw action there from August 1915. After that campaign he went to Egypt where he decided upon flying in preference

Captain H. T. Fox-Russell MC.

to trench warfare, and returned to the UK for pilot training. Having achieved this he was made an instructor before being posted to No. 64 Squadron forming at Sedgeford. Made a flight commander, he accompanied this unit to France in October 1917.

He saw action during the November battle of Cambrai flying DH5 fighters and on the 23rd, 64 were badly shot about. Fox-Russell had the tail of his machine blown off and was lucky to survive the subsequent crash. Another DH5 also came down nearby, its pilot breaking both legs, but he was rescued by Fox-Russell who carried him to safety despite heavy German gunfire. Sent home to recover from his experience he took the time to qualify for his Royal Aero Club Flying Certificate, No. 4649, on 27 December.

He was awarded the Military Cross, gazetted on 4 February, the citation appearing on 5 July:

For conspicuous gallantry and devotion to duty. He formed one of a patrol which silenced an enemy battery. He dropped bombs on two of the guns, silenced others with his machine gun and then engaged transport on a road. The operation was carried out under heavy fire and very difficult weather conditions. On another occasion he dropped bombs and fired 300 rounds on enemy trenches from a height of 100 feet. His machine was then hit by a shell and crashed in front of our advanced position. He reached the front line and while there saw another of our machines brought down. He went to the assistance of the pilot, who was badly wounded, extricated him under heavy fire and brought him to safety. He showed splendid courage and initiative.

His brother Captain John Fox-Russell MC of the Royal Medical Corps, attached to the 1/6 RWF, was awarded a posthumous Victoria Cross in Palestine during the Third Battle of Gaza on 6 November 1917. Completing his time with 64 Squadron, Henry returned to England to become an instructor at No. 4 Training Depot Squadron at Hooten in Cheshire, not too far from the family home. He continued to instruct, but just one week after the Armistice he was flying a Sopwith Dolphin (C4011). He somehow managed to get into a spin at 900 feet and failed to regain control. He died in the subsequent crash. It was thought he either fainted or had just become disorientated. He was 21 years of age.

* * *

Captain C. F. King MC, DFC, CdG, 24 January 1919

Cecil Frederick King was born in Sevenoaks, Kent, on 19 February 1899, son of Frederick Hamilton and Mrs Nora King, later of Springfield Dukes, Chelmsford, and later still, 'Lingwood', East Liss, Hampshire. He had one brother, one sister, and two step siblings from his father's first marriage. He was educated at Hildenham House, Broadstairs and finally Charterhouse. He enlisted as a private in the Sussex Regiment from OTC, moved to aviation in February 1917, and was gazetted second lieutenant in the Royal Flying Corps on 10 May 1917. Once his pilot training was complete he was sent to France where he joined No. 43 Squadron, flying Sopwith Camels.

Captain C. F. King MC, DFC. CdG.

He claimed his first victory on 12 November 1917, but really came into his own in the new year, shooting down four more in February 1918 and three more during March. By the end of June his score had risen to sixteen, by which time he had received the Military Cross, gazetted on 22 April:

> *For conspicuous gallantry and devotion to duty. On five occasions during a period of three months he has sent down four enemy machines completely out of control and has destroyed one other. Later, under very adverse weather conditions, he carried out a low reconnaissance, during which he engaged troops in a station, causing several casualties, fired into a body of the enemy entering a village from a height of 50 feet, attacked four gun limbers, causing the teams to stampede, and finally dived into a parade of troops who scattered in all directions. He has displayed exceptional daring and skill which, combined with a splendid dash and initiative, have set a fine example to his squadron.*

He had added three more victories to his tally by August, and when his squadron re-equipped with new Sopwith Snipe fighters, he downed a further three, to bring his score to twenty-two. On 3 August the *London Gazette* recorded the award of the Distinguished Flying Cross:

He is a fine leader who at all times shows great gallantry and skill in manoeuvring; his energy and keenness have brought his flight to a high standard of efficiency. He frequently descends to low altitudes to obtain good results from bombing and shooting, and on several occasions he has brought down enemy aeroplanes.

From the French he also received their *Croix de Guerre* with *Palme,* recognising his good work during the Second Battle of the Marne. With the coming of peace, King returned to England and, once a spot of leave had been taken, was posted to Sedgeford, Norfolk, as an instructor with No. 3 Flying School. The school was commanded by Major H. H. Balfour MC who had been in 43 Squadron too. At Sedgeford was another close friend from 43 Squadron, Lieutenant Hector Daniel MC, a South African. On 24 January 1919, Daniel and King were flying above the airfield in a formation but collided. Daniel, in H2724, crashed and survived, but King, in C8318, was killed. His funeral took place at Docking, near Sedgeford on 4 February with full military honours. He was one month short of his twentieth birthday.

*   *   *

Lieutenant E. G. Davies DFC & Bar, CdG, 6 February 1919

Edgar George Davies came from Islington, North London, where he was born on 4 November 1898, the son of George and Miriam Davies. However, when he joined the Royal Flying Corps on his 19th birthday, he was living in nearby Tufnell Park. His father owned a butcher's shop and young Ed would help out there; the family story is that he could kill and prepare a chicken with great ease by the time he was twelve. When war came, his first

2nd Lieutenant E. G. Davies DFC & Bar, CdG

attempt to join the colours was to enlist in the army shortly after his 16th birthday, by lying about his age, and even managed seventy days of service with the Royal Field Artillery before his parents tracked him down and forced his release.

Two years later, at 18, he joined the Westminster Rifles and obtained a commission into the RFC. By the time he began to fly, pilot training was far more extensive and comprehensive than it had been even a year earlier, so it was not until well into 1918 that he was deemed ready for active duty.

Davies went to France in late August 1918 and after a few days at a pilot pool, he was posted off to join No. 29 Squadron, based at St Omer, on 1 September. The squadron was equipped with single-seat SE5A fighters and on arrival his CO was no doubt pleasantly surprised to find he had over 100 flying hours in his log book.

Within a few days the squadron relocated to La Lovie and before the month was out Davies had scored two combat victories, a Fokker DVII shot down east of Lille on the 16th and a balloon which he flamed south-east of Comines on the 29th. In October he scored four further victories, all the dangerous Fokker DVIIs, Germany's premier fighter of the war. He downed these on the 2nd, 7th, 27th and 28th, thereby becoming an ace.

Then, in the final days of the Great War, he bagged a further four, by which time 29 Squadron were operating from Hoog Huys, east of St Omer, and finally at Calais/Marcke. On 3 November he shot down a DFW two-seater reconnaissance machine over Celles, following this by scoring a double on the morning of the 9th, firstly a Rumpler two-seater, followed by a Fokker biplane five minutes later. His 10th and final victory was yet another Fokker biplane over Moorleghen on the afternoon of 10 November. The next day, the Armistice was announced, effective from 11 am; Edgar Davies' war was over.

His CO, Major C. H. Dixon MC, recommended Davies for an Immediate Award on 27 October 1918, forwarding a recommendation to Wing Headquarters noting these combat victories:

> *Since 16.9.18 he has destroyed 4 E.A. and one balloon.*
> *On 16.9.18 he destroyed an enemy Scout E of Lille.*
> *On 2.10.18 he destroyed an enemy Scout E of Roulers.*
> *On 7.10.18 he destroyed an enemy Scout in the vicinity of Menin.*
> *On 27.10.18 he destroyed an enemy Scout near Renaix.*
> *On 29.10.18 he destroyed an enemy balloon in the vicinity of Comines.*

The resultant award of the Distinguished Flying Cross was announced, the citation appearing in the *London Gazette* on 8 February 1919:

> *Bold in attack and skilful in manoeuvre, this officer never hesitates to attack the enemy when opportunity occurs, without regard to disparity in numbers. On 7th*

October, with three other machines, he attacked seven Fokkers; four of these were destroyed, 2nd Lieutenant Davies accounting for one. Since 16th September he has to his credit four enemy machines and one kite balloon.

A Bar to this DFC was already in the pipeline and this was awarded and then gazetted on 3 June 1919. The recommendation for this award shows the following short citation:

A real fighting pilot. Since the award of the DFC (5.11.18) he has personally destroyed 5 E.A.

Major Dixon, no doubt prompted by Wing HQ, produced a list of further decorations on 16 November, now that the war was over. British, French and Belgian governments were always keen to give their counterparts the opportunity to suggest names of men who might be worthy of their country's decorations. Each RAF squadron would be asked to submit names, and 29 Squadron's CO put forward the names of Captains C. H. R. Lagesse DFC, C. G. Ross DFC, T. S. Harrison DFC and Lieutenant E. G. Davies DFC. The part of the recommendation relating to Davies read:

As regards 2/Lieut Davies, I recommended this officer for an immediate award on 27.10.18, at which date he had destroyed 4 E.A. and one balloon; and he was awarded the Distinguished Flying Cross. Since then he has destroyed a further 5 E.A.

On 26.10.18 he destroyed an enemy Scout E of Avelghem.
On 3.11.18 he destroyed an enemy two-seater near Grand Rejet.
On 9.11.18 he destroyed an enemy two-seater N.E. of Audenarde.
On the latter date he also destroyed an enemy Scout near Laethem St. Marie.
On 10.11.18 he destroyed an enemy Scout S.E. of Moorleghen.

Four days later Dixon added two more names to this list: Lieutenants E. O. Amm DFC and H. Holroyde. In the event all six pilots received the Belgian *Croix de Guerre.*

[NB. There is some dispute regarding Davies' victory dates but these are those recorded in the recommendations. They are essentially correct although the balloon is a whole month out.]

SE5A No. H7162 that Davies flew in October/November 1918, and in which he was killed on 6 February 1919.

By December 1918 the squadron had moved to Germany, as part of the Army of Occupation, settling into the air base at Bickendorf, situated on the edge of Cologne. On 6 February, Davies took off in SE5 H7162, coded with the letter 'E', a machine he had been flying since October and in which he had claimed at least seven of his combat successes. In all probability he was flying with a feeling of exuberance, but while performing a high speed roll across the aerodrome, the wings of his SE5 crumpled and the machine crunched into the ground, giving Davies no chance of survival. He was 20 years old and is buried in Cologne's South Cemetery.

*   *   *

Captain L. A. Payne MC, MiD, 19 February 1919

Lawrence Allan Payne was a South African, born in Barberton, Transvaal on 15 July 1894, the son of Alfred Harold and Mrs Sarah Payne. He received his education at the Barberton Public School, and began his working life as a revenue clerk in the Swaziland Administration Offices from May 1913 until October 1916. Being one of those recruited by Major A. M. Miller, he enlisted into the RFC in January 1917 as No. 60100.

Sent to England for training, he somehow became associated with Pulborough in Sussex, his address being recorded as 'Casa Bonnifoi', Little Hill, Pulborough.

He received a commission into the RFC via the General List in May 1917, received his pilot's wings, and in September was sent to France, joining No. 48 Squadron which flew BF2b Bristol Fighters. With his various observers, Payne accumulated ten victories between 29 October and 30 May 1918 and was made a flight commander. He was awarded the Military Cross, the citation appearing in the *London Gazette* on 26 July:

Captain L. A. Payne MC.

For conspicuous gallantry and devotion to duty. Volunteering to proceed on a special reconnaissance under adverse weather conditions, he penetrated for a distance of nine miles behind the enemy's lines at an altitude of 200 feet, despite the most intense machine-gun and rifle fire. He returned later, his machine riddled with bullets, with the required information. Previous to this he had bombed and engaged with machine-gun fire bodies of hostile infantry with the most effective results. He has destroyed one hostile plane and driven down two others out of control. He has at all times displayed great fearlessness and dash.

One of his observers, who also received the MC, was G. H. H. Scutt, who we shall read more about in Chapter Four.

Completing his tour with 48, he returned to England on 8 June and, following a period of rest, flew as an instructor for a short while before returning to 48 on 21 October, gaining his eleventh victory a week before the Armistice. After the war, 48 Squadron became part of the occupation forces in Germany, before a planned move to India, but Payne was not destined to go along. On 18 February 1919, he was lost following an aircraft accident, flying a Bristol Fighter (F4475). He and Lieutenant Ford had taken off at 10.45 am and crashed at 11.30, where the Rhine passes Merheim. It was suggested that they had hit an air pocket. One of his brother officers had received a letter from a family member and his reply, dated 31 March 1919, covers Payne's unfortunate end:

Bristol Fighters of 48 Squadron at Cologne, 1919.

While flying at a low altitude over the Rhine, north of Cologne, on Feb. 18th, with Lieut. L. Ford as observer, the machine struck the water throwing Ford over the top planes. He swam back to the machine which was in a floating but sinking condition. Capt. Payne stood and took off his trench coat and advised Ford that they had better both strike out for the bank. Here, I should add, the river is very wide with a fast current and as the broken ice had been floating down from the mountains, the water must have been intensely cold. Capt. Payne who was a good swimmer made more rapid progress than Ford who is only a boy and had almost reached the bank when he disappeared.

Ford utterly exhausted turned on his back, and allowed himself to be carried downstream and was rescued by two Germans who had seen the mishap and put out in a boat. All searches for poor Capt. Payne proved fruitless, although a strict watch was ordered to be kept, and motor boats patrolled the river.

Nothing further was heard until a month later when a message was received from the Belgian Headquarters that the body of a British Flying Captain had been recovered from the Rhine, some miles north of Düsseldorf. The doctor, another Flight Commander and myself immediately proceeded to the spot, and were able to identify the body of our chum. We made arrangements with the Belgian Headquarters at Crefeld for removal to Cologne where in the British corner of the cemetery in Marcus Strasse he was laid to rest on March 22nd, in the presence of his brother officers and friends from other squadrons.

His remains were enclosed in a coffin of dark polished oak which was conveyed to the cemetery on an aeroplane trailer. The coffin was draped with the Union Jack, and the many beautiful wreaths were eloquent of the universal esteem in which he was held in this and other squadrons. Two bugles sounded the 'Last Post', and it was with heavy hearts that we saluted the memory of a gallant gentleman who has made the supreme sacrifice as fully as if he had perished in actual combat with the enemy whom he had sallied forth to meet so many times.

I first made the acquaintance of Capt. Payne when I joined the squadron last spring, and I as one who followed him in those days cannot speak too highly of his gallantry as a pilot and leader, of his chivalry and modesty. None did more than he to maintain a spirit of cheerfulness and confidence when the clouds obscured the dawn of Victory as in those fateful days of a year ago, and many junior officers found inspiration in his unfailing courage and consideration. We did more than esteem "Ping" as he was more intimately known. We loved him.

A propeller cross is being erected over Capt. Payne's grave and Capt. C. the medical officer and a great friend has promised to take a photo and forward it on to you. Capt. Payne it may interest you to know lies beside a brother pilot, Lieut. Allen, who also came from Swaziland. All the effects including many photographs have been carefully packed and sent through the usual channels. I have not written to Capt. Payne's relatives in South Africa, so perhaps you could convey the information I have given. The whole squadron deeply sympathise with all to who he was so dear.

Payne was mentioned in Sir Douglas Haig's despatches of 16 March 1919, (LG 1 July). Whether this might have led to another decoration was not considered further due to his death.

* * *

Captain A. P. Adams DFC, MiD, 6 March 1919

Allen Percy Adams was born in 1898, the son of Percy and Leoni Adams of Halstead, north of Sevenoaks, Kent. During the First World War he had joined the Royal Flying Corps and became an observer with No. 47 Squadron at Mikra Bay, operating over Salonika, on the Greek front, in 1917. The squadron flew a variety of aeroplanes, including AWFK3s and BE2s engaged on reconnaissance missions. In due course his requests for pilot training bore fruit and having been sent across to Egypt for flight instruction, where most airmen serving in the Middle

East were trained, he became a pilot and on 6 August 1917 was posted to No. 30 Squadron at Baghdad. They had BEs and RE8s, as well as French Spad fighters.

He completed many operations during his time with this squadron, and in 1918 became officer commanding 'C' Flight. Flying a variety of aircraft, now including Bristol Scouts, RE8s and Martynsides, its crews were engaged in reconnaissance missions, sometimes bomb raids against the Turkish army, and they occasionally encountered hostile fighters. It often operated detached flights to several places in order to cover the large area for which they were responsible, flying from such places as Ramadi, Hamadan, Kifri and Zenjan,

Captain A. P. Adams DFC, MiD.

as well as their main base at Baghdad. Allen saw out the war with 30 Squadron, and during the first months of peace, continued to fly against dissident tribesmen in Southern Persia. For his work, Adams was awarded the Distinguished Flying Cross in the New Year's Honours List of 1919.

While no official citation appeared in the *London Gazette* for this award, it was no doubt prompted not only by his long and devoted service in air operations over Mesopotamia but also by his daring rescue of a downed fellow pilot on 25 October 1918. Lieutenant S. D. MacDonald was brought down by hostile ground fire and forced to make an emergency landing in hostile territory. Captured airmen were often killed by tribesmen or treated badly. They usually carried what they termed 'goolie chits', written in Arabic, promising a reward if the men were returned intact! There was little hesitation in trying to rescue brother pilots in these circumstances. Seeing MacDonald's plight, Allen Adams throttled back, glided down, landed, and picked up his downed comrade before he could be captured, bringing him safely home. Somerled Douglas MacDonald was to have a long and distinguished career in the Royal Air Force, retiring as Air Vice-Marshal, CB, CBE, DFC in 1947. His DFC was won while flying with No. 63 Squadron in Kurdistan in 1920. Later in his career MacDonald was attached to the headquarters of the Sudan Defence Force at Khartoum as a wing commander in 1937.

Adams, meantime, had become one of 30 Squadron's longest serving officers, operating out of Kifri, midway between Baghdad and Kirkuk, and he was no doubt overdue for a rest. In fact the squadron was due to be reduced to cadre in April

The crash-site where Adams fell. Note the undercarriage off to the left.

and its pilots sent home. However, on 6 March 1919, during a bomb raid, carrying sixteen 20-lb Cooper bombs, and flying near Khun Bushire, Southern Persia, in a Martinsyde G100 'Elephant' (7461) he was brought down by native ground fire, crashed and was killed. He was 21 years old and was buried in the Tehran War Cemetery. There is an inscription to him in the Halstead Parish Church: 'Allen Percy Adams, who fell in battle for King and Country, 1919.'

*   *   *

Captain D. McK. Peterson DSC and Oak Leaf, CdG, 16 March 1919

Despite the United States coming late to the war, in April 1917, there were many Americans keen to help France in her hour of need, and this included many who saw aviation as the best way to do it. Most well known were those who joined the French via the Foreign Legion, and were formed into the famed Lafayette Escadrille in 1916. Officially this unit was Escadrille N124, the 'N' denoting it as being equipped with Nieuport Scouts. One such man was David McKelvey Peterson.

Born on 2 July 1895 to Pierson B. and Louise W. (née Jadwin) Peterson, he came from Honesdale, Pennsylvania, and graduated from Lehigh University in 1915 with a BA in engineering. Once in France he worked with the US ambulance service as a driver, before volunteering to fly with the *Aéronautique Militaire.* Once trained, he was assigned to the Lafayette on 16 June 1917. With this unit he shot down a German Albatros DV Scout on 19 September over Monfaucon. When the United States Air Service arrived in France, several Americans were allowed to transfer, and Peterson was one, moving to the US 103rd Pursuit Squadron upon its formation with the rank of Captain. However, in April 1918 he was sent to the 94th Pursuit, and with this unit he claimed a further three victories in early May, one Scout and two Rumpler C-type two-seater reconnaissance machines.

In early May he was given command of the 95th Pursuit, both units being equipped with Nieuport 28 fighters, and before the month was out he had brought down two more enemy machines, an

Captain D. McK. Peterson, standing beside a Nieuport 28 fighter. The 'Hat in the Ring' insignia is that of the US 94th Pursuit Squadron.

LVG two-seater on the 17th and another two-seater on the 20th. The LVG was not confirmed initially, but in September a captured airman reported, during interrogation, that this particular LVG (serial number 14512/17), had indeed been forced to land after the action. The pilot landed at Woinville, and although he and his observer escaped injury, the engine had been on fire and the machine seriously damaged.

For these actions, Peterson was awarded the Distinguished Service Cross, the citation reading:

For extraordinary heroism in action near Luneville, France, on 3 May 1918. Leading a patrol of three, Captain Peterson encountered two enemy planes at an altitude of 3,500 metres and immediately gave battle. Notwithstanding the fact that he was attacked from all sides, this officer, by skilful manoeuvring, succeeded in shooting down one of the enemy planes and dispersed the remaining four.

Shortly afterwards, Peterson was awarded an Oak Leaf Cluster to his DSC, with the following citation:

> *For extraordinary heroism in action near Thiacourt, France, on 15 May 1918. While on patrol alone, Captain Peterson encountered two enemy planes at an altitude of 5,200 metres. He promptly attacked despite the odds and shot down one of the enemy planes in flames. While thus engaged he was attacked from above by a second enemy plane, but by skilful manoeuvring, he succeeded in shooting it down also.*

In addition to these decorations, Peterson received the *Croix de Guerre* from the French, and was cited on two further occasions, 9 November 1917 and 29 November 1918. On 29 August he was promoted to the rank of major.

He returned to the US with his squadron when the war ended; they were based at Gerstner Field, Louisiana. He was then sent to Dorr Field, Florida, where he became an instructor. On 16 March 1919 he was killed in a crash at Daytona Beach, Florida. His body was taken to his home town and he was buried in the Glen Dyberry Cemetery. He was 23 years of age.

* * *

Lieutenant A. B. Whiteside MC and Bar, 22 April 1919
Major T. A. Batchelor DFC, AFC, 22 April 1919

Arthur Barlow Whiteside was the son of the Reverend Arthur and Mrs Whiteside of 2538 Quadra Street, Victoria, British Columbia, Canada, born in Fort Qu'Appelle, Saskatchewan on 13 December 1990. He received his education at McGill University between 1912 and 1914 and as the war had begun enlisted in Quebec with No. 1 Canadian General Hospital as a private (50009) before transferring to the Princess Patricia's Canadian Light Infantry. Going to France with the Canadian Expeditionary Force, he saw action on the Western Front, receiving a commission. He appears to have been wounded at least twice.

Once his mind had turned to flying, he took lessons and gained his Royal Aero Club Certificate, No. 4763, on 5 June 1917, and once training was complete was gazetted as a flying officer on 1 July. He was posted to a night bombing squadron, No. 102, equipped with FE2d 'pusher' machines, aircraft designed for fighter-reconnaissance duties earlier in the war, but now relegated to night bombing raids. He began operations and, on nightly sorties in the pitch dark of night, flew a large

A Handley Page 0/400 bomber.

number of raids, commencing September 1917. In the early months of 1918 he was awarded the Military Cross, gazetted on 26 March, although the citation did not appear until 24 August:

> *For conspicuous gallantry and devotion to duty. He carried out several night-bombing raids with great success, attacking enemy aerodromes, trains and billets, often from a low altitude. On one occasion he attacked a train with his machine-gun from a height of 100 feet. He showed splendid skill and initiative.*

Citations were often shortened versions of a CO's recommendation, and so it was in Whiteside's case. The recommendation gives a far better picture of his war flying:

> *A. B. Whiteside. 102 Sqn 5/2/18: For gallantry and devotion to duty when carrying out night bomb raids during the period 20/10/17 – 2/2/18, notably on the following occasions. On 28/10/17 this Officer successfully bombed the railway east of Courtrai from a height of 2,000 feet. On 6/11/17 2/Lt Whiteside set out to attack troops, trains, etc, in the Cambrai area. He succeeded in dropping his bombs on troops at Moorslede in spite of machine-gun and rifle fire. On 7/11/17 his objective was Gontrude aerodrome. He bombed this from a height of 750 feet after which he followed an EA to the north-east of Theilt, making observations.*

He then proceeded to Lichtervelde and, descending to 100 feet, opened fire with his machine-gun on a train. On the night of 30/11/17 he made three trips to Marquion. He successfully bombed the village, afterwards firing many rounds at lights and other suitable targets. On 3/12/17 this Officer again found his objective – Honnecourtville – in spite of a strong wind and considerable haze. He obtained direct hits on the village and emptied two drums at ground targets. On the night of 18-19/12/17, 2/Lt Whiteside carried out a fine piece of navigation. He flew over Gontrude and, finding it deserted, returned to St. Denis-Westrem to drop his bombs. On 13/1/18 this Officer proceeded to bomb Menin. He experienced intense darkness, but eventually succeeded in obtaining direct hits. On 25/1/18 his objective was Marquion aerodrome which he bombed with great success, obtaining three direct hits on the hangars. He also obtained direct hits on EA which he located by means of a parachute flare. This operation was carried out at a height of 500 feet. He afterwards dropped a bomb on Scheldewindeke aerodrome with the aid of a parachute flare and dropped his bombs among the hangars. He also fired many rounds at trains and sent in a very valuable report. This Officer has done consistently good work since he has been with 102 Squadron. He has not been deterred by adverse weather conditions and his work has throughout been characterised by the greatest courage and determination to overcome difficulties.

Whiteside continued flying night raids and he narrowly escaped disaster on 23 May. His FE2, A5649, was hit by shrapnel from AA fire that damaged the engine, which stopped. To add to the dangers of flying with few aids in a black sky, Whiteside now had to try to find a spot to put his machine down and hope he had glided far enough to cross into Allied territory. Throughout the summer of 1918, raids continued, and soon his CO was again writing up a recommendation for a further award. This resulted in him being awarded a Bar to his MC, gazetted on 16 September:

For conspicuous gallantry and devotion to duty. This Officer has taken part in over fifty bombing raids, many of which, carried out at heights considerably under 1,000 feet, and in adverse weather conditions, were only successful through the skill and energy displayed by him in discovering his objective. One night in particular, after having successfully bombed a large ammunition dump, which was set on fire and blown up, he proceeded to drop bombs on a town which held large numbers of the enemy, also firing from a low altitude with his machine-gun on the roads leading to it. Returning to his squadron he obtained more bombs and ammunition, and with the same Observer, proceeded to drop bombs on a train behind the enemy's lines. On several occasions his machine was badly knocked about by enemy fire from the ground. The devotion to duty and disregard of danger displayed by this Officer have been admirable examples to all members of his squadron.

His observer on many of these raids had been Lieutenant E. F. Howard, a brother Canadian. He too received the Military Cross, his citation mentioning fifty-two bomb raids. Having completed a tour of duty, Whiteside was sent back to England and then allowed a spot of home leave to Canada. Upon his return he was sent to be an instructor at No. 2 School of Navigation and Bomb Dropping. Here he was introduced to the Handley Page 0/400 bombers, huge aircraft for their day. Then the war was over, but Whiteside's period of duty continued into 1919 while he waited for his release to return home.

The School began practising night flights from RAF Weyhill Aerodrome at Andover. On 22 April 1919, Major T. A. Batchelor DFC, AFC, selected a crew for another practice flight, with Whiteside as second pilot, along with four crew members, Lieutenant E. A. Westall, Flight Sergeant H. W. Smith (wireless operator), Flight Sergeant H. H. Heales and Corporal E. G. Ward. Another on board was Captain W. R. Adkins (formally RNAS), but whether he was a pilot under training, is not clear.

'With Full Military Honours'.

Batchelor took F3758 off at 02.30 am, but the twin-engined bomber failed to clear the roof of a low building, crashed and caught fire as the 400 gallons of fuel ignited. The engines had been tested earlier that day and been found OK, but one of the survivors said the aircraft did not appear able to climb, and felt sluggish. Three of the officers were killed in the crash, including Whiteside. Only Westall survived, although injured. Smith too was killed but the other two airmen had luckily been thrown clear.

Thomas Archibald Batchelor, aged 32, son of Captain T. Batchelor (4th Kings Own Royal Lancaster Regiment) and married to Una, living at 30 Hampstead Road, Preston Park, Brighton, had won his DFC flying with No. 214 Squadron in 1918. He had been operating with HP 0/400 bombers, so he was experienced on type. On one occasion he had been wounded in the arm and the consequent loss of blood had made it difficult for him to control his heavy aircraft, but he managed to get home. He had been flying since 1915.

Arthur Whiteside, aged 28, was buried in nearby Penton Mewsey (Holy Trinity) Churchyard, near Andover, Hampshire. The verdict from the court of enquiry merely said, 'Accidental Death while on Duty'. Major Batchelor was buried in the same churchyard.

* * *

Captain E. T. Hayne DSC, DFC, 28 April 1919

Edwin Tufnell Hayne came from South Africa, born on 28 May 1895 to Mr Tufnell Ward Hayne and Mrs Emily Ethel Hayne of Kerry Road, Park View, Johannesburg. Making his way to England, having been recruited in South Africa, he joined the Royal Naval Air Service, becoming a Flight Sub-Lieutenant on 5 July 1916. Completing pilot training he eventually wound up in A Flight of No. 3 Naval Squadron in 1917, flying Sopwith Camels.

Like many pilots it took time before he managed to down his first enemy aircraft, but he survived initial combats and, having done so, was to become a proficient air fighter for the next year. Although a Naval squadron, 3 Naval, like several others, was attached to the RFC rather than being restricted to operations over the Channel or French or Belgian coasts. Hayne had several encounters with hostile aircraft over the battlefront, one occurring on 30 May. He and Leonard Rochford were attacked by Albatros Scouts but both managed to evade them, and although Hayne fought with one for several minutes, he failed to get in a telling burst of fire.

Three pals with 3 Naval Squadron, with Hayne on the left. Art Whealy DSC, DFC is in the centre, and H. F. Beamish DSC is on the right. All three were aces.

He was also unsuccessful on 12 August, a day that 3 Naval were engaged in patrolling over the sea on a Fleet Protection Patrol. Suddenly they spotted Gotha bombers which had attacked Southend, but being low on fuel the four Camel pilots were unable to make a prolonged assault. Although the Naval pilots opened fire on the huge enemy machines, they did not appear to cause any damage. Hayne was lucky to get down at Manston, as faulty synchronisation gear had caused him to badly damage and splinter his propeller.

His first successful claim came on 22 August, south of Middlekerke, sending an Albatros DV down 'out of control'. On 10 September he was involved with other pilots in bringing down a Bavarian DFW two-seater of FA293(A) inside British lines at Adinkerke, capturing its crew. It would be some months before Hayne would score again, although he and Rochford drove off a two-seater on 1 October, believing they had killed or wounded its observer.

His scoring began in earnest on 18 March 1918. In the late morning he claimed an Albatros DV out of control and a short time later destroyed another DFW. On the 21st, he was again involved with his flight in destroying an Albatros two-seater east of Bapaume, to bring his score to five. Three days later he made it six by sending another Albatros Scout down in a spin over Vaux. During the German March offensive, Hayne carried out numerous ground-attack sorties.

On 1 April 1918 the RFC and RNAS were merged into the Royal Air Force, and 3 Naval became 203 Squadron RAF. Hayne did not score this month but claimed two Fokker Triplanes on 3 May. Two more two-seater reconnaissance machines were added to his score on 15 and 17 May, and then he downed two Pfalz DIII scouts on the 18th, one shared with one of the squadron's top pilots, Captain R. A. Little DSO, DSC, who was killed two days later. Another Pfalz on the 19th and an Albatros Scout on the 30th ended his May scoring, by which time he had been promoted to captain and flight commander. His sixteenth and final accredited victory came on 16 June, a DFW C-type over Estaires.

By this time he had been awarded the Distinguished Service Cross, in November 1917, and added a Distinguished Flying Cross after this run of successes. This award was announced in the *London Gazette* on 21 September 1918 with the following citation:

During the recent enemy offensive this officer carried out forty-eight special missions. Flying at extremely low altitude he has inflicted heavy casualties on massed troops and transport. In addition he has accounted for ten enemy machines, destroying three and driving down seven out of control; in these encounters he has never hesitated to engage the enemy, however superior in numbers. On one occasion he observed ten hostile aeroplanes harassing three Dolphins; he attacked three of the enemy, driving down one in flames.

The German offensive referred to was, of course, Operation Michael, in March 1918, the last major offensive mounted by the Germans in France. Fighter squadrons were heavily involved in ground attack sorties with bombs and machine guns, harassing advancing German troops. Hayne was no stranger to these types of low-flying sorties. Back on 16 August 1917 he had made a lone attack on a German aerodrome at Sparappelhoek, having initially flown out to sea in order to approach it from the north-west. Coming across the coast west of Ostend he fired into aircraft hangars and shot up three Albatros Scouts on the ground. Coming round he shot up buildings and then, flying along a road at 100 feet, strafed a horse-drawn wagon. Reaching Middlekerke he opened fire on more horse-drawn vehicles on the sea-front. He saw no drivers, who were either taking a break or taking cover, but he did see the horses stampeding away at a fast rate.

Hayne returned to England on 16 July, his war over France at an end. In 1919 he was flying with No.14 AAP (Aircraft Acceptance Park) and, on 28 April, he took off in a Bristol F2b fighter (E5098), with Major Maurice Nasmith Perrin RAF and RAMC in the rear cockpit. However, the 'Brisfit' suffered engine failure and, as

A Bristol F2b.

so often happens, even with experienced pilots, Hayne endeavoured to turn back to the airfield, stalled, and crashed. Hayne was killed immediately, and Perrin, seriously injured, did not survive the day. Perrin had been on active service since 1914. He was married to Susan Frances Perrin and was 32 years of age. His parents lived in Kensington. He is buried in Weybridge Cemetery, while Hayne lies in Castle Bromwich (St Mary and St Margaret) Churchyard, Warwickshire. He was one month short of his twenty-fourth birthday.

*   *   *

Captain B. P. G. Beanlands MC, 8 May 1919

Bernard Paul Gascoigne Beanlands, known more readily as Paul, was the son of the Reverend Canon Arthur John and Mrs A. T. Beanlands of Wickhurst Manor, Weald, Sevenoaks, Kent. He was actually born in Victoria, British Columbia, on 9 September 1897, where his father was rector and canon of Christ Church Cathedral. His father died in September 1917. Paul came to England when he was 11 years old and went to Oundle School in 1909. While there he joined the 1st Battalion of the Oundle Contingent and in August 1914 went to the Royal Military College, Sandhurst. From here he was gazetted second lieutenant to the 1st Battalion of the Hampshire Regiment on 23 December. He later moved to the 3rd Battalion.

In January 1915 he sailed for France and saw action during the Second Battle of Ypres, being wounded on 27 July, reportedly a hand injury from an exploding grenade. From a field hospital in Rouen he was shipped home and remained on sick leave until October. Transferring to the RFC in May 1916, he gained his RAeC flying certificate (No. 2473) in February 1916 and the first squadron he was sent to was No. 70 which was equipped with Sopwith 1½ Strutters (two-seaters). Flying both short and long range reconnaissance missions and fighting patrols, he obtained one combat victory on 6 September by downing a Roland two-seater in flames with his observer, Lieutenant C. A. Good and two other crews – an aircraft from KG1. He was then sent to

Captain B. P. G. Beanlands MC.

No. 24 Squadron as a flight commander, one of the few RFC squadrons equipped with the DH5 fighter, in 1917.

With this unit he gained a further six victories on this unusual machine that possessed a back-stagger top wing configuration that was not universally liked by its pilots, yet he achieved claims over two C-type observation machines and four single-seat Scouts. The two-seaters were downed while flying A9165 and the four fighters while in A9304. The first of these was an Albatros DIII that he forced down inside Allied lines on 13 November. Its occupant was a Marine pilot from MFJII who was killed. For his achievements Paul was awarded the Military Cross, recommended by his squadron commander on 18 November and supported by his 14 Wing CO, Colonel Joubert de la Ferte. The recommendation read:

On 25 August near Belle Eglise, while leading a patrol of four De Hav 5s, he dived on a formation of 2-seater EAs [enemy aircraft] *over the enemy lines. He attacked one but after firing about 30 rounds his gun jammed and he drew off to clear it. He rejoined the fight and observed one of the other pilots in difficulties with one of the EA on his tail, immediately attacked it and drove it down to 2,000 feet, when it fell out of control. Confirmation was received that this machine burst into flames and crashed. On 13 November near Nieuport, while leading a patrol of 8 De Hav 5s he engaged a formation of 7 DIII scouts. During the fight he drove one down out of control. He then attacked another DIII scout which was over our lines above the clouds and drove it down out of control. This machine crashed in our lines and the pilot was made prisoner. On several occasions Captain Beanlands has brought down EA out of control over the enemy lines, but unfortunately these have never been confirmed owing to poor visibility.*

However, in the way of things, this report was reduced to just two lines for the *London Gazette*:

For conspicuous gallantry and devotion to duty. He has brought down three enemy aeroplanes out of control and driven down several others over the enemy lines.

His squadron turned in its DH5s and re-equipped with SE5A fighters in December while he was on rest. Returning in the new year of 1918, he gained one further victory on 18 March, shooting down a two-seater in company with one of his flight. The German's huge offensive, Operation Michael, began on 21 March and Beanlands, flying low-level bombing and strafing sorties on this day, was badly shot up by ground fire and forced to land. The following day, in another SE5, he was again seriously hit by hostile fire and was himself badly wounded in the process. He was sent back to England for treatment but his recovery was delayed by the onset of septic poisoning.

Returning to duty he was made Wing Examining Officer to No. 18 Wing RAF where he saw out the war. Remaining in service, he was attached to No. 30 Training

Beanlands seated in a Spad while in England.

Depot Squadron at Northolt, but on 8 May 1919 he was killed in a flying accident in SE5A B109. According to the accident card, Beanlands zoomed off the ground, stalled, and spun into the ground. The court of enquiry assumed this to be so, and that he was too low to recover before he went in. He was buried in St Nicholas Churchyard, Sevenoaks, Kent. He was 21 years old.

* * *

Captain C. W. Warman DSO, MC, 12 May 1919

On the day Paul Beanlands was killed, Clive Wilson Warman was seriously injured in a crash. Clive was the son of Ralph and Jessie Warman who later lived in Bedingham, Horsham, Sussex, but Clive was born in Norfolk, Virginia, USA, on 30 June 1892. When the war began, he, like so many American-born lads, found it easier to join up in Canada rather than make their own way to England. Warman joined the Canadian Princess Patricia's Light Infantry, arriving in the UK in January 1915, then France in February. He was wounded during the Second Battle of Ypres in April 1915 and, after a period in hospital, found himself sent to Dublin, being engaged in the putting down of the Easter Rebellion. Feeling it was time to get away from soldiering, he

Captain C. W. Warman DSO, MC.

volunteered for and was commissioned into the RFC in August 1916, but was then given home leave to Canada, returning in early 1917. Completing his training and gaining his Royal Aero Club Certificate (No. 5395) on 1 April 1917, he was retained as an instructor at the air fighting school at Turnberry.

Finally posted to France, Warman joined No. 23 Squadron in June, one of only two RFC squadrons flying the French Spad fighter. Air fighters in the First World War might generally be fitted into certain categories. One was to fall in combat quickly, before they had a chance to learn how to survive. Another was those who flew for long periods at the front, and might either score very few victories, or steadily build a score over several months, even over a year. Then there were those, like Warman, who would shine like bright meteors across the skies of France for a comparatively short period.

His first claim came on 6 July 1917, destroying an Albatros DIII Scout near Houthoulst Forest. A week later he downed a two-seater C-type observation aeroplane. Two more victories came before the month was out, both Albatros Scouts, on the 27th and 31st. His fifth victory was over an observation kite balloon. These were balloons sent up some way behind the lines with one or two observers in a basket suspended below it. Their job was to observe enemy movements, such as troops, transport and artillery positions. They would report down to the ground by Morse code, giving map references so that gunfire could be directed to the target. They were vulnerable to attack by aircraft so were heavily defended by anti-aircraft fire or nearby fighter aircraft patrols. However, Warman flamed this one on 9 August. If balloons were attacked for specific reasons, rather than a chance engagement, the fighter's machine gun would be filled with Buckingham incendiary ammunition, designed to ignite the inflammable gas that made the balloon lighter than air. Warman's gun was armed with this on this day.

He scored twice on the 12th, both Albatros Scouts, one in the morning, shared with Lieutenant S. C. O'Grady, the second forty-five minutes after midday, the latter going down in flames. It was another double success on the 15th, two more Albatros single-seaters, during a long patrol that evening. One combat was recorded at 18.25, the other at 20.00 hours.

On the 16th he scored twice again, during an early morning patrol. The first was a DFW two-seater, shot down near the German airfield at Beveren. The second was another kite balloon suspended behind the Passchendaele battlefield. Then it was home for breakfast. But first he was set upon by three German fighters and during his manoeuvring discovered his gun had jammed. In his frustration, he threw the wooden mallet pilots used to hammer the cocking handle at the nearest fighter. He then managed to disengage and get back over the front line to safety.

His twelfth victory came two days later, on 18 August: another Albatros Scout, again above Passchendaele. However, his scoring spree abruptly ended on the 20th. During another scrap with German fighters he received a serious shoulder wound, an injury that would preclude him returning to combat flying.

So rapid had been his success that the rewards his squadron commander had recommended had no time to appear separately in the *London Gazette*, before he was commended again. So his Military Cross and subsequent Distinguished Service Order appeared in the same issue of the *Gazette*, 26 September 1917. His MC citation read:

For conspicuous gallantry and devotion to duty. He has on all occasions proved himself to be an exceptionally skilled and gallant pilot, having in the space of six weeks brought down six machines and destroyed a hostile balloon. He has also driven down five other enemy machines, displaying a consistent determination to attack at close range regardless of personal danger.

The DSO citation recorded that he had achieved his success '… under specially gallant circumstances'.

So severe was his wound that he was not released from hospital until 28 June 1918, but had been able to attend his investiture at Buckingham Palace for both awards, on 13 April. From hospital he was sent to a post at Air Ministry in London, but it was not until September that he was deemed fit to fly once more, and he was unable to return to France. In December, with the war won, he relinquished his Air Ministry appointment to go on a mission to Italy, not returning until February 1919. Once more on duty he was assigned to No. 81 Squadron prior to taking up an appointment with No. 1 Canadian Air Force Squadron.

However, perhaps a promising career with the Canadians came to an abrupt end on 8 May 1919. Taking off in an Avro 504 trainer he began a series of aerobatic 'stunts' over the Sewage Works at Edmonton, near Picketts Lane, Enfield, Middlesex. For reasons not explained, the aeroplane suddenly went out of control, crashed, and Warman was badly injured. He was taken to nearby Edmonton Military Hospital but died four days later, at 10.15 am on the 12th.

He was buried at Brookwood Military Cemetery in Surrey. The words carved on his headstone read: *Loved by all that knew him, most of all by Father and Mother*

*   *   *

Major A. D. Carter DSO & Bar, CdG, MiD (3), 22 May 1919

Following a distinguished flying career in the First World War, Albert Desbrisay Carter was to die tragically within months of the ceasefire, flying a German aeroplane. He had been born in Pointe du Bute, Westmoreland County, New Brunswick, Canada, on 2 June 1892, the only son of Leonard and Ettie Goodwin-Carter. Following his education he decided to join the Canadian army, being commissioned in March 1911. Coming to England and

Major A. D. Carter DSO & Bar.

then sent to France he served with the New Brunswick Regiment of the Canadian infantry, rising to the rank of major in February 1916. He was wounded in action and upon recovery decided, like many others, to continue the war in an aeroplane.

By the summer of 1917 he had become a pilot and for a while was engaged on coastal patrols, but that autumn managed a posting to 19 Squadron in France, one of only two RFC squadrons to be equipped with French Spad VIIs, and later Spad XIIIs. It was not long before he was scoring victories, his first two being on 31 October, a German two-seater and an Albatros DV scout, one in the morning the other in the afternoon. During November he scored six more times, with four two-seaters and two more Albatros Scouts.

His run did not abate in December, with a further seven claims, one two-seater, one Pfalz DIII Scout, and five Albatros DVs. Thus by the end of the year his score had risen to fifteen, which under the scoring rules of the First World War was logged as six destroyed (two in flames) and nine 'out of control'. He became a flight commander on 4 November and no doubt due to his rank received the DSO, thus bypassing the usual Military Cross for such actions. The citation records:

> *For conspicuous gallantry and devotion to duty. He destroyed two enemy aeroplanes, drove down several others out of control, and on two occasions attacked enemy machines from a low altitude. He showed great keenness and dash as a patrol leader.*

The squadron now changed equipment, receiving the new Sopwith 5F Dolphin fighters, an unusual design even for Sopwiths, the machine having an in-line rather than a rotary engine, and a back-stagger design of the top wing. As mentioned earlier, it was not always popular with pilots.

The squadron were ready to resume the fight as spring approached, and Carter scored a double with two Pfalz Scouts on 15 March, two days later adding an Albatros Scout to his tally. In March the massive German offensive Operation Michael began, and 19, like most squadrons, were heavily engaged in ground attack sorties, in an attempt to halt the enemy's advance. He and another pilot shared a two-seater 'out of control' on the 24th and his twentieth victory came on 10 April, yet another two-seater. By the end of April his score stood at twenty-four.

On 2 May he shot down a Fokker Dr.I Triplane, and six days later he got an Albatros DV. On 15 May he crashed another Triplane, and send down one of the new Fokker DVIIs 'out of control'. His twenty-ninth and last victory was achieved on 16 May, flaming a two-seater over Bucquoy in the late morning. This brought him the award of a Bar to his DSO, a rare event. He was still officially only a flight commander that carried the rank of captain. The citation for his second award stated:

> *For conspicuous gallantry and devotion to duty as a fighting pilot. In three and a half months he destroyed thirteen enemy machines. He showed the utmost determination, keenness and dash, and his various successful encounters often against odds, make up a splendid record.*

He was also the recipient of the Belgian *Croix de Guerre*, and had been mentioned in despatches on three occasions. Broken down he had been credited with 15 destroyed (including six shared with other pilots) and 14 'out of control' (two shared).

His run ended on 19 May. In action with fighters of Jasta 52, he was engaged by its *Staffelführer*, Leutnant Paul Billik, over Wingles. It was the German's nineteenth victory of an eventual thirty-one before he was himself shot down and taken prisoner in August. Carter came to earth inside German lines, wounded, and was taken into captivity, but at least he would survive the war, as would Billik.

Returning home from Germany he was sent to the newly formed Canadian Air Force that had an embryo fighter squadron and a similar bombing squadron. Carter was sent to the bombing unit as a flight commander. In fact both units had

Carter seated in the Fokker DVII which broke up in the air on 22 May 1919, resulting in his death. Note the unusual German cross. No doubt this was an attempt at changing the latin cross into something like the former Pattée cross.

The wreckage of the Fokker DVII at Shoreham.

former fighter aces as flight commanders. Although these two squadrons would later be numbered No. 1 and No. 2, at this early stage they were known as 93 and 123 Squadrons. There was any number of captured German aircraft to be had, both in England and in Germany with the Army of Occupation. The Canadian squadrons had some too – Fokker DVIIs.

One such Fokker, on the strength of 123 Squadron, was a machine built by O.A.W. (Ostdeutsche Albatros Werke), numbered 8482/18, with a Mercedes engine. On 22 May 1919, just over a year since he was shot down over France, Carter took off in this machine and began putting it through its paces. Coming out of a dive, the machine suddenly collapsed, spreading pieces across Shoreham airfield. Carter was killed instantly. He is buried in Old Shoreham Cemetery, Sussex. He was 26 years of age.

* * *

Captain M. R. James DFC, 29 May 1919

The date shown here is not the date of death, but the day Mansell Richard James disappeared. His exact date of death is unknown and could have been some days later according to some references.

James was born in Leamington, Ontario, on 18 June 1893, but was living in Watford, Ontario, when war began. Enlisting into the Royal Flying Corps, he was

Pilots of 45 Squadron in Italy. Left to right: Captain Lieutenant C. G. Catto, Captain M. R. James MC, Lieutenant Black, Lieutenant F. S. Bowles, Doc Smith, Lieutenant A. Rice-Oxley.

commissioned on 22 September 1917 in England and having completed pilot training was eventually posted to No. 45 Squadron in Italy on 12 February 1918, flying Sopwith Camels.

Fighting German and Austro-Hungarian airmen over the Northern Italian Front that summer, he achieved eleven combat victories and was awarded the Distinguished Flying Cross, gazetted on 2 November:

> *An excellent scout pilot who has at all times shown great skill, courage and determination in attacking enemy machines. During a short period of time he has destroyed nine enemy aeroplanes.*

In September James was promoted to captain but on 6 May 1919 resigned his commission and took a ship to America. A number of Sopwith Camels had found their way to the USA as war surplus machines, and somehow James managed to acquire one, flying it, some say, as the first of the type to fly in the US.

In late spring of that year, the *Boston Globe* newspaper put up a $1,000 prize challenge to be the fastest man to fly between Atlantic City, New Jersey, and Boston, Massachusetts. James was up for the challenge although he had never flown in the US before and certainly not over the route to be covered. Nevertheless, he was confident the Camel was the fastest machine around and duly took off from Atlantic City on 28 May to cover the 115 mile course. An earlier competitor, Melvin Hodgdon, had flown the distance at 90 mph, but the Camel was capable of 120 mph, so it seemed certain James would triumph. James did it at 115 mph, slowed somewhat by a headwind.

Using little else but a chart and compass, James landed at a flying strip eight miles north of Boston, identifying it because a lone aeroplane had been put in the middle of the field in order that James could spot it. At around 6 pm James climbed back into the Camel and took off for Mitchell Field, Long Island, a distance of some 240 miles, from where he would alter course towards Atlantic City. Once in the air, his exuberance tested the crowd's nerve as he turned his machine and dived straight down towards them, as if he was going to crash. They naturally scattered, and no doubt James was laughing to himself as he levelled out and flew away. Once airborne he had planned to follow the railway track to help navigate his way, but it appears he followed the wrong one, as he later landed at Tyringham, Massachusetts, near Lee, about 100 miles west of Boston, where he refuelled and stayed the night. The next day, the 29th, he took off at about 11.30 am. However, the story is clouded by the fact that another report indicates he took off from Lee on 2 June, heading south, before turning west. A crowd had again gathered – there were few aeroplanes to be seen in the air here in those days – and because of his direction it was thought he would soon fly back over the field, but he was not seen again.

What happened has never been satisfactorily explained. In early August a berry picker on Mount Riga, outside Millerton, New York, reported finding the wreckage of an aircraft in a ravine. Two years later it was reported that James could have gone down in a river at Poughkeepsie, New York. In December 1925, a hunter said he had discovered wreckage near Pittsfield, Massachusetts, which led to several search parties heading into the area, spurred on by a $500 reward for information offered by James's uncle. Nothing was ever found. In 1925 a US Coast Guard vessel found a floating wing of an aeroplane in Fort Pond Bay in Long Island Sound, but again nothing conclusive was ever discovered. A tragic end to this First World War ace, and one has to speculate if his remains will ever be found in the wreckage of a crashed Sopwith Camel, or did he manage to land somewhere, injured or not, and eventually succumb to the wilderness? He was 25.

*   *   *

Captain A. J. B. Tonks DFC & Bar, 14 July 1919

Adrian James Boswell Tonks was born in Solihull, near Birmingham, on 10 May 1898, the son of Arthur George and Mrs Alice Tonks. By the time the First World War began the family were living in Kensington, London. Adrian joined the Royal Naval Air Service in 1916 and trained to be a pilot, finally being posted to No. 4 Squadron RNAS on 17 August 1917.

Sent to France that same month his squadron was equipped with the Sopwith Camel and before the month was out 19-year-old Tonks had made his first combat claims during a morning offensive patrol. Flying Camel B3856 he sent down two Albatros DV Scouts 'out of control' south-east of Ostend on the 22nd. However, he did not score again until 9 November, claiming a DFW two-seater out of control north of

Captain A. J. B. Tonks in his RNAS uniform in 1917.

Pervijze. Another Albatros DV was claimed on 23 November.

Following a rest, he returned to France in the late spring of 1918, by which time the RFC and the RNAS had merged to become the Royal Air Force. No. 4 Naval Squadron RNAS now became No. 204 Squadron RAF. With his earlier experience, he was made a flight commander with the rank of captain.

The squadron was still equipped with Sopwith Camels, and Tonks gained his fifth accredited victory on the last day of June, claiming a Fokker DVII over Zeebrugge. 204 Squadron, along with several other former RNAS squadrons, was often in action with the aircraft of the German Naval Air Service, and particularly the German Marine units, especially the fighter aircraft of the *Marinefeldjagdstaffeln* (MFJ). These units were equipped with the same front-line aircraft used by the German Army Air Service, so Tonks and his pals were in combat at this time with the latest German fighter, the much vaunted Fokker DVIIs. In some ways this seemed to be a private war 'up on the coast' between former Naval squadrons and the German Marine boys.

Much of the air fighting developed around bombing raids on the German ports of Ostend and Zeebrugge, where Sopwith Camel squadrons escorted DH4 and

A Sopwith Pup, ordinarily a docile and gentle aeroplane to fly.

DH9 bombers targeting these German Naval bases. During August, Tonks scored a further five victories, all over Fokker DVIIs, including three in one early morning dogfight east of Ypres on 15 August. These, added to claims on 10 and 13 August, brought his overall score to ten, and he was awarded the Distinguished Flying Cross, the citation reading:

> *A brave and determined airman who has destroyed four enemy aeroplanes and driven down six out of control. In a recent engagement with twelve enemy scouts he destroyed one and drove off others who were attacking some pilots in his Flight. In these combats he expended all his ammunition, but seeing three enemy machines attacking one of ours, he, with great gallantry, dived amongst them with a view to distracting their attention. In this he succeeded. A courageous and meritorious action.*

On 28 September 1918 he fought another intense action with Fokker biplanes over Wercken and shot down two, bringing his total victories to twelve. This action brought him a Bar to his DFC. The citation for this action (*London Gazette* 3 December) reads:

> *Since 28th September this officer has led eleven low bombing raids, displaying courage and skill, and inflicting serious damage on the enemy from low altitude.*

During bombing raids Captain Tonks has destroyed two enemy machines, proving himself a bold and daring fighter.

In these low-bombing attacks, Camel pilots would dive and harass enemy ground forces as they were pushed back in the final weeks of the war. They usually carried four 25lb Cooper bombs and would continue attacks with their twin Browning machine guns, often until their ammunition was expended.

On 13 October 1918 Tonks was posted home and given a job at Air Ministry, a post he retained for the short time until the Armistice. He thereupon decided to remain in the RAF, and in the spring of 1919 he was posted out to the Middle East as a flight commander with No. 80 Squadron based at Aboukir, just along the coast east of Alexandria. Officially the squadron was equipped with the Sopwith 7F1 Snipe, so it was an easy transition from Camel to Snipe for Adrian Tonks. The squadron had one or two other aircraft as well, as either 'hacks' or training aircraft, one of these was a Sopwith Pup, C480.

This particular Pup was rather long in the tooth, having been part of a batch ordered in August 1917 when the type was no longer in front-line combat units. Just as the war in France was ending, C480 was shipped out to the Middle East and put on the strength of No. 22 Training Squadron, also based at Aboukir, and then taken over by 80 Squadron. On 14 July 1919, Adrian Tonks took off in this machine for a flight to Cairo but, for some unexplained reason, he crashed at his destination and suffered a fractured skull, an injury to which he later succumbed. An enquiry into the crash concluded that it was the result of an error of judgement on the part of the pilot. Tonks was buried at Alexandria; he was still only 21 years of age.

* * *

Captain H. A. R. Biziou DFC, 14 July 1919

On the same day Adrian Tonks was killed in Cairo, another First World War veteran died over southern England. Henry Arthur Richard Biziou was born on 18 September 1896, the son of Ernest A. Biziou, a French-born cook, and his wife Mary Jane (née Upton). They lived at The 'Maisonette', North Farnborough, Hampshire. Upon leaving school, Biziou, whose nickname was 'Weegee', became an engineering student at the firm of H. J. Spooner, at 311 Regent Street, London, from 1912 until the war began in 1914.

Joining the military with the Royal Navy as a mechanic in October 1914 he joined the Royal Naval Armoured Car Division and saw service in Gallipoli from April

1915, before moving to Egypt on New Year's Day 1916. Biziou then moved to the 6th Yorkshire Regiment from May 1916 and was gazetted second lieutenant to the General List. Volunteering to be an observer in the Royal Flying Corps in October, he flew as such with No. 42 Squadron. In 1917 he was serving in France with this squadron, which was equipped with RE8 reconnaissance aeroplanes. Following several months of active service he returned to England on 9 May 1917, selected as a possible scout pilot.

Captain H. A. R. Biziou DFC in front of a Sopwith Dolphin.

His pilot training commenced at Reading, and having gained his 'wings' was posted to 65 Squadron in August. This future fighter squadron was preparing for overseas duty, in what was known then as 'working up'. It had just started receiving Sopwith Camel fighters at Wye, Kent, north-east of Ashford. While all such Home Establishment squadrons were preparing for overseas, there was no guarantee that its pilots would remain with them, and so it proved in Biziou's case, for on 15 October he was sent to another unit that was 'working up' – No. 87 Squadron at Sedgeford, Norfolk. This must have been a bit demoralising for the 21-year-old as 65 Squadron flew to France just nine days later.

At this stage, 87 Squadron were flying various training-type aircraft, mostly Sopwith Pups and Avro 504s. He was with A Flight, commanded by Captain J. H. Larkin CdG, an Australian who had been an RE8 pilot in France. The rumour was that the squadron would receive SE5s but in the event 87 became one of only four units to be equipped with Sopwith Dolphins to see active duty in France. Meantime, Biziou was sent off to Gosport on the 29th for a course at the School of Special Flying.

The transition to Dolphins came once the squadron had moved to Hounslow in December. The CO was Captain C. J. W. Darwin, but as the squadron became operational, Major J. C. Callaghan MC arrived in January to take over. Casey Callaghan, often referred to as the 'Mad Major' was Irish and had won his MC flying FE2b aircraft in 1916. He had lost two younger brothers flying with the RFC and he too would not survive the war. On 8 February 1918 Biziou was posted up to Ayr, and the School of Air Fighting for some instruction on air-to-air firing and air fighting. Callaghan's observer on FE2s was Burton Ankers, who we shall read about in Chapter Five.

The squadron, after one false start caused by the German March Offensive, finally took their Dolphins to France on 24 April 1918, firstly to St Omer and then to Petite Synthe, near Dunkirk, three days later. It would remain there for exactly one month before moving to Estrée-lès-Crécy, west of Doullens.

The Dolphin was unusual in that it was one of the few designs to have a back-stagger top wing, situated so that the pilot's head was above it. It gave an excellent all-round view although at first pilots felt vulnerable should the machine turn over. In fact although this happened from time to time it caused few fatalities. The Dolphin had good high-altitude capabilities and initially the squadron were engaged against high-flying German reconnaissance aircraft that often flew over to photograph Allied positions.

Biziou was the first pilot to score a victory, downing a Rumpler two-seater on 6 May in Dolphin C4166 'B'. He had been part of a three-man late afternoon patrol that encountered the Rumpler and while its pilot immediately turned to head east, Biziou was able to attack it, sending it down in flames over Gheluvelt, east of Ypres. For this effort Biziou received congratulations from 65 Wing HQ. Biziou crashed this Dolphin on 6 June, turning it over, but he was not injured.

It was two months before he scored again, by which time his companions had racked up more than two dozen claims, the outstanding pilots being Jerry Pentland, Joe Larkin and 'Wiggy' Vigers, at least ten of which were two-seaters, which pleased their new masters, 13 Wing. Biziou had also been made leader of C Flight following Callaghan's death on 2 July, Darwin taking over the squadron. Just prior to this promotion, Biziou claimed his second victory, on 8 July, a DFW two-seater destroyed while on a lone patrol. Victory number three came on 21 August, this time an Albatros DV scout which he destroyed near Bapaume. The squadron was now operating from Rougefay, between Abbeville and Arras. On this day the squadron claimed eleven victories, Albatros and Pfalz Scouts as well as the new Fokker DVIIs.

Although Biziou had been slow to score since arriving in France, he more than made up for it during September, claiming five Fokker biplanes between the 16th and the 22nd – in fact scoring doubles on the 16th and 22nd. These actions resulted in the award of the Distinguished Flying Cross, gazetted on 3 December. The citation read:

A most successful leader of marked gallantry. During recent operations he has destroyed four enemy aeroplanes and driven down one out of control; two of these he accounted for in one engagement on September 16th with a number of Fokker biplanes. In addition he has driven down a hostile balloon.

An SE5A.

The balloon mentioned was not added to his personal score as it was generally accepted that a balloon needed to be flamed to have it included in a pilot's combat record. However, Biziou had survived the war following periods as a soldier, an observer and as a fighting pilot, with eight official victories and the DFC. He remained on active duty and on 18 February 1919 was sent to the Royal Aircraft Establishment at Farnborough to join its Experimental Squadron. At least he would be near the family home.

On Monday, 14 July 1919, he was flying above Farnborough in an SE5A (D7014) but somehow managed to collide with an Avro 504K (E3621), crashed and was killed. He is buried in Aldershot Cemetery. The occupants of the Avro were Lieutenant Leonard Arthur Herbert, from Richmond, Surrey, flying with a civilian mechanic, Mr C. Highly, both being killed. It was concluded that neither Biziou nor Herbert had observed each other's presence in what was termed misty weather conditions then prevalent over Farnborough. Henry Biziou was 22 years old.

*   *   *

Captain (The Hon) R. C. Cain DFC, 18 July 1919

The son of Richard and Harriat Georgina Cain, of Sulby, Isle of Man, Richard Claude Cain was born 29 May 1881. He attended King William's College on the Isle of Man between 1904 and 1910 before going to St. Catharine's College, Cambridge, 1910-1911. While at the latter he joined the Officer Training Corps.

Leaving Cambridge, he emigrated to Canada, working for the Government Land Officer until 23 September 1914, at which time he enlisted in the Royal Canadian Horse Artillery, attached to 'B' Battery. By March 1917 he had arrived in England where he joined the Royal Horse Artillery, but then volunteered to be an observer with the Royal Flying Corps. He was sent to No. 34 Squadron fighting on the

Captain R. C. Cain DFC.

Northern Italian Front, with effect from 11 February 1918, remaining so until he was wounded in the foot by an attacking Austro-Hungarian fighter on 27 October.

Cain had a busy day on the 27th. It was the start of the Allied assault across the Piave River, which began at 06.45 hours. It became known as the Battle of the Vittorio Veneto. No. 34 Squadron were tasked with flying contact patrols, that is, flying low over the battlefront in order to determine where British and Italian troops were in relation to the Austrians. In an early sortie, with RE8 No. D4906, observer to Second Lieutenant M. Nicol, a Canadian, they were shot up by ground fire and Nicol was wounded, but he got the aircraft home. In the same aeroplane, shortly before 10 am, with Second Lieutenant L. J. Shepherd MM, they were again over the battle when they were attacked by two Albatros DV Scouts, which was when Cain received his injury.

Returning to England, his long tour of duty was at an end, but it had already been acknowledged by the award of the Distinguished Flying Cross. This citation appeared in the *London Gazette* on 21 September:

By his skill and initiative as an observer this officer has on many occasions directed fire on enemy artillery, wagon lines and convoys, causing serious damage. His work has been most valuable, carried out at times under very difficult conditions. On a recent occasion he successfully bombed a bridge, obtaining a direct hit at low altitude.

A DH 10 bomber.

Following his recovery, his next appointment and posting was to No. 2 Air Acceptance Park at Hendon in May 1919. By this time he had become a pilot and on 18 July he was piloting a new DH10 bomber (E5557) on a test flight. With him were two crew members, Corporal John A. Gammie, from Inverness, and Aircraftman Second Class Thomas H. Griffiths, from Erdington.

After taking off, Cain began to make a turn at 150 feet, but the aircraft dived into the ground and burst into flames. All three men were burnt to death. An enquiry ruled that it had been an error of judgement on the pilot's part.

Twenty-seven-year-old Cain was buried in Kirk Malew (St. Malew) Churchyard, on the Isle of Man. His two companions were both buried, Gammie (aged 20), in Boharm Old Cemetery, Banffshire, Griffiths (aged 22), in St Barnabus Churchyard, Erdington.

*   *   *

Captain C. E. Howell DSO, MC, DFC, MiD (2), 10 December 1919

Cedric Ernest Howell, known to everyone as 'Spike', came from Adelaide, Australia, born 17 June 1894. His father Ernest was an accountant, married to Ida Caroline (née Hasch). There was also a daughter. Spike was educated at the Church of England Grammar School in Melbourne from 1909 and, upon leaving, trained as a draughtsman while holding a commission in the 49th (Prahran) Cadet Battalion, Citizens Military Forces. His first attempt to join the colours failed but finally in 1915 he was accepted in the Australian Imperial Forces as a private, and after training sailed for Egypt as part of a reinforcement contingent for the 14th Battalion. He saw action at Gallipoli as a sniper before being struck down with malaria, but, once recovered, sailed for France, serving with the 46th Battalion on the Somme front.

Requesting a transfer to aviation in 1917 he became one of 200 men recruited from the AIF and gazetted as a second lieutenant

Captain C. E. Howell DSO, MC, DFC, MiD.

to the RFC via Special Reserve, on 17 March. He obtained his RAeC certificate (No. 4517) on 18 April and, once he had completed his training, was posted to France as a Sopwith Camel pilot, going to No. 45 Squadron in October. However, his CO thought his pallor suggested he was still suffering from malaria and returned him to England; but he returned in November.

His squadron was now sent to the Italian Front, where his skill as a fighting pilot was quickly recognised. His victory score began in January and by May he had shot down six Albatros Scouts. With a total of eleven victories on the morning of 12 July, and sixteen by sundown, awards began to arrive. His Military Cross was gazetted on 16 September 1918:

> *For conspicuous gallantry and devotion to duty. He bombed an electrical power-house with great skill, obtaining three direct hits from 100 feet. With two other machines he carried out a most dashing attack on a formation of twelve enemy aeroplanes. Although badly hampered by frequent jams in both of his machine-guns, he destroyed three and drove down one out of control. He is a most successful and gallant patrol leader, and has destroyed six enemy aeroplanes and shot down one out of control.*

This was soon followed by the announcement of the Distinguished Flying Cross, gazetted just five days later, on the 21st:

> *On a recent occasion this officer, leading his patrol of three machines, attacked nine enemy aeroplanes, destroying six and driving down one out of control; he*

himself accounted for two of these. On a former occasion he destroyed three enemy aeroplanes in one flight. He is a fine fighting pilot, skilful and determined.

With a total of nineteen victories by mid-July he ended his tour but a further award was presented to him, the Distinguished Service Order, this citation appearing in the *London Gazette* of 2 November 1918:

This officer attacked, in company with one other machine, an enemy formation of fifteen aeroplanes, and succeeded in destroying four of them and bringing one down out of control. Two days afterwards he destroyed another enemy machine, which fell in our lines, and on the following day he led three machines against sixteen enemy scouts, destroyed two of them. Captain Howell is a very gallant and determined fighter, who takes no account of the enemy's superior numbers in his battles.

In addition to this, Howell received a mention in the despatches of General Rudolph Lambart, 10th Earl of Cavan, on 26 October 1918, and was further mentioned on 6 January 1919.

Howell returned to England in August 1918, becoming an instructor at the Central Flying School at Upavon for the rest of the war. In March 1919 the Australian Government, keen to promote links with Great Britain, proposed a competition. A prize of £10,000 was offered for the first successful flight from Britain to Australia. A number of people applied and Howell felt fortunate to be sponsored by the Martinsyde Aircraft Company to fly one of their A Mark 1 biplanes in the race. George Henry Fraser, from Coborg, Australia, was chosen to accompany him as the navigator and flight engineer. Fraser had served with the Australian Flying Corps during the war.

The Martinsyde A 1 biplane, the type in which Howell and Fraser were lost.

On 4 December 1919 they were the sixth contestants to start out on the first leg from London to Paris. The following morning they were off again, to Pisa and got there despite continued bad weather. From Pisa to Naples followed but on the next hop to Salerno they were forced to return because of the weather. Once better weather came they headed for Taranto and then off to Athens on 8 December. They were last seen in the semi-darkness over St. George's Bay, Corfu, thought to be trying to make an emergency landing on the island. Somewhere here they came down in the sea. It is estimated they were no more than 500 metres off shore and people on the beach reported hearing cries for help, but the sea was too rough for any rescue attempt until daybreak. Following a prolonged search the Martinsyde was finally located in about twelve feet of water by an Italian naval search ship. Howell's body was washed ashore later, but Fraser was never found.

Howell had been married during the war to Cicely Hallam Kirby, on 12 September 1917, and she was on the SS *Orsova* on her way to greet him in Adelaide. The news of his loss was broken to her by Howell's father when the ship finally docked. Howell's body was taken home and buried with full military honours at Warringal Cemetery, Heidelberg, Victoria. Several hundred people attended the ceremony and former airmen acted as pallbearers. His parents and sister also attended as he journeyed there on a gun carriage from the Royal Australian Garrison Artillery. In 1923 a stained-glass window to Howell's memory was unveiled by General Sir Harry Chauvel at St. Anselm's Church in Middle Park, Howell having attended there in his youth. In 2001 it was moved to St. Silas's Church, Albert Park.

*   *   *

Captain Sir John W Alcock KBE, DSC, 18 December 1919

In the annals of flying the name of John Alcock is well known for his famous flight across the Atlantic in 1919, along with Arthur Whitten Brown, the first men to successfully make this perilous journey. Less well known is Alcock's service career with the Royal Naval Air Service in the First World War.

John William Alcock (known also as Jack) was born in Seymour Grove, Old Trafford, Stretford, Manchester, on 5 November 1892, to John and Mary Alcock. He grew up with one sister and three brothers and began his education at St Thomas's Primary School in Stockport. Upon leaving school he was employed at the Empress Motor Works in Manchester and in 1910 was made assistant to Mr Charles Fletcher, the Works' Manager. Fletcher galvanised Alcock's interest in aviation and with another worker, Norman Crossland, they were the founders of the Manchester Aero Club. Another powerful influence was the French aviator Maurice Ducrocq, a pilot and the UK sales representative for aero engines.

Ducrocq hired Alcock as a mechanic at Brooklands, where he learnt to fly at the Frenchman's flying school, gaining Aero Certificate No. 368 on 26 November 1912. Jack then became a racing pilot for the Sunbeam Car Company and in the summer of 1914 competed in an air race on a course Hendon–Birmingham–Manchester–Hendon in a Farman biplane. When war came he immediately joined the Royal Naval Air Service as an instructor, being commissioned in December 1915.

Captain J. W. Alcock DSC.

In 1916 he was posted to Mudros, on the Greek island of Lemnos, to fly with No. 2 Wing RNAS. He flew a variety of missions and aircraft types but then, in early 1917, a Sopwith Triplane (N5431) arrived and for a while Alcock flew it extensively until 26 March. On this date Alcock unfortunately ran it into a ditch at Mikra Bay airfield, Salonika. He was unhurt but the fighter was badly damaged, although later repaired. Once it was so, Alcock added a Lewis gun above the cockpit, set to fire over the propeller, while still retaining the type's

Alcock's Sopwith Triplane after its repair. Note the mounted Lewis gun added to the machine's normal single Vickers gun.

single synchronised Vickers gun. He also made several other modifications with bits taken from other aircraft, and called it the 'Sopwith Mouse', also the 'Alcock A.1'.

Continuing operations, Alcock also began to fly a Sopwith Camel and was not averse to flying bomb raids in a large Handley Page 0/100 bomber (3124). On 7 August he attacked Panderma and its harbour, and on 1 September attacked Adrianople. On the way he spotted a submarine, dropping two bombs in its direction, and then dropped two more on an AA battery at Kuleli Bargas, finally reaching Adrianople to drop more bombs on the main railway station and buildings.

On 30 September he took off in a Camel in company with Lieutenant H. T. Mellings in the Triplane, with another pilot in a Sopwith Pup. They found and engaged two enemy seaplanes that were escorting a reconnaissance machine. In the fight, Mellings went for the two-seaters but was attacked by a seaplane. Alcock attacked one of the fighters which began to stream smoke and Mellings fought the other one which eventually crashed into the sea. Alcock finished off the other fighter before having to break off with engine trouble. Mellings and the Pup pilot chased the two-seater, leaving it low over the water with its pilot obviously in trouble.

However, the day was not yet over and that afternoon he flew the Handley Page on a raid against Constantinople, with 112lb bombs and some Thermite incendiaries. As he overflew the lines near Gallipoli, anti-aircraft fire opened up and although it didn't appear to have caused damage, the bomber's port propeller later flew off and petrol began to leak away. Alcock headed for home on one engine, gradually losing height. Eventually he decided to ditch five miles north of Suvla Bay. Alcock and his two crewmen survived but came under rifle fire from the shore. Nevertheless they successfully swam to a beach area and remained under cover until noon the next day; then they were located and taken prisoner. They remained guests of the Turks until the war's end. However, for his efforts, Alcock was to be awarded the Distinguished Service Cross, the citation in the *London Gazette* of 19 December 1917 reading:

For the great skill, judgement and dash displayed by him off Mudros on 30th September 1917, in a successful attack on three enemy seaplanes, two of which were brought down in the sea.

After the war, and his release, Jack Alcock remained in the RAF until March 1919, at which time he become a test pilot for Vickers Ltd. The *Daily Mail* had offered £10,000 for the first successful crossing of the Atlantic by air and Alcock teamed up with Lieutenant Arthur Brown. Brown, a Glaswegian, was six years older than

Arthur Brown and John Alcock.

Alcock and as an RFC BE2c observer with No. 2 Squadron, had, with his pilot Lieutenant H. W. Medlicott, been shot down over France on 10 November 1915 and taken prisoner. Brown was eventually repatriated to neutral Switzerland in January 1917, although Medlicott had been shot dead attempting an escape in May 1918. Brown was a proficient navigator whose skill would be essential for the Atlantic attempt.

The plan was to fly from Canada in a Vickers Vimy. Despite last-minute delays and the threat of another crew in a Handley Page 0/1500 about to make the attempt too, Alcock and Brown took off from St John's, Newfoundland on 14 June. After 16 hours and 12 minutes, the Vimy crunched down in Ireland, having flown the 1,890 miles to take the prize. Both men found their place in aviation history and both were knighted for their achievement. They became Knight Commanders of the Civil Division of the Most Excellent Order of the British Empire, announced in the *London Gazette* on 27 June:

> *In recognition of distinguished services to aviation, in connection with the successful flight from St John's, Newfoundland, to Clifden, Co. Galway, on 14–15 June, 1919.*

Sadly, although Jack Alcock's fame would not die, he himself did not last out the year. On 18 December he took the prototype Vickers Viking amphibian aeroplane

The Vickers Viking that Alcock was flying to Paris on 18 December 1919.

(G-EAOV) to the Paris Air Show, but near Rouen encountered foggy conditions and one wing hit a tree causing the machine to crash. Alcock was badly injured and although he was taken to No. 6 General Hospital in Rouen was pronounced dead. His body was taken back to England where he was buried in the Southern Cemetery, Charlton-cum-Hardy, Greater Manchester. He was 27 years old. Arthur Brown died in October 1948, aged 62.

Oddly, his fame does not seem to have reached RAF records, for on his RAF casualty card he is listed only as Captain John Wm. Alcock DSC, RNAS (RAF) and his unit is still shown as 2 Wing.

Chapter Two

1920–21

Captain F. E. Kindley DSC and Oak Leaf, DFC (Br), 1 February 1920

Born on a farm at Pea Ridge, Arkansas, on 13 March 1896, Field Eugene Kindley was the son of George C. and Ella Kindley. When he was 2 years old his mother died and his father took a position as supervisor of an agricultural school in the Philippines, so Field was left with his grandmother, Cynthia Kindley, who lived in Bentonville, Arkansas, until he was 7. He then joined his father in Manila, where he lived until 1908, whereupon he moved back home, to Gravette, Arkansas, to live with an uncle, A. E. Kindley. He completed his education and moved to Coffeyville, Kansas, where he became a partner in a motion picture theatre.

Captain E. F. Kindley DSC, DFC(Br).

While living in Coffeyville, he joined the Kansas Army National Guard and eventually transferred to the aviation branch of the US Army Signal Corps, attending the School of Military Aeronautics at the University of Illinois. Despite a series of accidents and mechanical failures, not to mention poor landings, he succeeded in becoming a pilot and, along with several others, sailed for England in September 1917.

Completing his flight training in England with No. 4 TDS, he was commissioned in April 1918. His first official mission was to ferry a Sopwith Camel to France on 5 May, but encountering heavy fog crashed into the White Cliffs of Dover. Recovering from his injuries he was posted to France, joining the RAF's 65 Squadron, equipped with Camels.

He was to claim one victory with 65 Squadron, a Pfalz DIII on 26 June. The pilot was the *Staffelführer* of Jasta 5, Leutnant Wilhelm Lehmann, who had been credited with four victories before his death. Kindley was then posted to the 148th Squadron, which had been formed at Kelly Field, Texas, in late 1917. Arriving in France in

1918, it came under British control on 20 July. Among its pilots were a number who would gain fame in the First World War, including Elliot White Springs, Jesse Creech, Henry Clay Jr., Clyde Bissell, Larry Callahan and Orville Ralston.

Kindley was credited with the 148th's first official victory, on 13 July, downing an Albatros DV Scout, following this with two Fokker DVIIs shot down in August, six more during September, plus a kite balloon, and then a Halberstadt CL two-seater. His twelfth and final victory was another Fokker biplane on 28 October, shared with Jesse Creech.

One Fokker DVII, shot down on 13 August, was flown by the brother of the great Baron Manfred von Richthofen, Lothar von Richthofen. Kindley was only able to claim an 'out of control' victory, meaning it was not seen to crash or burn, but appeared certain to hit the ground. Lothar survived this combat, Kindley seeing his machine gun bullets tearing into the Fokker before it nosed down in what appeared to be an uncontrolled dive. Lothar had scored his fortieth victory the previous day, and was so seriously wounded in this fight with Kindley, and subsequent crash, that he did not see further combat.

For his actions over France, Field Kindley received the Distinguished Flying Cross from the British, the citation reading.

On September 24th, Lt. Kindley led his flight down on seven Fokkers north of Bourlon Wood one of which he followed down and saw crash and burst into flames. On September 26th while working in conjunction with another of our flights, Lt. Kindley's flight accounted for two EA crashed, one of which he got. On September 27th this officer on low flying duty dropped bombs on railways near Marcoing, then attacked a balloon near Noyelles-sur-l'Escaut, driving same down and compelling the two observers to jump. He then, at an altitude of 600 feet, attacked and silenced an enemy machine-gun and shot up troops. Being then attacked by a Halberstadt he engaged it and brought it down in flames. Lt. Kindley's ammunition then being used up, he started for the lines but on the way back he saw two EA which he dived on. They turned and went east. This officer has been on active service in France since 23 May 1918. His work in this squadron has been consistently good and since 30 July, he has been leading 'A' Flight with marked success. He has accounted for a total of seven and one half EA destroyed and driven down out of control, three.

The USAS also awarded him the Distinguished Service Cross:

For extraordinary heroism in action near Bourlon Wood, France, 24 September 1918. Lt. Kindley attacked a formation of seven hostile planes (Fokker type) and sent one crashing to the ground.

Later he received an Oak Leaf Cluster to this DSC:

> *For Extraordinary heroism in action near Marcoing, France, 27 September 1918. Flying at a low altitude, this officer bombed the railway at Marcoing and drove down an enemy balloon. He then attacked German troops at low altitude and silenced a hostile machine-gun after which he shot down in flames an enemy plane (Halberstadt type) which had attacked him. Lt. Kindley has so far destroyed seven and one half hostile aircraft and driven down three out of control.*

He was confirmed in the rank of captain in early 1919 and it was not long before he was posted back to the United States where he did some flying but also some public relations work. On 17 December 1919 he became the commanding officer of the 94th Pursuit Squadron, at Kelly Field, San Antonio, Texas. Due to a planned visit to the air base by General John J. Pershing, head of the American Air Service, in early February, a flying display was arranged. On the 1st, the day before the general's visit, Kindley took to the air in a British SE5A fighter to rehearse a simulated bombing run. Diving onto the target he discovered a group of enlisted men wandering into the danger area. He quickly pulled back on the control column, causing the fighter to stall. Also a control cable appeared to have snapped, making the machine impossible to manage. The SE5 nosed into the ground from 100 feet, killing Kindley instantly. The official cause is recorded as 'structural failure'.

His body was taken back to Gravette for burial in Hillcrest Cemetery. There is a simple stone with the words (minus his surname):

Capt. Field E.
son of
G. C. & Ella Kindley
Mar. 13, 1896
Feb. 1, 1920

Several monuments and memorials exist in his honour. Gravette's city park has one, Coffeyville High School another. In the Second World War the air base in Bermuda was named after him, while a small auxiliary airstrip at Corregidor, Philippines, was also named for him. The Arkansas Air Museum in Fayetteville has some of his personal effects on display. He was 23 years old.

*   *   *

Captain C. R. Pithey DFC & Bar, 21 February 1920

Croye Rothes Pithey came from Scheepersnek, Natal, South Africa, where he was born on 19 August 1895, son of Sydney Herbert and Louise Mary Pithey. He had four brothers and four sisters. After his schooling (he also learnt fluent Zulu) he became an accounts clerk in a firm of Chartered Accountants in Johannesburg, between February 1916 and May 1917, at which time he enlisted into the Royal Flying Corps in South Africa, signed up by one of the many recruitment officers touring the colonies for would-be aviators.

He sailed for England where he began his flying training and, gaining his RFC wings, was posted to France, being assigned to No. 52 Squadron. The squadron was equipped with RE8 two-seat reconnaissance machines, referred to by some First World War airmen as 'flying coffins'. Like a number of aircraft built by the Royal Aircraft Factory, it was wonderfully stable in the air, so ideal for its crews looking down to observe movements on the ground, or from which to take aerial photographs of the terrain, or to direct artillery fire. Unhappily, its inherent stability was a liability if German single-seat fighters made hostile moves against them, or even if confronted with an opposing enemy two-seater.

The RE8, by 1918, was far from being a new machine. Its beginnings had emanated as far back as the spring of 1916, from the need to replace the ageing and outdated series of

A 12 Squadron group photo taken in 1918. Croye Pithey is seated in the second row, 4th from the right (inset: Croye Pithey).

BE2 machines. Despite some misgivings as to its ability to deal with any opposition in the air, the RE8 was built in numbers and equipped virtually all the Corps two-seater reconnaissance units throughout 1917-18. It had a maximum speed of nearly 100 mph at 6,500 feet, reduced to 92 mph at 10,000, but as its service height was around 11,000 feet, it did not have to prove itself faster above this.

However, Pithey was not destined to stay with 52 Squadron for very long and records show that he was taken into hospital just three weeks after his arrival, on 24 March. Whatever the problem was it was soon overcome, and by 12 April he was out and posted to 12 Squadron, at Soncamp, between Doullens and Arras. Pithey was crewed with his own observer, an Englishman by the name of Hervey Rhodes (later Lord Rhodes).

Hervey Rhodes, Pithey's observer. Later Lord Rhodes.

The two men teamed up as a crew just as the German March Offensive opened up along the Arras-St Leger-Doullens front. Despite their inexperience they managed to survive this period of aerial turmoil and gradually began to form an impressive team, undertaking all manner of tasks over the battle areas. As it turned out, both were experts with a machine gun and this became more than apparent during the next few months. They spent their spare time coordinating their fire, practising methods of engaging enemy aircraft and making certain that all angles of attack could be covered between them. Ordinarily the RE8 crews were not supposed to engage in aerial combat except in order to protect themselves. The best method, of course, was to head for home as soon as any danger was spotted. However, for some reason, Pithey and Rhodes much preferred to tackle an opponent rather than turn tail and run.

While engaged on a reconnaissance mission on 7 May, some 8,000 yards behind the German front line, they saw an observation balloon on or near to the ground, either having just been pulled down, or about to be sent aloft. Without hesitation, Pithey headed for it, diving to around 1,700 feet, allowing Rhodes to fire three bursts with his rear Lewis gun, whereupon the balloon burst into flames. Kite balloons were never the easiest of targets, indeed they were very dangerous things to attack. Many pilots avoided them at all costs unless ordered to try to stop their activities of ranging artillery into Allied lines. On 4 June the team managed to flame another at 08.45 hours. For this and other efforts, both men were recommended for a decoration, resulting in each receiving the Distinguished Flying Cross, gazetted on 3 August 1918. Pithey's citations read:

> *When on reconnaissance 8,000 yards behind the enemy lines he saw a hostile balloon on the ground: descending to 1,700 feet, he and his observer engaged and destroyed it. He then completed his reconnaissance. On another occasion, when on photography work, he was attacked by nine hostile scouts. By skilful manoeuvring he enabled his observer to shoot down three; the remaining six dispersed. He displays the greatest courage and determination in photographic and reconnaissance work.*

Their continued daring and disregard for danger resulted in Bars to their DFCs, and their joint citations appeared in the *London Gazette* on 3 December:

> *Lieutenant Pithey and his observer, Lieutenant Rhodes, have crashed five enemy aeroplanes and driven down five out of control; in addition they have shot down two balloons in flames, displaying conspicuous courage and skill on all occasions. On 1st September they attacked an enemy two-seater on contact patrol; this machine at first retired east but returned, accompanied by six scouts, to the attack; after a short engagement they were driven off, and Lieutenant Pithey, although his machine was badly shot about, continued his patrol and brought back a most valuable and accurate report.*

Operations continued into September and both men were constantly flying the usual variety of sorties demanded in Corps squadrons until both men were wounded from ground fire on 27 September. Pithey managed to fly the machine back to the airfield and landed safely. Several men rushed to the machine when it became obvious there was a problem. Willing hands extracted the two wounded flyers. Rhodes was covered in blood and his cockpit was awash too. But they survived. It was the end of an incredible run of good fortune having survived so many air fights not to mention the many other sorties they had flown during the last five months.

Croye Pithey was granted a permanent commission in the RAF immediately after the war ended, and had also served briefly with 106 and then 105 Squadrons in 1919. He then appears to have been a founder member of No. 2 Squadron, reformed on 1 February 1920 at Oranmore, Southern Ireland, with two-seat

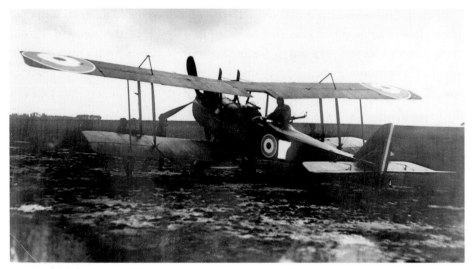

The RE8 Corps reconnaissance machine.

Bristol F2b Fighters. Its specific task was to support troops dealing with the riots there. It was based at RAF Digby as well as Belfast.

On 21 February, Pithey led two other pilots in a ferry flight from Shotwick near Chester, to Baldonnel, near Dublin, taking off just after 2 pm, a more or less straight east to west flight across the Irish Sea, about 130 miles, with an ETA of 4.30 pm. They were in two-seat BF2bs (H1567, H1612 and H1621) without anybody being carried in the rear cockpits. None of the three Bristol Fighters arrived. The weather was fine and the three aircraft were seen between Denbigh and Rhyl shortly after take-off, seemingly on course, but that was the last anyone saw. At around 4.30 pm, an aircraft was reported to have fallen into the sea some 85 miles south-west of the Scilly Isles, a message being received from the Master of the *Norfolk Rang,* and although a lifeboat was launched, no trace was found of pilot or plane. If it was one of the three missing machines, what was it doing around 300 miles south of Dublin?

Pithey's two companions were both experienced pilots. Horace Lloyd Holland, from Bournemouth, was 21 years old and had been in the RFC since April 1917. He had served with 141 Squadron on Home Defence duties. Hardress de Warenne Waller, from County Tipperary, was 22 and a former student at Malvern College. He had joined the RFC in November 1916 and although he had been injured in September 1917, appears to have spent some time as an instructor before serving in 117 and 105 Squadrons in 1919. Both men had been granted short service commissions in October 1919.

Their bodies were never recovered and they are remembered on the Hollybrook Memorial at Southampton. This memorial commemorates 1,900 men and women of the Commonwealth land and air forces who have no known graves and who have been lost at sea. Among them is the name of Lord Kitchener, Secretary of State for War, lost in the battle-cruiser HMS *Hampshire*, mined and sunk off Scapa Flow in 1916.

* * *

Captain C. B. Ridley DSC and Captain J. D. De Pencier MiD, 17 May 1920

In the skies over Germany on 17 May 1920, two successful wartime fighter pilots died in a collision with another aeroplane. As the date shows, these were not hostile skies, the war having ended 18 months earlier.

Captain C. B. Ridley DSC.

Cyril Burfield Ridley came from Esher, Surrey, born on 15 January 1895. Upon leaving school he lived in Toronto, Canada, but soon after the outbreak of war in Europe, joined the Royal Naval Air Service and trained to become a pilot, obtaining his aviator's certificate No. 2474 at Hendon. He joined No. 1 Squadron RNAS in the summer of 1917, a unit flying Sopwith Triplane fighters, and between April and September claimed four German aircraft shot down, three Albatros Scouts and one DFW two-seater. 1 Naval then re-equipped with Sopwith Camels and his fifth victory came on 6 December, another Albatros Scout.

After a bit of a break in early 1918, Ridley scored on 12 March, sharing a kite balloon with several members of the flight, and on 8 April he flamed a balloon in a lone attack. These victories led to the award of the Distinguished Service Cross on 17 April. His citation records:

For distinguished services as a pilot and for courage in low flying expeditions during which he attacked enemy trenches with machine-gun fire from a height of

30 feet. On 9 March 1918, he attacked a formation of enemy scouts, selecting one which was attacking one of our machines. The enemy aircraft dived down with a quantity of smoke issuing from it, but it appeared to flatten out at 2,000 feet and disappeared in the mist. He has previously destroyed several enemy machines, and has at all times led his flight with great skill and courage.

His next four claims after 8 April were all over German fighters, one Pfalz DIII, two Fokker Triplanes and a Fokker DVII, the latter on 4 July, being his eleventh and final claim. He was then sent home for a rest and saw out the war in England. He was now an RAF officer following the amalgamation of the RFC and RNAS on 1 April 1918, and in 1919 he received a posting to Cologne, Germany.

*   *   *

John Dartnell De Pencier was Canadian, born on 12 November 1898 in Manse, Vancouver, British Columbia. His father, the Most Reverend Adam Urias De Pencier DD, became the bishop of the nearby town of New Westminster, living at The See House, Nanton Avenue. His mother was Nina Frederika De Pencier, at one time living at 1346 Pendrell Street, Vancouver. They had four sons and two daughters.

A captain of his school's Rugby XV 1915–16 John was 'an excellent "half"; is splendid on defence; has much improved in making openings; was a very efficient Captain.'

Captain J. D. De Pencier MiD.

Soon after war came, John enlisted, at age 17, with the 12th Battalion, 68th Depot Battery of the Canadian Field Artillery. His father served with the 6th Canadian Chaplain Service, attached to the 62nd Battalion, CEF. A notable boxer, he became known as 'The Fighting Bishop' to the troops and, for his war work, became an MBE in 1917 (later OBE).

Transferring to the Royal Flying Corps, De Pencier trained to become a pilot and in October 1917 was posted to No. 19 Squadron in France, which was flying the French Spad VII scouts. On the 30th of that month he and another pilot shared in sending down a DFW two-seater 'out of control' west of Dadizeele, but it was almost two months before he claimed his second victory, this time an Albatros DV scout that went spinning down over Houthoulst Forest, Belgium.

A BF2b.

The squadron now re-equipped with the new Sopwith Dolphin fighter, and his first success with this machine came on 26 February, a Fokker Dr.I Triplane. Another Albatros Scout went down on the afternoon of 21 April, the day Manfred von Richthofen was killed, and number five was a Pfalz DIII he destroyed northeast of Estaires on 20 May. Two more shared claims in June, another Fokker Triplane and a DFW, brought his score to seven, and then a Fokker DVII biplane on 13 July made it eight.

He did not survive totally unscathed, for after one action he returned in some discomfort and the doctor and some pals noted a mark on his stomach and assumed it had been made by a spent bullet. After lunch he decided to have a nap and, when he awoke, discovered his bed soaked in blood. In fact he had been hit by a bullet that had passed right through him without causing serious damage. He was given seven days leave in England to recover.

By this time he had been made a captain and now returned to England where he later took a posting to the newly formed No. 1 Squadron, Royal Canadian Air Force. However, with the war's end, he was sent to Germany as part of the Army of Occupation, joining No. 12 Squadron at Cologne, part of the Rhine Forces. He received a mention in despatches.

It was here, on 17 May, with 12 Squadron, that he and Ridley, flying a routine training sortie in a Bristol F2B fighter, D8059, collided with another Bristol (H1566) flown by Flying Officer Toomes, falling from around 450 feet. The squadron was engaged in a practice formation flight and the court of inquiry determined that the cause of the accident, in their opinion, was mainly due to Ridley diving away from the formation and then zooming up underneath again, and leading the formation at a height contrary to standing orders. It was also partially due to Flying Officer

Toomes not keeping his leader in sight. Whatever the reason, both Ridley and De Pencier were killed in the resultant crash. Both were buried in Sudfriedhof Cemetery, Cologne, aged 25 and 21 respectively.

* * *

Captain J. R. Swanston DFC & Bar, 28 June 1920

John Romilly Swanston was born in Pakistan on 3 May 1898. He joined the Royal Navy early in the war and, deciding to fly, took his Royal Aero Club Certificate (No. 4497) on 21 March 1917, in order to fly with the Royal Naval Air Service. His actual date of joining the flying service is given as 28 November 1915. Following a long period of duty, he was awarded the Distinguished Flying Cross, while serving with No. 213 Squadron, on Sopwith Camels, gazetted on 2 November 1918 with the following citation:

A very capable flight commander. On a day last month he led a formation of twenty machines on a low bombing raid on an enemy aerodrome, and by skilful management succeeded in effecting a complete

Flight Sub-Lieutenant J.R. Swanston RNAS.

surprise, which resulted in great damage being done. Captain Swanston has carried out twenty-two valuable reconnaissance flights over the line, has personally obtained a direct hit on an enemy aerodrome, set fire to a railway truck containing enemy anti-aircraft guns, destroyed two enemy aeroplanes, and helped to destroy another. During his three periods of employment on active service he has been in the air 310 hours.

Often the wording of these citations varies slightly from the original recommendation. Of interest is the actual wording, dated 19 September 1918:

On 15th September 1918, led a formation of 20 a/c on a low Bomb Raid on Uytkerke aerodrome. His leading was splendid and enabled the attack to be a complete surprise. Great damage was done to the aerodrome, this officer obtaining a direct hit on a shed with his bombs. He also, assisted by another Camel, shot up some A/A guns on a railway truck. The guns ceased fire and the truck burst into flames as a result of his fire. He has done 22 valuable reconnaissance flights over the lines, has destroyed 2 enemy machines single handed and helped to destroy a two-seater E/A. Took part in low bomb raid on 13.8.18 and silenced an A/A battery with m.g. fire. He is a splendid leader and has [a] wonderful personality which helps to keep the whole squadron keen.

Uytkerke aerodrome is just inland from the Belgian town of Blankenberge.

In the *London Gazette* dated 11 February 1919, Swanston's name was among RAF officers the Belgian Government made *Chevaliers Ordre de la Couronne.*

After the war he remained in the RAF, going to No. 60 Squadron in India, in April 1920, seeing action in the Waziristan Campaign. The squadron were flying the DH10 bomber biplane, which was not a popular aeroplane, in fact those flying it thought it dangerous. There were several accidents involving these machines, and in one, on 28 June 1920, John Swanston lost his life.

According to a squadron history he was assigned to fly a reconnaissance mission from Risalpur on this day, taking with him 19-year-old Aircraftman Second Class F. C. Oliver (149907), from Dartford, Kent, son of Mr and Mrs H. J. Oliver. The RAF casualty card (form 559) notes however that they were on a flight test at 06.00 hours that morning. They had only just become airborne when the bomber got into a spin, crashed and caught fire, both men being killed instantly. The card also notes: 'Cause of accident not apparent'. Swanston and Oliver were popular and

A DH10 bomber of No. 60 Squadron.

able members of the squadron. Their names are on the Karachi War Memorial. Swanston was 22 years old.

A Bar to Swanston's DFC was later announced for his part in the Waziristan Campaign, noted in the *London Gazette* for 29 April 1921, by merely stating, 'For gallantry and distinguished service in Waziristan, 1919-1920'. However, the actual recommendation for the award, dated 20 May 1920, states:

Recommended for conspicuous gallantry and devotion to duty during recent operations. This officer has set a high example of energy and skill. He invariably descended to low heights to drop his bombs, although his machine (D.H.10) is not suitable for low bombing over this country. He has also carried out raids by night.

* * *

Captain J. W. Pinder DFC and Bar, MiD, 16 August 1920

Following both world wars, there were many airmen who simply never flew in an aeroplane again, while others, totally bitten by the flying bug, continued as aviators for as long as their health allowed. The airmen in this book are all of the latter variety, who simply had to continue flying. For each of them it became a way of life, although sadly, it also became a way of death. John William Pinder is as much an example as any, and the account of his death was, like all of them, tragic to read about.

John Pinder was born in Deal, Kent, on Saint Valentine's Day, 14 February 1898. As soon as he was old enough he enlisted into the Royal Naval Air Service, as a probationer, on 22 October 1916, and did his ground work at the RNAS shore establishment school, HMS *President*. In early 1917 he began flight training, but on one of his first flights, in a Curtiss J4 Jenny (No. 8820), on 3 January, with Flight Sub-Lieutenant S. Webb in the pilot's seat, they crashed while landing at Redcar, although both men survived the experience.

Once he became a pilot, he eventually found himself with No. 9 Naval Squadron in France, which was equipped with Sopwith Triplanes. His first successful combat occurred on the evening of 5 June, claiming an Albatros DIII Scout shot down 'out of control'. It was another month before his second success, this time flying a Sopwith Pup, claiming another Albatros Scout. The reason he was flying a Pup was that 9 Naval were in the process of changing over from Triplanes to Sopwith Camels, Pups helping the transition from three wings to two. On 25 July, he shot down a two-seater reconnaissance machine for victory number three, but his first in a Camel.

By early autumn he was posted to No. 13 Naval Squadron, based on the North Sea coast, operating over this part of France and Belgium. He was now a flight commander, and downed a German seaplane on 17 October north of Zeebrugge. By the end of 1917 his score had risen to six. In April, 13 Naval became 213 Squadron RAF with the merging of the RFC and RNAS, and during the summer of 1918 he brought his score to twelve. He had already been awarded the Distinguished Flying Cross, gazetted on 3 June.

Pinder was then rested, at the end of August, sent to take a post at the Air Ministry in London prior to an appointment with the Grand Fleet, but in October he was returned to France to join 45 Squadron. This unit had recently returned from the Italian Front, and now became part of the RAF's Independent Air Force, its long range bombers tasked with attacking German targets in both eastern France and into Germany itself. Not that it meant fighter escort work, but a number of enemy two-seater reconnaissance aircraft were encountered. Pinder gained five more victories during these last weeks of the war, including two Rumpler C-types, both brought down inside Allied lines, one on 23 October, one on the 28th.

With seventeen victories, a number having been shared with his men, he was awarded a Bar to his DFC, gazetted on 3 June 1919, exactly one year from the date

Pilots of No. 213 Squadron RAF in 1918, with John Pinder standing in the raincoat, 4th from the left.

of his DFC, and also received a mention in despatches. On 17 June 1919 he was elected to the membership of the Royal Aero Club and, on 24 October, was given a permanent commission in the RAF. However, this was cancelled on 24 October, and, while the reason is obscure, it may have been because Pinder had found a new career.

Having joined the RAF's unemployed list on 6 December 1919, he turned up in South America the following year, with the Brazilian Air Force, at Içara in Brazil. No doubt he could see endless possibilities for pioneering air work in that country, but this all ended tragically on 16 August 1920.

That day, he and Lieutenant Aliatar Martins of the Brazilian Air Force, attempted to make the first direct flight from Rio de Janeiro south to Buenos Aires, some 1,000 miles along the eastern Brazilian coast. They flew a Maachi 9 flying boat. Soon after taking off, they suffered damage to a propeller blade and, rather than land on the sea, put down on an inland lagoon, Lagoa dos Esteves. What happened next is speculation but is probably near to the truth.

The Maachi flying boat was what is termed a 'pusher' aircraft, in that the engine and propeller faces to the rear. Once on the water, they repaired the damage and prepared to take off. Ordinarily one man would take the controls while the other

A Maachi 9 flying boat, similar to that used by Pinder and Martins on their ill-starred trip on 16 August 1920.

would start the engine, normally with a handle, much like one used to start a motor car. Whether the engine 'kicked', or whether Martins got too close to the propeller is not known, but he was hit by it, broke an arm, and was hurled into the water. Pinder was quickly out of his seat and headed back to the rear hatch and, seeing his injured friend drifting away, dived in to attempt a rescue. The attempt failed and, drifting too far away from the Maachi, they were both drowned.

When a search began for the missing machine, it was eventually found on the lagoon on 27 August, and some distance away were the two bodies of Pinder and Martins. A truly sad and unusual turn of events. John Pinder was 22 years old.

*　*　*

Flight Lieutenant F. Nuttall MC, DFC, AFC, MiD, 18 September 1920

The son of W. T. and Mrs H. C. Nuttall of New Brighton, Christchurch, New Zealand, Frank Nuttall was born on 16 November 1887. Deciding to answer the call to arms after the First World War began, he came to England and joined the Royal Flying Corps, being gazetted second lieutenant via the Special List on 6 April 1916. He gained his flying certificate three weeks later and for a while was retained as an instructor before being posted out to Egypt to continue instructing others. Finally he was sent to No. 30 Squadron in April 1917. It was equipped with Martinsyde G.100 Elephants, using various landing grounds around Baghdad, but soon it began to equip with Bristol Scouts, BE2es and even Spad VIIs. He was later made captain and flight commander and by the end of 1917 the squadron was flying DH4 bombers.

Flight Lieutenant F. Nuttall MC, DFC, AFC, MiD.

Before that, on 31 October 1917, fellow pilot Lieutenant A. P. Adams was shot down and forced to land in the desert where he set fire to his Martinsyde. Nuttall landed nearby and rescued Adams, saving him from capture or even worse at the hands of hostile tribesmen. (Almost a year later, on 25 October 1918, Adams also rescued a downed pilot, now flying an RE8. Adams received the DFC in the 1919 New Year's Honours list, but was killed in action in March 1919. See Chapter One.)

On 25 January 1918, Nuttall and his observer Lieutenant R. B-B. Sevier suffered engine trouble, being forced to make a landing in the desert; Nuttall knew only too well what it had been like for Adams. They burnt their machine and then began to trudge for twenty-four miles in two days to eventual safety, carrying their two Lewis guns and their ammunition drums. For his October rescue of Adams, Nuttall was awarded the Military Cross, the citation appearing in the *London Gazette* in March 1918:

For conspicuous gallantry and devotion to duty. Seeing another machine driven down by hostile fire in the enemy's lines, he glided to the ground under heavy fire and dispersed the enemy with his machine gun. He took the stranded pilot on board and got away safely. By his prompt and courageous action he saved his comrade from being taken prisoner.

Nuttall's Martinsyde was shot up during a low-bombing raid near Kirkuk on 27 April and he was wounded. For this and other actions, he was awarded the DFC, belatedly, in 1919:

An RE8.

A gallant flight leader, who had rendered valuable services in carrying out the most arduous duties in action, and had commanded his Flight with great skill under exceptionally difficult conditions. On the 27th April 1918, near Kirkuk, while engaged in attacking enemy troops from a low altitude, he was shot down, wounded.

He remained in Egypt for a while but in 1919 was posted out again to Mesopotamia, this time going to No. 63 Squadron, staying for three months. Going back to Egypt again he was then sent home to England, having in the meantime been mentioned in despatches. Then came his third award, the Air Force Cross, gazetted on 10 October 1919, regrettably with no published citation. Back home he acquired a permanent commission in the RAF and once more returned to the Middle East in January 1920, initially to 30 Squadron, then back to 63 Squadron in Persia (Iran), as a flight commander.

On 6 September Nuttall was flying an RE8 (D4699) but was forced to land at Izam Zadi Achem, near Manjil, through engine failure. While attempted to take off, the engine again failed causing the machine to crash into a river bed where it and its engine were written off.

His luck finally ran out while flying an RE8 (D4698) now used as a light day bomber, on 18 September 1920. On this day, flying with 22-year-old Londoner, Leading Aircraftman Leonard Alfred Dellow as his observer, they were killed in a flying accident at Kasvin, returning from a reconnaissance mission. Frank Nuttall now lies in Tehran War Cemetery. He was 33 years old when he died.

* * *

Captain I. D. R. McDonald MC, DFC, 22 September 1920
Lieutenant H. C. E. Bocket-Pugh DFC and Bar, 22 September 1920

During the early 1920s, the Royal Air Force was engaged in operations in the Middle East, especially in India and Iraq. These were often flown in difficult circumstances, and in not very pleasant operating conditions. The main antagonists were dissident tribesmen railing against no end of problems they felt they had with the British. The British Army often had to drive into the unforgiving territory to quell various uprisings, and had to be supported from the air. If members of aircrew got into difficulties and were forced to come down in 'hostile' country, it was rarely a question of surrendering to these native forces. A quick death would be greatly preferable to the horrors some military personnel were to experience.

British military personnel, especially flyers, carried details of rewards to those who returned captured men to the nearest British base or military formation, printed in the various native dialects. However, not everyone was seen as a chance for a rewarding bag of gold coins.

Ian Donald Roy McDonald hailed from St John's, Antigua, British West Indies, having been born there on 9 September 1898, of English parents. His father Donald was a member of the Legislative Council of the Leeward Islands, BWI, and Ian received his early education at King's College, Antigua, and later at Denstone College, Uttoxeter, Staffordshire, from 1913, and where he was a member of the OTC. Leaving school in 1916 he joined the RFC as a cadet before being commissioned in February 1917.

Flying Officer I. D. R. McDonald MC, DFC.

Completing his pilot training he spent time with 39 Home Defence Squadron before being sent to join No. 24 Squadron in France, flying DH5 fighters, and soon began his considerable victory score by downing an Albatros Scout on 15 November. After two more victories the squadron converted to SE5s. McDonald continued his run of victories and became a flight commander in March 1918 – all at the age of 19!

During April, May and June, McDonald amassed a total score of twenty combat claims, the last of which, on 17 June 1918, he and two of his flight shared. The German pilot was the ace Kurt Erwin Wüsthoff, *Staffelführer* of Jasta 15.

Lieutenant H.C.E. Bocket-Pugh DFC and Bar.

Wüsthoff had a victory tally of twenty-seven, scored while flying with Jasta 4 in the Richthofen *Geschwader*, mostly in 1917. He came down inside Allied lines and was captured. McDonald had already been awarded the Military Cross, and then the Distinguished Flying Cross, and, strangely, his DFC was published in the *London Gazette* on 2 July 1918 – ahead of his MC which was not gazetted until 16 September. His MC citation read:

For conspicuous gallantry and devotion to duty. With seven scouts he attacked eighteen enemy machines, of which three were destroyed and one driven down completely out of control. When driven down to within 200 feet of the ground by two enemy machines owing to a choked engine, he turned on them and drove one down. He has in all destroyed eleven enemy aircraft and carried out valuable work in attacking enemy troops on the ground.

The citation to his DFC recorded:

A dashing fighting pilot. In the past two months he has destroyed five enemy machines and brought down two others out of control. At all times he shows a fine offensive spirit and complete disregard of danger.

Returning to England on 21 June he took up less arduous duties and he did not return to France before the Armistice. After the war he returned to Antigua suffering from eye strain but was unable to settle so returned to England and the Royal Air Force. He was granted a permanent commission and took up a post as a flying instructor at RAF Cranwell. He was then posted overseas, joining No. 84 Squadron, flying DH9A bombers, based at Baghdad, in that constant trouble spot Mesopotamia, or Mespot as British troops called it, soon to become better known as Iraq. He began flying operations against insurgents and against troublesome uprisings.

On 20 September 1920, the squadron were requested to drop food supplies to a British River Gunboat, HMS *Greenfly*, stranded and under siege by rebel tribesmen at Samāwah on the Euphrates River, 230 miles south-east of Baghdad; the ship had run aground on 10 August. Flying Officer H. C. E. Bocket-Pugh DFC and Bar, had only recently been awarded this Bar decoration for operations in Somaliland, his earlier DFC awarded for work in Russia. He was assigned the task and McDonald went too in the observer's cockpit. They took off in a DH9A F2838 and, in company with another aircraft, they located the ship and proceeded to fly in low to drop their load, while coming under heavy ground fire. Aircraft of the day had no armour protection for either crew members or sensitive parts of the engine, and obviously something vital was hit, possibly the fuel tank or fuel line. Sailors aboard the ship saw the bomber plunge into the water and also watched as the two men swam clear to wade ashore. Exactly what happened to them is not clear but it was known that downed airmen or captured soldiers were rarely treated well. Air Ministry later revealed that a report had been received telling them that both men had been murdered – believed shot – at a place called Dangatora. It was

A DH9A bomber.

hoped that they did indeed die in this way, for many others would be despatched in a far less humane way by native tribesmen. The ship's crew were later forced to surrender due to lack of food, and all non-Indian personnel aboard were murdered, while the Indians were held as hostages.

MacDonald's body was never recovered so his name is commemorated on the Basra Memorial, Iraq, along with Bocket-Pugh. He was only 22 years of age.

Lieutenant Henry Charles Edward Bocket-Pugh was also 22 years old, and had seen active service with the RAF in Italy during the First World War. He had been flying with No. 224 Squadron based at Alimini, Italy, from April 1918, which had been part of 6 Wing, RNAS, but then the RAF's 67 Wing.

On 11 May, six DH4 aircraft from the squadron took part in a raid on the Austrian naval base at Kumbor, in Cattaro Bay, Turkey, a 400-mile round trip from 224's Adriatic base. The DH4 flown by Bocket-Pugh was shot down and he, with his observer, was taken into captivity. He was repatriated on 29 November 1918.

The following year he was in North Russia, and the award of the DFC appeared in the *London Gazette* for 22 December 1919. During January and February 1920 there was unrest in Somaliland; the Dervish forces of Mohammed Abdullah Hassan, the Somali religious leader, also referred to as the Mad Mullah, were in continuing revolt. Eventually Hassan was defeated, ending his twenty years of resistance. Bocket-Pugh had been part of a force of twelve aircraft of 'Z' Force. His work here resulted in the award of a Bar to his DFC. The recommendation for this was jointly with his observer, Oswald Robert Gayford, already the recipient of the DFC and Bar; in the event, while Bocket-Pugh received a Bar to his DFC, Gayford only received a mention in despatches, and not the recommended second Bar to his DFC:

For their consistently excellent work in bombing and shooting up the Mullahn strongholds, forces and stock. On one occasion after the Mullah had been reported to have broken south they discovered the Mullah's own party with 150 ponies. To ensure good results and to allow time for the Camel Corps to come up, they came down to less than a hundred feet and bombed the ponies and men, this at great risk to themselves as flying fragments pierced their machine in many places. They then shot up and chased the party north, having killed 38 ponies & 19 men. This killing of ponies etc, so disorganised the Mullah's own party that later practically all their important people were captured.

(Gayford had been an observer in the RNAS in the First World War, receiving a DFC in 1918, and a Bar in 1919 for operations in South Russia. He became a pilot in 1921 and rose to the rank of Air Commodore in the Second World War. In 1933 Squadron Leader Gayford and Flight Lieutenant G. E. Nicholetts (a future AVM) broke the record for a long distance flight from Cranwell to Cape Town in a Fairey Monoplane. He died in 1945.)

No sooner had Bocket-Pugh finished operations in Somaliland than he was sent to 84 Squadron, meeting up with Iain McDonald and their mission on 22 September. Captain B. S. Thomas, the squadron's intelligence officer, made this report on their loss:

Aeroplane No. H.58[1] was shot down from a height of a few hundred feet and crashed into the river – 1 mile above Khidr and turned over on her back. The two pilots, Lieutenant Bocket-Pugh and Lieutenant McDonald, were observed from an escorting machine to scramble onto the bank and neither appeared wounded though Bocket-Pugh was walking up and down in an agitated manner. The escorting aeroplane was obliged to leave at this point, owing to the danger of crashing itself, it being hit by six bullets in a vital part of the machine. The escorting pilot remarked that what appears to them to be extraordinary is that when their own machine went down to a few hundred feet to see it if was possible to render assistance, the ill-fated pilots on the ground did not look up or seem to take the slightest notice of their presence – a fact which would be accounted for if the pilots had been blinded. This evidence is not borne out by Arab evidence.

According to Arab reports, following the crash, one pilot was shot, immediately on coming ashore by desert Arabs of the Al Juabir tribe. He fell, but was not killed outright, so they attacked him with their native daggers. This officer, presumably, was McDonald. The body was then stripped. The Arabs say they discovered he

---

1. Both serial numbers appear in reports, so perhaps H.58 was the escort machine which returned damaged, noted as Cat.W.

was circumcised, which indicates that the body was foully treated or at any rate mauled.

Stories conflict as to the time which elapsed between the two murders. The second officer, Bocket-Pugh presumably, is said to have offered the Arabs a large sum of money if they would give him safe conduct to Greenfly. This did not avail. The village Arabs of Shaikh Haji Siffir arriving on the scene almost at once, their leader a nephew of Haji Siffir, one Bin Mghamis himself shot the pilot dead. The ears were then cut off and sent to Khidr where they were delivered to the Holy Man – Shaikh Abdul Ali and Shaikh Caldhim. The head was smashed by a 'maghwar', the native 'knob-headed' weapon, and teeth were removed. There is a story that an arm was also cut off one of the bodies but this lacks confirmation.

The bodies of the officers are at present reported to be lying stark in the open on the bank of the river, the leading man being too weak or depraved to order their tribesmen to bury the corpses.

At midday a third plane which went out with letters for the Shaikh and with sun helmets for the officers, arrived over Khidr and dropped its cargo. It was however too late to be of assistance. The letters and helmets were duly taken into the chief men, Haji Siffir, Shaikh Abdul Ali and Shaikh Caldhim, who with most of the villagers had gathered in the house of Abdul Ali and the letters were read out with fiendish delight.

The cause of the crash is assumed by the pilots of the escorting machine to be that the bomb rack, to which the Greenfly's rations were attached, failed to function; this accounts for the plane flying at a low altitude for a long time, where she was a vulnerable target to rifle fire from the ground. Colour is added to this theory by the fact that tinned milk and fish were on the 23rd being sold in the Khidr bazaar. Those things would be readily salved from the plane which was 'undercarriage upwards' in the river. The Arabs also claimed to have dismantled the Lewis Gun which they now have with them at Khidr. Those parts of the aeroplane above water were gutted and what remained of the planes and fuselage were taken as trophies to the villages. Only the engine now remains in the river.

*   *   *

Flying Officer W. Sidebottom DFC, 8 December 1920

William Sidebottom came from Hyde, Greater Manchester, where he was born on 11 October 1893. He joined the Royal Naval Air Service on 11 October 1917 and trained to be a pilot. Once he had attained this goal the RNAS and RFC had merged into the Royal Air Force on 1 April 1918, so that when he was finally sent to France it was as an RAF second lieutenant.

He was posted to No. 203 Squadron (formerly 3 Naval) where on 16 June he and Lieutenant E. T. Hayne destroyed a DFW two-seater over Estaires. On 20 July he shared another of this type with his flight commander, Captain L. H. Rochford DSC and Bar, and before July was out he had scored over two Fokker DVII fighters. His fifth victory, another Fokker biplane, he shot down on 11 August. He shared his sixth victory with another 203 Squadron ace, Captain A. T. Whealy, on the 22nd, a DFW.

Lieutenant W. Sidebottom DFC.

In September he scored twice, a Fokker on the 24th, with another pilot, and yet another Fokker on the 28th. In October he really got into his stride, downing a DVII on the 1st, another on the 2nd, then shared a Rumpler two-seater with Leonard Rochford on the 9th which went down in flames to crash near St Aubert. Shared victories in the First World War gave numerical credit to both pilots, and this was Rochford's twenty-eighth. His twenty-ninth and last victory came on 29 October, by which time 'Titch' Rochford had been awarded the DFC to add to his RNAS awards. Sidebottom, by this time, had become Rochford's deputy flight leader, and led the flight when Titch was away on leave.

Sidebottom's last three victories came in late October, two Fokker biplanes in the late afternoon of the 23rd over Vertain, and another Fokker on the 29th over Bruay. This brought his score to fourteen. These achievements, plus numerous low-bombing sorties against German troops and transport, brought him the reward of the Distinguished Flying Cross. The following citation was recorded in the *London Gazette* dated 8 February 1919:

> *This officer has carried out numerous offensive and low-bombing patrols with courage, skill and judgement. He has also proved himself a bold and resolute fighter in aerial combats, having nine enemy machines to his credit.*

The recommendation for this award had been written following his 1 October success, hence the note of just nine victories. One such bomb raid was against the German airfield at Lieu St Amand, Sidebottom leading his flight in a massive attack by Camels of 203, SE5s from 40, and Bristol Fighters of 22 Squadrons.

Officers of 203 Squadron in July 1918, commanded by Major R. Collishaw. Sidebottom is sitting far left front row. Collishaw is centre of second row with Leonard Rochford on his left.

Like several RAF officers who had started their combat careers late in the war, William Sidebottom jumped at the chance of further action in 1919. There was conflict going on in Russia, with the White Russian forces clashing with the Bolsheviks, or Red Russian forces. Britain had sent some troops to help the White Russians, under General Anton Denikin, as well as an RAF Squadron, No. 47. The well-known Canadian ace, Raymond Collishaw DSO and Bar, DSC, DFC, who had been Sidebottom's CO in 1918, was asked to command 47 Squadron, and Collishaw had rounded up a number of men he had known, including some from 203 Squadron, Sidebottom being one of the eager volunteers. 47 Squadron operated three flights, two with DH9 bombers and one with Sopwith Camels.

Little is known of Sidebottom's time in Russia, but upon his return to England he had accepted to continue service with the RAF and, with his DH9 experience recently gained, was posted to No. 30 Squadron, operating these types in north-west Persia (Mesopotamia) against dissident factions. On the morning of 8 December 1920 the squadron mounted a bombing raid against these forces, Sidebottom taking off in DH9A E780, with an observer in the rear cockpit, 333697 Aircraftman Second Class Liston Wilkinson. Fifteen miles from Rustamabad, they came under ground fire that hit the DH9, forcing Sidebottom to make a landing. He tried to get as near as he could to what might be called the front line, before coming to

A DH9A bomber of 30 Squadron. Note the spare wheel fixed to the fuselage, useful in the event of a forced landing in rough country.

earth. As they came to rest, hostile fire continued, hitting and killing Sidebottom, although his observer managed to race to safety without injury.

His mother Sarah, living in Stockport Road, Hyde, Cheshire, duly received the telegram informing her of William's death in action. Sadly his mortal remains were not recovered so with no information as to where he was buried, his name is inscribed on the Tehran Memorial in Iran. He was 27 years of age.

* * *

Flight Lieutenant J. A. Le Royer MC, 3 April 1921

A Canadian from Quebec City, born on 28 January 1890, although the year 1889 is recorded elsewhere. His parents were Charles Eugene and Celinas (née Bernard) Le Royer of St Claire, Dorchester County, Quebec.

In 1914 Joseph Achille Le Royer became a civil engineer in Montreal and Toronto, and in 1915 he joined the colours, being commissioned into the 163rd Battalion of the French/Canadian Infantry. Sailing to England, he was promoted

to captain on 26 May 1916, and seconded into the
Royal Flying Corps the following February.

On 15 February he went to No. 1 School of
Aeronautics, then to Hythe on 2 March where
he trained to be an observer. Next he was sent to
France as a probationary flying officer joining No.
11 Squadron, equipped with two-seat 'pusher'
FE2b aircraft. He was soon confirmed as an
observer, and received his 'wings' on 25 March.

His squadron was engaged in fighting patrols,
his position being in the front cockpit of the
gondola, with his pilot seated behind him. Behind
the pilot was the engine, which pushed the aircraft
forward. From the front cockpit, Le Royer had an
excellent all-round 180-degree view of the front,

Flight Lieutenant J. A. Le Royer
MC CAF.

but if attacked from the rear by an enemy aircraft, he would have to undo his seat
belt, stand on the seat, and turn to face the rear where there was a mounted Lewis
gun on a pole which he could use to fire rearwards. Its use was generally as a sort
of scatter-gun, to hopefully unnerve the attacker.

His squadron had many roles, including air fighting, patrolling, taking
photographs and bomb dropping. German fighters had little fear in engaging
the large FE2 machines and often the FE crews would, in a formation, fly into a
defensive circle, each observer being able to protect the tail of the aircraft in front.

Le Royer gained his first combat victory flying with Second Lieutenant G. A.
Exley, on 14 April, sending down an Albatros DII scout 'out of control'. On the
27th, the squadron were involved in some heavy air fighting over Vitry, Le Royer
and his pilot, Second Lieutenant D. S. Kennedy, claiming two Albatros DIIIs
shot down in flames, and another sent spinning down 'out of control'. Both men
received the Military Cross for this action. Le Royer's citation, gazetted on 18 July
1917, states:

> *For conspicuous gallantry and devotion to duty. He has constantly shown great
> skill and courage when acting as Observer. His accurate shooting and coolness
> under fire have largely contributed to his successful aerial combats against superior
> numbers.*

As is often the case, the published citation varies from the actual recommendation
for an award, and so it proved in this case. The recommendation says:

For skill and gallantry. On 27th April, 1917, while on patrol, he attacked three scouts, who were attacking a Sopwith and an FE, with 2/Lt Kennedy as pilot. These were dispersed, one HA being shot down in flames near Izel-lès-Equerchin, and another driven down. A second formation, of four, which attacked the FE, was also dispersed, one being shot down and seen to crash near Vitry. Previously, on 14 April 1917, he drove a hostile scout down out of control.

Douglas Kennedy's MC was gazetted the same date, and part of the citation mentions the 27 April action:

While on a close patrol he attacked three hostile scouts and succeeded in dispersing them. A second formation of four enemy machines then attacked but were also dispersed, two of them being driven down.

Kennedy later flew Bristol Fighters with 62 Squadron but his unit found itself battling the Richthofen Circus on 12 March 1918, Kennedy being shot down and killed by the Baron's brother, Lothar.

Le Royer was wounded by ground fire on 5 July and returned to England for treatment. Once recovered, he returned to 11 Squadron in mid–August, but he had applied for pilot training, was accepted, returned to England again on 11 November, and qualified in February 1918. After a brief posting to No. 199 (N) Training Squadron on 8 March, he was posted to No. 33 Squadron three days later, and then on 10 May was sent to France to join 102 Night Bombing Squadron. No doubt the posting was influenced by the fact that 102 Squadron flew FE2 aircraft, with which he was familiar, the FEs having been withdrawn from day flying by this time, but used extensively for night bombing.

By early September 1918 he had completed his tour of duty with 102, and received a posting back to his native Canada. However, by this time he had become a husband, having married Madeleine Beatrice Vidal, daughter of the late Inspector General Beaufort Henry Vidal and Beatrice Hermione Taschereau, on 22 July 1918. They would have a son and a daughter.

Le Royer was still in Canada when the war ended, and he received a posting to the National Defence Headquarters in Ottawa to join the Canadian Air Force, formed in 1920. In 1924 it would become the Royal Canadian Air Force. However, Joseph Le Royer would not see that event.

On 1 April 1921 (the third anniversary of the formation of the RAF) he was at Camp Borden, Ontario, being shown the Avro 504K, by now the standard training aeroplane both in Canada and the UK. After instruction from Flight Lieutenant

A. L. Cuffe, Le Royer took off on his first solo on the type (in H9744 which also had the civilian serial G-CYBD) and made two successful landings. Taking off again, eyewitnesses watched as he appeared to stall during a right-hand turn, went into a spin from 200 feet and hit the ground. Badly hurt he died of internal injuries two days later and was buried in Notre Dame Cemetery, Ottawa.

It is recorded that his flying times were: one hour on the DH1, 12 hours on the DH6, 108 hours on the FE2, and 82 hours on the BF2b. His last day's flying on the Avro was 1 hour, 45 mins. He was later inducted into the Canadian Hall of Valor. He died at the age of 31.

*   *   *

Flying Officer H. M. Coombs DFC, 8 June 1921

After the Great War, the Royal Air Force had a substantial presence in the Middle East, including Egypt, Iraq (Mesopotamia) etc, and with a variety of aircraft, most of which had seen service during the war. One of the squadrons was No. 216, based at Heliopolis, Egypt, and one of its pilots was 23-year-old Herbert Milbourne Coombs DFC.

A De Havilland 10 bomber.

Coombs was the son of the late Dr Milbourne L. B. Coombs and his wife Maude (née Foster) of Kenilworth, Cyprus Road, Newport, Isle of Wight. They also had a daughter. Immediately before the war, Herbert Coombs had been a motor engineer, but once war came he enlisted into the 2nd Wessex Brigade, and later transferred to the Royal Flying Corps. Following his pilot training, he was sent to No. 100 Squadron, a night bombing unit equipped with FE2d bombers and then, from August 1918, Handley Page 0/400s.

Coombs joined the squadron in May 1918, and made his first night raid on the Railway Station at Metz on the night of the 30/31st. This would be in an FE2, his observer being Second Lieutenant W. Rogers. The next night they bombed the Thionville rail junction and station.

In June he made four more raids. Important targets at this stage were anything to do with railways or aerodromes. Therefore in June his raids were upon the Metz-Sablon railway, the Boulay and Frescaty aerodromes, plus the blast furnaces at Maiziers. He had various observers: Lieutenants H. T. Ross, R. P. Keely, G. L. Pollard, and L. A. Naylor.

During July he flew six raids, five of which were upon the aerodrome at Boulay, and one on Saarburg rail junction. His observers were W. G. P. Dyson, S. N. Bourne (twice), F. C. Sawyer (twice) and G. L. Pollard. On 22 July he was confirmed as a full lieutenant, and on 1 September he was made acting captain. On 1 August he had to relinquish his territorial rank with the Wessex Brigade upon taking up a commission with the RAF.

There was a break for Coombs during August with some home leave, and while he was away 100 Squadron changed its FE2s for the larger twin-engined HP 0/400. Coombs would now have two crew members, the main one being Second Lieutenant P. Wilkins MC, who would fly with him on the next nine bomb raids as second pilot, and again a variety of gunners, named as Lieutenants E. Mason, A. Cooper and A. Lister, and Sergeant C. Crutchett.

On 15/16 September came his first HP 0/400 raid, against the aerodrome at Lorquin. Two more that month saw bombs go down on one of four assigned for the 20/21st and then against Mézières rail junction. On the last night of September, it was his first of four raids on rail junctions at Burbach and Mézières; slowing down German rail traffic to the front was important at this stage of the enemy's retreat.

Metz-Sablon railway was bombed on the 18/19th and his last raid was against targets in Germany on the night of 23/24 October, although in the event, due to weather, Coombs actually bombed the railway junction at Sarreburg. This brought his total raids to twenty-one.

With the end of the war, most squadron commanders were asked to submit any requests for awards that were either pending or where special recommendations should be forwarded to wing headquarters for consideration and approval. One name that went forward was for Herbert Coombs, his Distinguished Flying Cross appearing in the New Year's Honours List for 1 January 1919.

Coombs elected to remain in the RAF and was posted to 216 Squadron in Egypt, flying there in a Handley Page bomber. There he found himself back on a smaller bombing machine, the De Havilland 10, which was fast gaining a bad reputation in flying circles.

He was engaged in testing aeroplanes, and on Wednesday, 9 June 1921, flying DH 10 No. E9061, without a crew member aboard, he took off at 09.30 am for a practice flight, over the Abbassia rifle range area. During this flight he crashed and suffered fatal injuries. The subsequent court of enquiry reported:

Due to an error of judgement on the part of F/O Coombs, who attempted a flat turn with insufficient flying speed, resulting in a spin from which he was unable to recover.

A.O.C. Egyptian Group concurs but considers accident was due to inexperience of the pilot on handling this type of aircraft.

Herbert Coombs DFC is buried in the Cairo War Memorial Cemetery.

* * *

Captain A. F. W. Beauchamp Proctor VC, DSO, MC & Bar, DFC, 21 June 1921

Many of the airmen whose names appear in this book are not too well known except to the aviation historian or enthusiast, but a handful will be. The one we now read about is one of them.

Andrew Frederick Weatherby Proctor, known as Anthony, was born on 4 September 1894 at Mosel Bay, a small port on the east coast of Cape Province. His father was John James Proctor, a former army officer and then a teacher. Anthony had an elder brother. Andrew was educated at his father's school at George, and then at Mafeking before becoming a boarder in the old South African College in 1911 (which became the Cape Town University). In 1913 he began studying for a diploma in engineering but his studies were, as with so many other young men, interrupted by the start of the First World War.

On 1 October 1914 he enlisted into the Duke of Edinburgh's Own Rifles, despite his diminutive height of only five foot two inches, becoming No. 6348 Signaller Proctor, A. W., for active duty in the German South-West Africa campaign. This early experience was fought against the elements rather than any German opposition. In 1915 he moved to the South African Field Telegraph and Postal Corps, before being demobilised in August.

Captain A. W. Beauchamp Proctor VC, DSO, MC and Bar, DFC, BSc.

Returning to his schooling he passed his Third Year Studies but decided now was the time to return to active duty. He was recruited by Captain A. M. Miller DSO, an RFC officer sent to South Africa to gather eligible men interested in flying. In March 1917 he became an air mechanic, 3rd class, and soon found himself on a ship for England to undergo flight training. As he was leaving, his father suggested he added the name Beauchamp before his surname, knowing that young men of that era often tried to show a double-barrelled name for effect. His father said: 'the English like that.' It was also thought appropriate to drop the Germanic sounding name of Frederick, so within the RFC he became known as Andrew Weatherby Beauchamp Proctor, although on occasion this was written as Beauchamp-Proctor.

He began training at South Farnborough in March, and then Oxford School of Military Aeronautics at Oxford the following month, followed by flight training in May at Castle Bromwich. Further training at Netheravon and the Central Flying School brought him to 'wings' standard by July, following which he was posted to the newly formed No. 84 Squadron at Beaulieu, Hampshire by the 29th. His squadron was equipped with SE5A fighters and his mechanics needed to adjust seat and instruments in the cockpits of the machines he flew due to his height.

He and his squadron moved to France in September, but although he had a few combats as the year ran down, his first official kill did not occur until 3 January 1918 when he downed a two-seater observation aircraft 'out of control'. In February he scored four times, four more in March, and his tenth came in April. On 17 March he scored at least three enemy fighters in one action. May 1918 proved his most productive so far, and he was known by now as being a natural fighter pilot. On 31 May his score had risen to twenty-one, all but two being fighters. The award of the Military Cross was gazetted on 22 June:

Beauchamp Proctor with some of 84 Squadron. Left to right: Lt. Simpson, Capt. S.W. Highwood DFC, Proctor, Lt. J. E. Boudwin USAS.

For conspicuous gallantry and devotion to duty. When on offensive patrol he observed an enemy two-seater plane attempting to cross our lines. He engaged it and opened fire, with the result that it fell on its side and crashed to earth. On a later occasion, when on patrol, he observed three enemy scouts attacking one of our bombing machines. He attacked one of these, after firing 100 rounds into it, it fell over on its back and was seen to descend in that position from 5,000 feet. He then attacked another group of hostile scouts, one of which he shot down completely out of control, and another crumpled up and crashed to earth. In addition to these, he destroyed another hostile machine, and shot down three completely out of control. He has at all times displayed the utmost dash and initiative, and is a patrol leader of great merit and courage.

Proctor continued in this aggressive fashion through the summer of 1918, with seven victories in June, four of them balloons, giving him a taste for downing these dangerous targets as they hung suspended not far behind the German front lines, their crews ranging artillery fire and observing Allied troop movements. After a spot of leave in July, he returned to claim fifteen further victories during August, four of them balloons. He received a Bar to his MC:

For conspicuous gallantry and devotion to duty when leading offensive patrols. He has lately destroyed three enemy machines, driven down one other completely out of control and carried out valuable work in attacking enemy troops and transport on the ground from low altitudes. He has done splendid service.

Oddly, this citation appeared in the *London Gazette* for 16 September, but by then he had been awarded the Distinguished Flying Cross, gazetted on 2 July 1918:

A brilliant and fearless leader of our offensive patrols. His formation has destroyed thirteen enemy machines and brought down thirteen more out of control in a period of a few months. On a recent morning his patrol of five aeroplanes attacked an enemy formation of thirty machines and was successful in destroying two of them. In the evening he again attacked an enemy formation with great dash, destroying one machine and forcing two others to collide, resulting in their destruction.

During September he flamed four balloons, and in the first eight days of October, he destroyed three more and shot down three Fokker DVIIs and a Rumpler two-seater, which brought his overall score to fifty-four, nineteen of these being balloons. His amazing run of victories stalled after downing the Rumpler on 8 October, for flying home he was hit by ground fire and wounded in the arm, but managed to fly back to his base. He was invalided back to England and to the Northumberland Hospital near Newcastle-upon-Tyne.

The award of the DSO was already in the pipeline, and this came through, gazetted on 2 November. Although welcome, it was about to be over-shadowed by the award of the Victoria Cross, promulgated in the *London Gazette* for 30 November. The citations for these two awards read:

A fighting pilot of great skill, and a splendid leader. He rendered brilliant service on the 22nd August, when his Flight was detailed to neutralise hostile balloons. Having shot down one balloon in flames, he attacked the occupants of five others in succession with machine-gun fire, compelling the occupants in each case to take to parachutes. He then drove down another balloon to within fifty feet of the ground, when it burst into flames. In all he has accounted for thirty-three enemy machines and seven balloons.

Between August 8th, 1918 and October 8th, 1918, this officer proved himself victor in twenty-six decisive combats, destroying twelve enemy kite balloons, ten enemy aircraft, and driving down four other enemy aircraft completely out of control.

Between October 1st, 1918 and October 5th, 1918, he destroyed two enemy scouts, burnt three enemy kite balloons and drove down one enemy scout completely out of control.

On October 1st, 1918, in a general engagement with about twenty-eight machines, he crashed one Fokker biplane near Fontaine and a second near Ramicourt; on October 2nd he burnt a hostile balloon; on October 5th, the third hostile balloon near Bohain.

On October 8th, while flying home at a low altitude, after destroying an enemy two-seater near Maretz, he was painfully wounded in the arm by machine-gun fire, but, continuing, he landed safely at his aerodrome, and after making his report was admitted to hospital.

In all he has proved himself conqueror of over fifty-four foes, destroyed twenty-two enemy machines, sixteen enemy kite balloons, and driven down sixteen enemy aircraft completely out of control.

Captain Beauchamp-Proctor's work in attacking enemy troops on the ground and in reconnaissance during the withdrawal following the battle of St. Quentin from March 21st, and during the victorious advance of our Armies commencing August 8th, has been almost unsurpassed in its brilliancy, and, as such has made an impression on those serving in his squadron and those around him that will not be easily forgotten.

Proctor with 84's CO, Major W. Sholto Douglas MC.

Capt. Beauchamp-Proctor was awarded the Military Cross on 22nd June 1918; D.F. Cross 2nd July 1918, Bar to M.C. on 16th September 1918, and Distinguished Service Order on 2nd November 1918.

Discharged from hospital in March 1919 he was sent to the USA on a four-month lecture tour before returning to England, qualifying as a seaplane pilot, and being granted a permanent commission in the RAF. He received his VC from the king at Buckingham Palace in November 1919. Proctor was also given a year's leave in South Africa in order that he might complete his BSc degree in engineering.

Back in England he was posted to No. 24 Squadron and attended an engineering course at RAF Henlow. At this time an RAF pageant was being arranged, an event which developed into annual RAF displays during the interwar years. Proctor was chosen to be one of the demonstration pilots, his role being that of attacking a kite balloon.

On 21 June 1921, flying a Sopwith Snipe (E8220) he was practising for the display, which he started with a loop. As the Snipe became inverted at the top of this manoeuvre, it suddenly fell away into a vicious inverted spin, which continued unchecked into a Wiltshire meadow. It was thought that during this final manoeuvre he was pushed upwards in his harness, and the cushion necessary for him to sit on because of his height slipped forward and jammed his controls. Unable to get into his normal flying position he suffered the final agony of not being able to do anything about his spinning nosedive.

His body was returned to South Africa by sea where it was afforded a state funeral, then sent by train to Mafeking and its final resting place. He was 26 years of age.

*   *   *

Captain W. E. Shields DFC & Bar, 1 August 1921

Born in Toronto, Canada, 15 October 1892, William Ernest Shields, known as 'Will', was the son of W. H. Shields. A later address found him in Lipton, Saskatchewan. Not particularly tall of stature, his attestation papers note his height as five foot five inches. He did not, like Anthony Proctor (above), let that stop him becoming a successful fighting pilot.

Leaving school, he was occupied as a grain buyer before the war until he joined the Canadian Expeditionary Force on 23 March 1915, becoming a private with the 46th Infantry Battalion. His choice of arms, however, was an aeroplane, so he joined the RFC and, completing his flight training in England, went to France, posted to No. 41 Squadron, which flew SE5A fighters.

He began scoring on 12 June 1918 and by the war's end had achieved twenty-four combat victories, including the destruction of five German kite balloons. On 3 July he claimed three Pfalz DIII fighters in one dogfight. On 21 September, in a scrap with Fokker DVIIs, two of these collided, credited as his victories fifteen and sixteen. He was rewarded with the Distinguished Flying Cross and Bar, the first gazetted on 2 November 1918:

Captain W. E. Shields DFC & Bar.

A gallant officer who inspires others by his courage and dash. In six weeks he destroyed six enemy aircraft and drove down three others out of control. On one occasion he, single-handed, engaged three scouts, driving down two of them.

The Bar to this DFC appeared in the *London Gazette* on 8 February 1919:

Bold in attack and skilful in manoeuvre, this officer is conspicuous by his success and daring in aerial combats. On 22nd September, when on offensive patrol, he was attacked by fourteen Fokkers; he succeeded in shooting down one. On another occasion he was attacked by six scouts and destroyed one of these. In all since 28th June, this officer has accounted for fourteen enemy aircraft.

With the war over, he returned to his native Canada but continued to fly. Living in Portage la Prairie, Manitoba, he moved to High River, Alberta, after taking a position with the Dominion Air Patrol, becoming an acting sub-station superintendent. They flew air patrols, watching out for forest fires over the vast eastern Rocky Mountains, including the Red Deer area. On 22 June 1921 he married a Miss Nicholson of Andover, New Brunswick.

Just a few weeks later, on 1 August 1921, Shields and a wireless operator, G. H. Harding, were going to fly a patrol west of Red Deer, taking off at 07.37 am. Their aircraft had only reached some fifty feet when it side-slipped into a nosedive and crashed. Harding only received minor injuries but Shields suffered a fracture to the back of his skull, expiring a few minutes after being pulled from the wreckage. He was 28 years old.

*   *   *

Flight Lieutenant O. M. Sutton MC, 16 August 1921

Oliver Manners Sutton was the fourth and youngest son of Algernon Charles and Mrs Winifred Alice Sutton (née Fell) of Tunbridge Wells, Kent, although he was born in Chidham, Sussex, on 13 March 1896, and later lived in Chesterfield, Derbyshire. Sutton had a sister as well as three brothers. He received his education at Tonbridge School between 1910 and 1913, and at the Central Technical College in South Kensington during the last year before the First World War began, as an engineering student. He enlisted into the 19th (2nd Public School) Battalion, Royal Fusiliers, in September 1914, and commissioned into the 3rd (Reserve) Battalion, South Lancashire Regiment, and seconded into the 1st Battalion of the Loyal North Lancashire Regiment, serving in the trenches in France from May 1915. However he was both gassed and wounded in September on the first day of the Battle of Loos and the next month, after initial hospital treatment, he was evacuated to England.

Flight Lieutenant O. M. Sutton DFC.

Having recovered, he transferred into the Royal Flying Corps in July 1916, trained to become a pilot, and received his Royal Aero Club Certificate on 23 September. By October 1916 he was back in France with 21 Squadron, flying both as a pilot and observer in BE2-type reconnaissance and artillery observation machines over the Somme area. After a period on these corps duties he managed a transfer onto single-seat Scouts, joining No. 54 Squadron that was equipped with Sopwith Pups. He claimed his first fighter victory on 2 April 1917, a German two-seater driven down 'out of control'. In May he claimed two more hostile machines, another two-seater crashed on 11 May and then an Albatros Scout on the 24th. The second two-seater was shared with five other pilots, but the Scout was an unusual claim. In a dogfight he suddenly found this German pilot heading straight for him and it was only at the last moment he avoided a direct collision. His right-hand top wing hit the Albatros, the German machine then disintegrated in the air, and Sutton managed to get down safely. The enemy pilot was Leutnant Willi Schunke of Jasta 20, who was killed.

On the first day of June, Sutton destroyed another Albatros and possibly a second 'out of control'. June 3rd saw another Scout go down out of control and, two days later, yet another. On the 6th he destroyed another Albatros DIII Scout, which brought his score to between six or eight. These actions brought him the Military Cross, gazetted on 26 July:

> *For conspicuous gallantry and devotion to duty. On at least eight separate occasions he showed great determination in attacking hostile aircraft destroying them or driving them down out of control, and he has also done very good work in other flights preventing hostile aircraft from getting on the tails of other machines. On one occasion, though his gun jammed, he dived three times and drove off an enemy machine.*

By mid-June he had completed his time with 54 Squadron and returned to England to spend time as a flight instructor, with both 91 and 93 Training Squadrons. During the summer of 1918 he was posted overseas to the Italian Front, where he took command of a flight of Sopwith Camels in No. 28 Squadron, in 14 Wing, flying on the Piave Front. On 15 August he shot down an enemy fighter out of control, bringing his score to nine. He continued to lead his flight until he was wounded in action on 3 November, just over a week before the Armistice.

The year of 1919 found him in Germany as part of the Inter-Allied Commission Control, and that August he was granted a permanent commission in the RAF. The following year he became a test pilot, with the rank of flight lieutenant, flying a variety of aeroplanes at RAF Martlesham Heath, Suffolk. On 16 August 1921

The Bristol Braemar II (C4297) in which Sutton was killed on 16 August 1921.

he was down to make a test flight in a large, three-winged, twin-engined Bristol Braemar aircraft (C4297). During take-off he appeared to lose control of all forward momentum, swung to one side and collided with an aircraft hangar. Both he and his passenger, 21-year-old Aircraftman First Class Charles Sheridan, were killed. Oliver Sutton is buried in the south-west corner of St. Michael's Churchyard, Withyham, Sussex. He was 25.

Sutton had been behind the invention of the Sutton Harness, used by the RAF. According to fellow 54 Squadron pilot, Oliver Stewart, he and Sutton had been the first to experiment with Sutton's invention, that kept the upper body more secure in case of a crash and kept the pilot securely in his seat during inverted manoeuvres. The first examples were made by squadron fitters and riggers to Sutton's instructions and used operationally by 54's pilots. With only a few modifications, the harness was used continually by RAF pilots until the arrival of the ejector seat.

*   *   *

Captain E. R. Tempest MC, DFC, 7 December 1921

Edmund Roger Tempest was the third son of William Francis & Florence Helen O'Rourke Tempest of Ackworth Grange, Ackworth, Yorkshire, born on 30 October 1894. Edmund's famous elder brother, Wulstan Joseph Tempest (born 1890), would be awarded the Distinguished Service Order in October 1916 for famously shooting down the Zeppelin L31, and then won the Military Cross in January 1917 for other work on Home Defence duties with the Royal Flying Corps.

Captain E. R. Tempest MC, DFC.

Edmund and his brother were both farming in Saskatchewan, Canada, when the First War began, but they returned home, both boys being gazetted as second lieutenants to the 6th Battalion, King's Own Yorkshire Light Infantry, in November, although Edmund quickly transferred to the Royal Flying Corps. Wulstan went with his regiment to France, seeing action in the battles of

A DH10 bomber.

Hooge and Loos in 1915. By late 1915 Edmund had become a pilot, achieving his Royal Aero Club Certificate No. 1604 on 18 August. Posted to France, he began flying BE2cs with No. 6 Squadron, and the following summer flew with 29 and then 15 Squadrons. At the beginning of July 1917 he moved again, this time to No. 64 Squadron, a unit equipped with DH5 fighters. These machines, as already mentioned, had an unusual back-stagger upper wing arrangement, not universally liked as the pilot's head poked out between the upper wings.

Edmund shot down his first enemy aircraft on 30 November, an Albatros DV scout over Bourlon Wood, and soon afterwards the squadron changed its equipment to the more effective SE5A fighter. In March 1918, he began to score victories in earnest and by the end of April his total reached eight. Scoring steadily during May, June and July, his score rose to twelve. The award of the Military Cross came in May, his citation reading:

For conspicuous gallantry and devotion to duty. He attacked a formation of seven enemy machines, firing on one from a distance of only a few feet and destroying it. On another occasion with his patrol he engaged 13 enemy machines. Though both of his guns were out of action, he continued fighting for 15 minutes in order to enable the rest of his patrol to keep up the fight. Having driven off the enemy, he brought his patrol back safely. He showed splendid courage and initiative.

By this time he had become a proficient patrol leader, commanding the squadron's A Flight, and with a further five victories in August he brought his overall score to seventeen, of which twelve were categorised as destroyed and the other five classed as 'out of control'. He now received the Distinguished Flying Cross (*London Gazette* 2 November 1918). The citation read:

Since March this officer has destroyed nine enemy machines. A daring and most capable officer, who never hesitates to engage the enemy. By brilliant leadership he achieves success with the minimum of loss.

At the end of the First World War, many hundreds of men who had seen action during the war years were more than happy to return to civilian life, but there were also many who wished to continue flying. A large number who applied were unlucky because the RAF had to quickly downsize, but several of course needed to be retained and remained in the service of their country and the Royal Air Force. Edmund Tempest, with his war record, was among them. For a time post-war he flew at Martlesham, as a test pilot with the experimental establishment there.

By 1920 he was sent overseas. Britain was to be engaged in a number of areas of unrest in the 1920s and 1930s, Russia, the North West Frontier in India, Mesopotamia (now known as Iraq), Waziristan, and so on. The RAF was tasked with supporting ground forces whose job it was to suppress rebellious native tribesmen and other dissident factions within the bounds of Britain's Empire. Tempest ended up as a bomber pilot, firstly in Egypt with No. 216 Squadron, equipped with DH10 twin-engined aeroplanes, but then in January 1921 he was sent to No. 6 Squadron to fly the Bristol F2b two-seat fighter-reconnaissance-bombing aircraft, based at Baghdad West. In the recent war the Bristol Fighter had made its name in air-fighting over France, but had now changed its role to cover all manner of operational demands made on the service.

It was also interesting that Tempest had now returned to his old squadron from 1916. He came to 6 Squadron as a flight commander and arrived with the reputation of being a pilot of exceptional ability. The downside was that he was far from pleased at leaving 216, whose DH10s, as far as he was concerned, had a far better performance than the Bristols. He soon became known as 'Tempo' on the squadron.

While the squadron had to make a number of raids upon dissident tribesmen, it also flew demonstration flights over native encampments or small towns, in order to show them the power of the RAF should they try to start any trouble, and Tempest led some detachments to various parts of the country in this role, such as to Sulaimaniya in Kurdistan. Shortly before Christmas 1921, a DH10 from his old squadron arrived at Baghdad, bringing the mail from Cairo. Unluckily, the pilot, when ground testing his machine, had stuck out an arm from the cockpit whereupon the propeller had hacked off a fingertip. With the pilot incapacitated for a few days, Tempest saw the opportunity of flying his beloved DH10 back to Cairo, and also the opportunity to visit his old pals.

On 17 December, therefore, he decided to fly an air test with the bomber prior to arranging the trip to Cairo. One of the senior pilots with 6 Squadron at this time was Flight Lieutenant D. D'Arcy Greig DFC who, upon hearing of this, asked Tempo if he could have a ride in the De Havilland, to which Tempo readily agreed. Ordinarily, the DH10 had a crew of three, but there was only a need for the pilot on a test flight, plus anyone keen for a flip. With Tempo in the pilot's seat, D'Arcy Greig settled himself down on the seat in the rear, rather than be exposed to the slipstream by sitting in the forward gunner's position.

Shortly before midday, Tempest took the DH10 up and cruised around for about fifteen minutes before the engines were throttled back and a landing approach begun. D'Arcy Greig later recorded:

> *The leeward side of the airfield was approached in a cross wind glide, a final and rather steep left-hand gliding turn into wind being made at an altitude which I estimated as being around 200 feet. I did not feel happy about the final turn and had the impression that Tempo had left it a bit late. We had reached the stage of flattening out for the touch down, the left wing was still depressed and we had a pronounced drift to starboard. It was then that I realised that unless the engines were immediately opened up, a crash was inevitable. I reckoned that we would hit with the port landing wheel and wing tip first, swipe the undercarriage off and slither to a stop, to the accompaniment of all the usual sounds of rending timber and metal.*
>
> *The initial stages of the crash followed this pattern, but the slither came to an abrupt stop, the machine tilted vertically on its nose, throwing me half out of my cockpit. I would have come completely out but a portion of broken aeroplane caught me in the back, pinning my body firmly against the Scarff gun mounting. There was a sudden 'woomf' and my world was transformed into a sea of flame. By merciful providence my feet found a solid footing and I pressed down with force and shot through the fire and dropped over the centre of the machine and onto the ground.*

Greig's coat was on fire so he ran, as he put it, like a stag, frantically taking the burning garment off. Only then did he look back at the raging inferno, hoping that

Tempo was dead and not still alive amidst the mass of flames. But to his horror he suddenly saw his friend emerge from the flames like an animated torch. Greig yelled for him to throw himself to the ground as he retrieved his smouldering coat, then, running to the burning figure, did his utmost to smother the flames, but it was hopeless. Eventually the fire tender and ambulance raced up, another squadron pilot jumping down and spraying Tempest with an extinguisher. By now Tempest was sitting up, supporting himself with one hand; every stitch of clothing had burnt away, except his flying helmet, goggles and field boots.

Tempest must have known he was finished for he kept calling for a priest both in the ambulance and at the hospital, his voice little more than a hoarse whisper. Mercifully he died six hours later. He was buried in the Baghdad (North Gate) War Cemetery. He was 27 years old.

Chapter Three

1922–23

Lieutenant H. B. Richardson MC, 14 February 1922
Lieutenant F. J. Ortweiler MC, BA, 14 February 1922

These two former fighter pilots had survived the First World War and gone into civil aviation, although they had very different war experiences. Herbert Brian Richardson came from Ashford, Kent, born 27 May 1898, although he was living in Oxford as the war began. He was the third son of Walter M. and Ellen Richardson of Eastholme House, Ashford, his father being a brewer and maltster. Richardson was educated at Oxford High School between 1910 and 1914, and enlisted as a private soldier into the Oxford and Bucks Light Infantry, but after a brief month in France in September 1916, moved to become a trooper with the Queen's Own Oxfordshire Hussars (TF), and gazetted second lieutenant to the Royal Flying Corps in June 1917.

Lieutenant H. B. Richardson MC (left) with Major A. D. Carter DSO & Bar on the right.

Once trained, he was sent to France to join No. 24 Squadron, flying SE5A fighters from 14 November and despite a slow beginning, soon became a proficient air fighter, achieving fifteen combat victories between February and April 1918. These included six Pfalz DIII Scouts, two Albatros DV Scouts, three Fokker Triplanes and four two-seaters. His reward was the announcement of the Military Cross, promulgated in the *London Gazette* on 22 June. The citation began with the almost obligatory sentence:

For conspicuous gallantry and devotion to duty. While on patrol he attacked a formation of eight enemy aircraft, one of which he destroyed. On another occasion he engaged two enemy two-seater machines, and destroyed one of them. He has destroyed six enemy machines and driven down five others out of control, and has done valuable work in attacking enemy troops on the ground. He has consistently displayed great courage and skill.

Three of his claims were in a single fight which lasted five minutes above Bellicourt against a gaggle of Pfalz Scouts.

Following a period as an instructor, the war ended and he left the service, but continued his interest in flying. He was granted a short service commission on 23 September 1920 which he resigned on 18 May 1921. Still associated with flying, his path would cross with that of F. J. Ortweiler early in 1922, by which time Richardson was working for the Spanish government as a flying instructor. He had also married.

*   *   *

Frederick John Ortweiler, as the name might suggest, had German parents. They were Simon and Matilda Ortweiler, who lived at 13 Cavendish Road, Brondesbury, London NW6, and he was born on 25 February 1898. His parents had come to England in 1886, becoming naturalised the year before Frederick was born.

Lieutenant F. J. Ortweiler MC.

Educated at Brondesbury Preparatory School, and then at St. Paul's, Westminster (1911-1916), he felt it his duty to serve his parents' adopted country's war effort upon leaving school in December 1916. He immediately joined the Royal Flying Corps, and it is interesting to learn that within the Public Archives at Kew there is a note in his personal file suggesting that British Intelligence officers had become satisfied that the senior Ortweilers were not British 'sympathisers' so their son could be trusted to fight against the Germans.

Accepted as a flight cadet in March 1917, he received a commission in May, gained his RAeC Certificate No. 4681 on 19 May and, having achieved his 'wings', was confirmed as a flying officer that August. Prior to going to France he was with 69 and 81 Training Squadrons before overseas service saw him posted to No. 29 Squadron in September, where he would fly Nieuport Scouts. People often say the average life of a pilot on the Western Front was about three weeks, and this is more or less the time Ortweiler survived combat until he was brought down on 16 October, by the German ace Erwin Böhme, his twentieth victory.

The German's fire must have only damaged the Nieuport's engine, for he was able to glide to earth and make a good forced landing, after which he was captured by German soldiers. He was taken to Lendelede for interrogation which was the start of being held in various prisoner of war camps, including Karlsruhe and Bruf, before finally arriving at Halle on 16 December. No doubt he had wondered if his RFC colleagues had thought he had defected because of his ancestry, and if so he quickly made a point of being a nuisance to his captors by making continued efforts to escape.

His first break for freedom occurred on 7 January 1918 but he was recaptured near the Dutch border the following day. Detained at Aachen and then imprisoned in Halle's civil jail, he was later moved to Fort Zorndorf and finally to Clausthal. His second escape was from here in April, but again he was retaken and moved to Holzminden in July and Stralsund in August. His third escape, on 12 October, was successful. For this and his previous efforts he received the Military Cross, gazetted on 16 December, in what was called the *Escaper's Gazette*:

> *… in recognition of gallantry in escaping from captivity while Prisoners of War.*

Ortweiler's Camel, marked as Eduard Böhme's twentieth victory.

Returning home in April 1919 he took a shortened degree course at King's College, Cambridge, gaining a BA in 1920. Deciding a career in aviation was his way forward he became chief pilot at the Cambridge School of Flying. He flew an SE5A in the 1921 Derby aerial display and got a job representing the De Havilland Aircraft Company, travelling to Spain for the aeroplane manufacturer on several occasions. On 14 February 1922, he was a passenger in a Bristol machine that crashed at Cuatro Vientos aerodrome near Madrid.

People watching from the ground reported that the Bristol appeared to stall during a steep turn over the airfield and then dived into the ground. Ortweiler and two others on board were killed, one of the latter being Brian Richardson MC. Ortweiler's body was returned to England for burial. He was eleven days short of his twenty-third birthday, while Richardson was 22 years old.

*   *   *

If Ortweiler had felt any guilt about his loss in combat, this would no doubt have been accentuated by the way he was captured. With his engine either knocked out or at least spluttering its last, and with a German fighter behind him, Ortweiler held up his hands and waved at the German as he descended. Not only did he descend safely, but actually landed on the German airfield at Rumbeke.

Upon his return from Germany, Ortweiler, like every other returning RAF airman was given a sheet of Gestetnered paper, with a number of questions about their capture. He would not be the only one to report that once down inside enemy lines he had managed to set light to his machine so it would not be taken. Ortweiler said this too, never thinking that much later, photographs of the undamaged and captured Nieuport would find their way to England. Erwin Böhme had described the events in a letter to his girlfriend:

His name is Mr Ortweiler. His family comes from Frankfurt and he is now biding his time in a German PoW camp. I recently came upon an English Nieuport single-seater at the front, in which our friend was sitting. Naturally I invited him to pay us a visit. As he did not promptly descend, I became somewhat more urgent in my efforts to compel him to descend. Yet, as he continually waved at me 'with his hands', I did not want to do anything to him. Then he landed safe and sound at our airfield. We laughed until we were blue in the face. Moreover, it was my victory number 20.

*   *   *

Captain J. B. Fox MC, 3 March 1922

The RAF were still flying operations in the Middle East post-war, and losing people to dissident tribesmen, and would do so for a few more years. Another casualty was John Bertram Fox, the son of the Assistant Postmaster General of Ceylon (now Sri Lanka), while employed in the Indian Civil Service. Born in July 1893, he was educated both there and at the Dollar Institution, Dollar, Scotland, until 1911. Not long afterwards he went to Canada to work but with war beginning in August 1914 he immediately joined the Canadian Infantry as a private in the Machine Gun Section of the 3rd Battalion. He served in France with the Canadian Expeditionary Force until July 1915 at which time he became a despatch rider but then responded to a call for men to join the Royal Flying Corps.

Captain J. B. Fox MC.

Accepted for pilot training in April 1917, once qualified he was off to join 55 Squadron, flying DH4 bombers. For several months he flew almost continually over the battlefront as well as bombing targets behind the lines, such as ammunition dumps, troops concentrations, railway stations, and so on. He and his observer, on one occasion in September 1917, even shot down a German fighter that was attacking them.

This event found its way into the RFC *Communiqués* (known to the rank and file as 'Comic Cuts') for 5 September:

When returning from a bomb raid, DH4s of 55 Squadron were attacked by ten EA scouts, two of which were shot down out of control; one by 2nd Lt J Heading & Lt A Sattin, and the other by 2nd Lt J Fox & 2/AM Leyland.

Raids continued, especially during the March Offensive by the Germans that pushed the British army back during Operation Michael.

In May 1918 came the announcement of the award of the Military Cross. His citation read:

For conspicuous gallantry and devotion to duty. During a period of two months he led his formation on six long distance bombing raids into enemy territory. On the last occasion, although engaged by three separate hostile formations, he dropped his bombs with excellent effect over his objective and brought the whole of his formation back to the aerodrome intact. His formation accounted for three enemy aeroplanes destroyed and four driven down out of control. He has carried out upwards of forty successful operations, his skill and leadership being of the highest order.

Airman S. L. Leyland, who came from Wallasey, Cheshire, received the Military Medal in December 1917.

John Fox was another RAF pilot who was granted a post-war commission, but sadly his career did not have long to run. In 1922 he was a pilot with No. 20 Squadron, based at Ambala, India. This unit was flying the long-serving and reliable BF2b, at a time when the RAF was engaged in the Third Afghan War. Fox was also engaged in flights over dissident tribesmen, encouraging them to follow a more peaceful way of life under British rule.

In the early spring of 1922, HRH the Prince of Wales was visiting India and on 3 March, Fox was engaged in a flight in conjunction with the Prince's tour. At 12.20 pm, some twenty-three miles from Lahore, while in formation with other squadron aircraft, Fox and another pilot collided. Fox was in BF2b E2442 with Flight Sergeant Hemmings in the rear cockpit and was hit from behind by another Bristol (H1548) flown by Flying Officer J. Buckley, with AC2 Richardson in the back. Both aircraft fell to the ground, killing all four airmen.

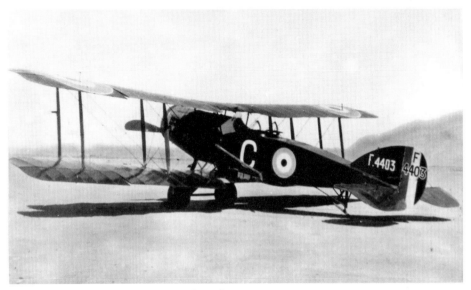

Bristol F2b of No. 20 Squadron RAF in India.

The initial court of enquiry came to the conclusion that Flying Officer Buckley was, in all probability, examining his instruments and did not see that he was running into Fox's machine ahead of him. However the AOC, RAF India, later stated that as there was no evidence to show what the actual cause of the collision was, he was unable to concur with the court's findings and decided that it be recorded as an open verdict. John Fox was 28 years old.

*   *   *

Captain W. W. Carey-Thomas MC, MiD (2), 10 March 1922

Former First World War airmen did not have to fight dissident tribesmen to run into hostile ground fire. There were troubles all over the place. William Warren Carey-Thomas was the son of Mr and Mrs Charles Carey-Thomas, and was born in Cardiff, South Wales, on 14 November 1885. Having been educated at Rossall School, Fleetwood, Lancashire, he went to South Africa in 1907, working with Rand Mines Limited, eventually becoming a senior mine official. With the coming of war he immediately volunteered to serve with South African forces in the hope that he could get into flying.

Major W. W. Carey-Thomas MC.

Along with several other like-minded men, he was sent to England in order to undertake flight training, being gazetted a second lieutenant to the RFC via the Special List on 31 July 1915. At his own expense he achieved his Royal Aero Club Certificate, No. 1918, on 15 October. This enabled him to complete his formal pilot training, being made a flying officer on 6 January 1916. His reward was a posting back to South Africa in order to join 26 (South African) Squadron in June which was operating in East Africa.

Here, Carey-Thomas served under Kenneth Reid Van de Spuy, occasionally acting as his observer (Van der Spuy was a future Major

Colonel H. A. (Pierre) van Ryneveld DSO, MC.

A DH9A aircraft.

General and a founder member of the South African Air Force). There was no comparison with operations in East Africa to that of the Western Front. For example, when Carey-Thomas was engaged on a reconnaissance in a BE2c, he ran short of petrol and decided to land on a remote emergency landing strip. He and his observer took a walk down to a nearby river in order to collect some water. As they pushed their way through long grass they suddenly came face to face with two lions. Beating a more than hasty retreat they ran back to their aircraft to spend a very uncomfortable and sleepless night listening to the sounds of wild animals all around them, clutching their revolvers.

Carey-Thomas was awarded the Military Cross for his work with 26 Squadron, gazetted on 3 June 1917. He was also twice mentioned in despatches. Completing his tour of duty with 26 Squadron, he returned to England at the beginning of 1918 but did not see further front line service.

After the war he returned again to South Africa where he joined the newly formed South African Aviation Force, which became the South African Air Force, and with the rank of major was given command of a squadron. In 1922 the country was torn apart by the Rand Industrial Revolt, in which gold miners staged an all-out strike which eventually turned to violence, bordering on civil war. As Carey-Thomas was familiar with the area around Witwatersrand from when he had been a mine official, the now Lieutenant Colonel K. R. Van der Spuy, by then a senior officer in the SAAF, assigned Carey-Thomas to make a reconnaissance on the first day of military air action, 10 March 1922. He took the rear seat in a DH9A aircraft, the pilot being Colonel Sir Pierre van Ryneveld KBE, DSO, MC.

In order to gather every bit of intelligence they could, van Ryneveld dived to a low altitude to identify what the two men thought was a 'commando of about 200 men in the trees near the corner of Brakpan.' They saw nothing positive so Carey-Thomas instructed van Ryneveld to fly lower but still nothing could be seen. However, upon looking round, van Ryneveld saw that Carey-Thomas was crumpled up in the rear cockpit, and so he quickly headed for home. Upon landing it was discovered that Carey-Thomas was dead, having been shot through the heart by a single bullet which had killed him outright. He was buried in Thaba Tshwane (Old No. 1) Military Cemetery, Pretoria. He was 36 and was the SAAF's first casualty.

*　*　*

Captain Sir R. M. Smith KCB MC & Bar, DFC & two Bars, AFC, 14 April 1922

This famous airman, Ross Macpherson Smith, came from Semaphore, Adelaide, Australia, born 4 December 1892. His father came from Scotland and his mother was Australian, from New Norcia, Western Australia, although she was the daughter of another emigrating Scotsman. He had a brother, Keith, two years his senior. Both boys received their education as boarders at Queen's School, Adelaide, and for two years at Warriston School, Moffat, in Scotland.

When war came Ross enlisted into the 3rd Light Horse Regiment and saw action at Gallipoli and Sinai against the Turks. Transferring to the Australian Flying Corps in early 1917, he first flew as an observer with No. 67 Squadron AAF, operating in Palestine and Egypt. He was soon to make an impression and his Military Cross was gazetted on 11 May:

Captain R. M. Smith MC, DFC, AFC.

*For conspicuous gallantry and devotion to duty, when his pilot descended to rescue
an officer who had been forced to land. On landing he held the enemy at bay with
his revolver, thus enabling his pilot to rescue the officer and safely fly away his
machine.*

The pilot was Lieutenant R. F. Baillieu, who also received the MC.

Smith then trained to become a pilot, which he achieved by July, and back with
67 Squadron, still with BE2 machines, took his duties seriously, not even fazed
when confronted with hostile aircraft. He was by this time known to everyone as
'Hadji'.

His squadron then became No. 1 Squadron AFC and his continued good work
resulted in a Bar to his MC:

*For conspicuous gallantry and devotion to duty. He was one of two pilots who
carried out a remarkable series of photographs in one flight, completely covering
an important area of 45 square miles. On a later occasion he successfully bombed
an important bridgehead from low altitude, and his work throughout, as well as*

Ross Smith and one of his observers, Lieutenant E. A. Mustard DFC.

his photography, has been invaluable and characterised by the most consistent gallantry.

The squadron had now re-equipped with Bristol F2b fighters which enabled more combat with enemy aircraft, and to be on better terms, indeed. Ross Smith achieved a total of eleven victories in air fighting. One victory in particular is worth mentioning, occurring on 19 October 1918. Having forced a DFW two-seater to land inside its own territory, he landed nearby. Covered by his observer's machine gun, Smith sauntered over to the enemy machine and ordered the crew out. He then set fire to the aircraft before returning to his Bristol and flew back to base. For these actions he received the DFC and two Bars, all gazetted on 8 February 1919:

During the months of June and July these officers accounted for two enemy machines, and they have been conspicuous for gallantry and initiative in attacking ground targets, frequently at very low altitudes. The keenness and fine example set by these officers cannot be over-estimated.

This was a joint citation with his observer, Lieutenant W. A. Kirk:

During the operations prior to October, 1918, he took part in numerous engagements involving flights of 150 to 200 miles, and succeeded in doing extensive damage to the enemy's hangers, railways, etc. Captain Smith displayed the most consistent gallantry and marked ability in all his work, whether bombing by night or day or in personal encounters in the air. While operating with the Sheriffian forces he destroyed one enemy machine and brought down two others out of control in the desert.

On 19th October, this officer, with Lieutenant A. V. McCann as observer, engaged and drove down an enemy two-seater. As it appeared to land intact he descended to a low altitude and, with machine-gun fire, forced the occupants to abandon the machine; he then landed alongside it, and while his observer covered the enemy officers, he set light to their machine and completely destroyed it. To have effected a landing in an unknown country, many miles in rear of the enemy's advanced troops, demanded courage and skill of a very high order.

McCann also received the DFC. Another of his observers, Lieutenant E. A. Mustard, received the DFC too, and later became a well-known figure in aviation for air surveys with the RAAF, although his wife persuaded him to change his name to Mustar. He later became the MD of Australian Transcontinental Airways.

Among his other feats, Smith was also held in high esteem by Lawrence of Arabia, and flew several occasions in support of him and his Arab forces.

Going back to Egypt, Smith made a historic flight from Cairo to Calcutta, for which he received the Air Force Cross. This brought on the idea of further long distance flights. In this he was encouraged by the announcement by the Australian Prime Minister, Billy Hughes, that an Air Race, with a prize of £10,000, would be given to the first man to fly from London to Australia in thirty days or less.

Ross Smith employed his brother Keith, also a pilot, to help make the attempt, and they persuaded the Vickers aircraft company to let them have a Vickers Vimy bomber for the race. Enlisting the help of two RAF mechanics, Sergeants Walter H. Shiers and James M. Bennett, they made the flight, starting from Hounslow, in twenty-seven days, twenty hours, landing at Darwin. They shared the prize money and both Ross and Keith were knighted KBE, gazetted on 26 December 1919. Both sergeants received Air Force Medals.

In 1922, Ross and Jim Bennett, recently commissioned, were preparing for a round-the-world flight in a Vickers Viking FB27A amphibian, but on 14 April, during a test flight, they crashed in Byfleet, Surrey, soon after taking off from Brooklands.

Ross Smith's body was transported to Australia and buried on 15 June at the North Road Cemetery, Adelaide. Brother Keith remained in aviation until his death from cancer the day before his sixty-fifth birthday in 1955.

*   *   *

The Vickers IV Viking amphibian in which Ross Smith was killed on 22 April 1922.

Flying Officer E. G. Green MC, 24 May 1922

Ernest George Green, from Jesmond, Northumberland, was born on 2 February 1892. When the war began he joined the army and was commissioned into the Royal Engineers, Signal Service (TF) on 11 December 1915. He then transferred into the Royal Flying Corps and became an observer on FE2b machines with No. 25 Squadron in November 1916, his first pilot being Second Lieutenant W. D. Matheson, but he was also assigned to others, including E. V. A. Bell and Alexander Roulstone.

Engaged in a variety of operations, including reconnaissance, aerial photography and fighting patrols, he was credited with at least four victories by the end of April 1917. For his good work he received the Military Cross, gazetted on 26 May:

> *For conspicuous gallantry and devotion to duty as an Observer. He has on several occasions brought down hostile machines and has carried out many successful photographic reconnaissances. He has at all times set a fine example of courage and initiative.*

Like many observers, he soon decided he could fly an aeroplane just as easily as his pilots were doing, so he applied and was successful in requesting flight training. Once he qualified and had been awarded his 'wings', he then returned to 25 Squadron. However his unit had exchanged its old FE 'pushers' for De Havilland 4 bombers. Green was now engaged in bombing targets behind the enemy lines. However, the German fighter pilots were always keen to engage and bring down British aeroplanes and on 3 February 1918, they succeeded in shooting down Green and his observer, Lieutenant Peter Clifford Campbell-Martin, flying DH4 No. A7873.

Taking off at 07.40 am, they had headed towards the railway sidings at Melle but were spotted by German fighters which attacked over Mariakerke. The first attack was made by some Fokker Dr.I Triplanes, Green, at the back of the formation, being hit early on. After a brief fight they had their fuel line shot through and some control wires were severed. Green was also wounded in the side by an explosive bullet which also fractured his hip. Three Albatros Scouts now joined in as Green, suffering from severe stomach and hip wounds, endeavoured to get down. His observer was also hit in the neck.

Nevertheless, Green made a successful forced landing and both he and Campbell-Martin were taken prisoner. The German pilot credited with their downfall was Leutnant Otto Löffler of Jasta *Boelcke*. It was his second victory and he would go on to achieve fifteen by the war's end. Returning from prison camp after the war, Green made the following report upon his repatriation:

I left the aerodrome at Boisdinghem, near St. Omer, at 8 am on Sunday 3 February flying a DH4 with Lieutenant P. C. Campbell-Martin as my observer. Four other similar machines completed the formation, our orders were to drop bombs on Melle railway sidings near Ghent. After crossing the lines we were followed by six German Triplanes who attacked my machine at 15,000 feet when near Ghent. I was rear machine in the formation, observer opened fire on enemy machines while I flew machine in order to give him good firing positions. After ten minutes we were cut off and surrounded by Fokker Triplanes and I dropped my bombs at this point and decided to turn for our own lines.

With my Vickers gun I attacked two enemy machines in rear. After clearing a jam in the gun and fighting again I was hit in the side by an explosive bullet which besides fracturing my hip, cut the main petrol pipes and tail adjusting wires. Two enemy Triplanes were seen to go down out of control from the fire of my Vickers gun. The result of observer's shooting are unknown to me as he was taken away immediately we landed.

A Bristol F2b.

Engine stopped owing to loss of petrol and we were forced to land near Ghent. Machine was surrounded by German soldiers who lifted me out of the cockpit and a car took me to hospital where I had an operation immediately to remove a bullet. Lieutenant Campbell-Martin was taken away to an officer's camp.

Back home, Green was given a short service commission with the Royal Engineers, but left the service on 30 September 1921. However, it seems he decided to rejoin the RAF for, on 24 May 1922, he was flying a BF2b (J6673) of No. 2 Squadron based at RAF Digby on a practice flight. In the rear cockpit was 200158 Sergeant Walter John Stivey, aged 32. For some reason Green decided to beat up the airfield but stalled the aircraft in a sharp turn near the ground and dived into the ground. Both men were killed instantly. A court of enquiry decided that due to an error of judgement, Green, during a left-hand turn, had stalled and in a dive to rectify this did not have sufficient height to do so. Green was 30 years old.

*　*　*

Flying Officer L. C. Hooton MC & Bar, MiD, 26 May 1922

The RAF's No. 6 Squadron, operating out of Baghdad in 1922, lost two First World War MC winners in three weeks, one was Flight Lieutenant F. N. 'Babe' Hudson, the second was Flying Officer Lionel Conrad Hooton.

Hooton came from Winchmore Hill, London, but had been born in Barnet, Middlesex, on 21 May 1891. Leaving school he emigrated to Canada where he worked in the Forestry Service and then took up ranching in British Columbia, also taking time to join a pre-war volunteer unit – the 88th Victoria Fusiliers. Rather than paying his own fare home, he joined the 3rd Canadian Pioneers as war in Europe was declared. In March 1915 he sailed for England and became a signaller to the Fort

Flying Officer L. C. Hooton MC in Iraq, 1922.

Garry Horse, a unit of the 5th Cavalry Division. Selected for a commission, he chose the Royal Flying Corps in May 1917, trained as an observer, and within two months was in France with No. 8 Squadron, flying in BE2 machines. It was not long before he requested pilot training and, having gained his 'wings', returned to 8 Squadron.

He and his regular observer, Russian-born Lieutenant Harry Wisnekowitz, who had become a naturalised British citizen while living in South Africa, were in the thick of the air fighting in March 1918 at the time of the German offensive known as 'Operation Michael', and on two occasions they returned to base badly shot up by ground fire in their Armstrong-Whitworth FK8 reconnaissance machine that the squadron now operated. These actions led to both men receiving the Military Cross, gazetted on 11 June:

> *For conspicuous gallantry and devotion to duty. On one occasion, during a very thick mist, he and his observer by flying very low, despite very heavy machine gun fire, succeeded in locating the enemy's position. Though their machine was hit in all the vital parts, it was flown back to the aerodrome in safety. On a later occasion, when on contact patrol during failing light, they succeeded in locating accurately the position of the enemy. They have shown the utmost gallantry and skill during recent operations, and have carried out their duties with the greatest courage and determination.*

These contact patrols were extremely dangerous missions during ground offensives, whether the army was retreating or advancing. In such fluid situations

A BF2b of 6 Squadron in Iraq.

where enemy troop locations were unclear, these sorties were flown out at low level and generally the only way to locate forward enemy soldiers was when the aircraft came under rifle fire. As may be imagined, it was imperative to know where forward elements of both Allied and hostile troops were located, especially if considering artillery fire on hostile troops.

On 7 April, this time with 2nd Lieutenant Eric Wells in the rear cockpit, Hooton again came under intense ground fire at low level and had his petrol tank holed. Other damage made the AWFK8, known as the 'Big Ack' by the airmen, almost uncontrollable, Wells having to climb out onto one wing to help stabilize it. This enabled Hooton to turn and fly back to friendly territory, where he just managed to land, 100 yards inside British lines. Hooton's luck ran out on 27 May, however, when he was wounded during a low-bombing sortie. Hooton and Wells both received decorations, Wells the MC, Hooton a Bar to his. Gazetted on 26 July the citation read:

For conspicuous gallantry and devotion to duty. When flying at a 1,000 feet his petrol tank was shot through and immediately afterwards his left aileron control was shot away. He tried to turn his machine without success, and it was side-slipping down out of control into the enemy's lines. Realising the danger, his Observer climbed out onto the right wing, enabling him to turn and land just within our lines. It was owing to his extraordinary coolness he was able to land the machine in safety. He has also done fine work on reconnaissance and in attacking enemy infantry.

Hooton also received a mention in despatches on 15 October 1918.

Lionel Hooton did not see further action, although he was attached to a Home Defence Squadron and soon after the war ended he was posted to No. 123 (Canadian) Squadron, seeing active service with the Allied Intervention Force in Russia in 1919. Remaining in the RAF, he went out to the Middle East to fly Bristol F2b aircraft in Iraq.

On 26 May 1922, shortly before midday, he was asked to test the engine of Bristol D7845. Taking off from Baghdad West airfield, with Aircraftman First Class G. T. Butler in the rear cockpit, they discovered they had a problem with the petrol flow. People on the airfield were immediately aware of a problem too as the Bristol's engine began coughing and spluttering. Everyone expected the pilot to shove the stick forward to keep up his flying speed, locate a flat patch of ground and make a forced landing – straight ahead! However, with the engine failing, Hooton made the fatal error of trying to turn back to the airfield while only at 150 feet and almost immediately the machine lost flying speed, stalled, and dived into the ground, bursting into flames as it hit. Both men died instantly. Hooton was buried with Air Force Honours at Hinaidi Cemetery three days later. He was five days short of his thirty-first birthday.

*   *   *

Flight Lieutenant F. N. Hudson MC, MiD, 6 June 1922

Another 6 Squadron casualty was Frank Neville Hudson, the son of a provisions merchant, Frank Hudson, and his wife Annie, from Beckenham, Kent, where he was born on 4 November 1897. The family later moved to Mells Lodge, Halesworth, Suffolk and Frank received his final education by attending Bradfield College, Reading, between 1912 and 1915. When war came he was accepted for military training at Sandhurst and was gazetted a second lieutenant to the 1st Battalion of the East Kent Regiment (The Buffs) but desiring to fly he was

Flight Lieutenant F. N. Hudson MC.

immediately seconded into the Royal Flying Corps. Learning to become a pilot he gained his Royal Aero Club Certificate No. 1830, on 6 October 1915, and by November he had completed his RFC flight training.

Posted as a 'founder' member of No. 15 Squadron in December he went with this unit to France, flying the BE2c aeroplanes as a corps squadron to the 2nd Army. It was not long before the danger of aerial warfare was impressed upon him, for on 19 January 1916 he was attacked by some Fokker Eindekkers and a spent cartridge case from his observer's gun jammed in an aileron. With manoeuvrability seriously restricted it was only the timely intervention of a friendly FE8 fighter that drove off their attackers and Hudson was able to get back home. This action was not written up in the RFC *Communiqués*, but another encounter on 7 February was:

2/Lt Hudson and 2/Lt [E. A.] Pack (BE2c 15 Sqn) on escort to 2nd Army reconnaissance, were attacked by one Fokker, firing through his propeller, about 50 yards in the rear. The Fokker was eventually driven off.

By now 'Babe' Hudson (as he was called) was in the forefront of many dangerous actions over the front lines. He had already been forced to land a crippled BE following engine damage from Fokker attack on 25 January, and then on 21 February Hudson received a wound in the head by a lump of shrapnel from anti-aircraft fire during a reconnaissance mission. As a reward for these and other actions he received the Military Cross, the citation reading:

For conspicuous gallantry and skill on several occasions, notably when, although severely wounded in the head, he successfully completed his aerial reconnaissance. After re-crossing the lines and landing at an aerodrome, he at once lost consciousness. This young officer is only eighteen years of age, but has many times driven off enemy machines and twice forced them to the ground.

Due to his age and youthful looks, it was little wonder he was known as 'Babe'. Hudson recovered from his injury and was back with the squadron in June 1916 and was soon being recorded in the *Communiqués* once more, on 26 September,

2/Lt Hudson and 2/Lt Manville, 15 Sqn, on three separate occasions engaged and dispersed small bodies of infantry with machine-gun fire. Many were seen to fall.

27 September,

2/Lt Buckingham with Lt Clark, Capt Binning with Lt Carre, 2/Lt Hudson with 2/Lt Bradford, and 2/Lt Binson with 2/Lt Laird, all of 15 Sqn, attacked infantry, horse and motor transport, from heights varying from 1,000 to 2,000 feet with machine-gun fire.

and 14 November:

Capt Hudson and 2/Lt Laird, 15 Sqn, brought artillery fire to bear, and fired with their Lewis guns, on 2 parties of hostile infantry in trenches.

Then he was again hit in the head by AA fire, rendering him unconscious. Fortunately he regained his senses with urgent shouts from his observer just before a crash seemed inevitable, and he managed to recross the lines safely.

Recovering from this near disaster, he received a posting to a fighter squadron, No. 54, which flew Sopwith Pups. Now a flight commander by the end October 1916, Hudson achieved six aerial combat victories between 27 January and 11 July 1917.

Two days after his last victory, 13 July, he and his flight were escorting a reconnaissance aircraft over the Belgian town of Bruges. AA fire exploded nearby and Hudson's engine was hit and promptly stopped. As he began to glide down, German aircraft of Jasta 20 attacked, and a defenceless Hudson was hit and wounded by Leutnant Gerhard Wilhelm Fleckern, south-east of Haan. Hudson was forced to go down, crash-landing on a beach inside enemy territory, and taken prisoner. It was some time before his family heard that he was alive and a prisoner, locked up in Karlsruhe Prisoner of War camp. Even then he was a plague to his enemies, becoming quite a nuisance to his captors.

He was repatriated back to England shortly before Christmas 1918 and was later given a mention in despatches:

> … *for gallantry while a Prisoner of War in escaping, or attempting to escape, from captivity, or for valuable services rendered in the Prison Camps of the Enemy.*

After the war Frank Hudson was able to remain in the Royal Air Force (surviving an influenza scare in March 1919) and, like so many others, was soon in receipt of a posting to the Middle East where he was sent to No. 6 Squadron based at Baghdad East, flying Bristol F2b fighter-reconnaissance aircraft. For two years he flew against dissident tribesmen in and around Mesopotamia, but his luck finally ran out on 31 May 1922. This day he had flown out to an army column marching against hostile elements near the Hawraman mountain range, taking a photographer from HQ at Baghdad with him. Coming back, several people on the ground saw Hudson making his landing approach in a series of right S-turns, the final one being carried out just short of the airfield boundary and at low level. The Bristol was just about at its maximum angle of bank, and pointing dead into wind when it stalled, hitting the ground with a sickening crash on its port wing tip. As rescuers arrived, thinking both men were dead, they were surprised to discover both alive but unconscious, Hudson having a very nasty, triangular, depressed fracture of the skull right in the centre of his forehead.

It was thought that Hudson had not allowed for the height of the airfield, which at 3,600 feet above sea level in a hot climate made the air particularly thin, and with the sub-tropical temperature on this hot sunny day, reduced the buoyancy of the air around him, thus raising the stalling speed well beyond normal. In England it would have not been a problem, but out in the desert climate it proved fatal. Babe Hudson was on the critical list and lingered for six days, but finally passed away on the morning of 6 June and was buried that same evening. He was 24 years old.

* * *

Flight Lieutenant R. St.C. McClintock MC, 22 June 1922

Ronald St.Clair McClintock came from County Carlow, Ireland, born on 13 July 1892, the son of Arthur George Florence McClintock JP DL and Mrs Susan McClintock (née Heywood-Collins). He was the McClintocks' fifth and youngest son and was probably born in Rathvinden. His grandfather was Lieutenant Colonel G. A. J. McClintock of the 52nd Regiment of Foot and the Sligo Rifles, while his great-grandfather, John McClintock, had been Sergeant-at-Arms to the Irish House of Commons and High Sheriff of Louth.

When war came, Ronald was working in Ceylon and enlisted as a rifleman in the Ceylon Planters' Rifles, his unit arriving in Egypt on 17 November 1914. Just eleven days later he was commissioned into 'A' Battery, 3rd West Lancashire Brigade of the Royal Field Artillery, as a second lieutenant. After service in the Middle East, he volunteered

Flight Lieutenant R. St.C. McClintock MC.

for the Royal Flying Corps, and became an observer with No. 2 Squadron in France, from December 1915, and was confirmed as such in April 1916, before requesting pilot training.

Once a pilot and having completed his training he was posted to No. 64 Squadron in July 1917, becoming a flight commander due to his previous operational experience. The squadron was equipped with DH5 fighters, the much-maligned machine that had back-stagger top wings. The squadron saw limited aerial fighting, being mainly used in the ground attack role, especially during the Battle of Cambrai that November. However, early in 1918 he was moved to No. 3 Squadron, flying Sopwith Camels. During March and especially during the build-up and then the eventual German March offensive, McClintock claimed five enemy aircraft shot down, starting with an LVG two-seater on 10 March, two German scouts on the 23rd, another C-type the next day, and finally an Albatros DV on 2 April. For his work he received the Military Cross, gazetted on 22 June:

For conspicuous gallantry and devotion to duty. On one occasion he shot down two enemy machines and on the following day he attacked and shot down a hostile two-

seater machine at a height of 100 feet. He has led upwards of forty patrols and has performed much valuable work on low-flying reconnaissance and bombing patrols. As a flight commander he has been untiring in his care of personnel and machines, and as a patrol leader he has displayed the greatest courage and resource.

On 20 April 1918, his squadron commander, Major R. Raymond Barker MC, was shot down and killed by Manfred von Richthofen, following which McClintock was given command of the squadron, a post he held until the end of the war. By this time he had been married, on 20 December 1916, to Mary (Molly) Gordon Laird, a union that produced a son, John Arthur Peter McClintock.

McClintock decided to remain in the Royal Air Force after the war, and by 1922 he was flying with No. 1 School of Technical Training. On 22 June 1922, he took off in a Sopwith Snipe (F2409), a machine that is recorded as being recently on the strength of No. 24 Squadron and used with the award-winning relay flying team at the 1922 Hendon Pageant. This day, at RAF Northolt, Middlesex, shortly after 1 pm, McClintock was killed in this machine. The RAF casualty record says that he fell from his machine having probably forgotten to fasten his safety harness, although another source suggests the Snipe collapsed during a manoeuvre at height and McClintock fell to his death. It was noted that the weather conditions were exceptionally bumpy and this is possibly why he was thrown out, but the

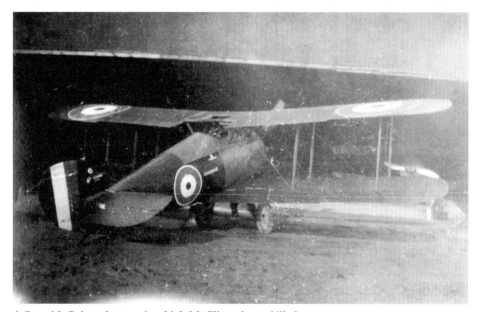

A Sopwith Snipe, the type in which McClintock was killed.

machine failing in the air seems more plausible. The Snipe had been the machine usually flown by Flight Lieutenant Francis L. Luxmore, another wartime fighter pilot who would receive the DFC in Iraq in 1924.

Whatever the cause, McClintock was killed, less than a month short of his thirtieth birthday and just four months after the birth of his second child, Pamela May, in February. Had the Snipe been over-strained during its acrobatic time with 24 Squadron? Was that why it was preferable to say he merely fell out, despite his vast experience of flying? We will probably never know.

His son John, as a pilot officer in the Royal Auxiliary Air Force, lost his life in a flying accident on 25 November 1940, with No. 615 Squadron. He and another pilot were flying in a Miles Magister (N3976) which lost a wing over Sunningdale, Surrey.

*   *   *

Captain Z. R. Miller CdG & Palme, 22 July 1922

Zenos Ramsey Miller was born in Pao Ting Fu, China, on 13 September 1896, of American parents who were missionaries. They were the Reverend James A. Miller and Mary McGraw Miller. He had four brothers also born in China, the youngest in 1907. Miller had two nicknames, Red and Zee.

Miller began his education at the Chefoo Boys School in Shandong Province, Northern China, and when the family returned to the States, he went to Wooster Academy and Wooster College, Ohio. In sport he had success in soccer, basketball and tennis. Planning a medical career, he was guiding his education that way until he enlisted into the USAS.

Joining the American Air Service in March 1917, he completed his flight training in France,

Lieutenant Zenos R. Miller of the 27th Pursuit Squadron.

but he was far from a natural pilot and had several narrow escapes. On one unfortunate occasion he was coming in to land at Toul and decapitated a French workman cutting the grass who he failed to see. He also accidentally set his aircraft on fire in a hanger, which was also destroyed.

Once his training was complete he was assigned to the 27th Aero Squadron on 24 November. In the summer of 1918 he shot down two kite balloons on 16 July, one in the afternoon, the other that evening. Three days later he shot down a Fokker DVII and, during a patrol on the 20th, was credited with two more DVIIs. The patrol became a disaster due to bad weather causing three American Spads to come down inside German lines, two of the pilots being killed. Miller was the third, and he was taken into captivity.

Sent to Trausnitz Castle, near the Bavarian town of Landshut, then to Villingen near the Swiss border, he saw out the war; but he had been decorated by the French with the *Croix de Guerre*. His French citation read:

As a patrol leader, has always shown very fine courage and very great self control. On 16 July 1918, over Gland, in the course of a patrol, brought down an enemy kite balloon and fired on troops on the ground. The same day he forced down an enemy balloon after a combat against three Fokkers.

Miller was also the recipient of a Silver Star Citation, 3 June 1919:

By direction of the President, under the provisions of the act of Congress approved July, 9, 1918, First Lieutenant (Air Service) Zenos R. Miller, United States Air Service, is cited by the Commanding General, American Expeditionary Forces, for gallantry in action and a silver star may be placed upon the ribbon of the Victory Medal awarded him. First Lieutenant Miller distinguished himself by gallantry in action while serving with the 27th Aero Squadron, A.E.F., in action near Braisnes, France, 20 July 1918, while on a voluntary reconnaissance patrol.

He was also recommended for the DSC but presumably this was not acted upon due to him failing to return from combat on 20 July 1918.

Returning from captivity, he returned to Boston, where he was enrolled into Harvard Medical School, and later graduated from Princeton on 21 Feb 1920, still with plans to become a doctor. By this time Miller was living at 131 Schofield Avenue, Carthage, Illinois. Prior to his death he had been working at the children's hospital in Boston.

A friend and colleague, Doctor Clarence Gamble, also a Princeton graduate, purchased an old Italian Savoia-Marchetti aeroplane in 1921 and, enlisting the help of Miller and one of his brothers, Ralph K. Miller, also a medical student, they planned to make a transcontinental flight across America. Gamble was the son of James N. Gamble, the soap manufacturer connected to Proctor and Gamble of Cincinnati, Ohio.

The aeroplane was flown from New York to Mineola on 21 July, from where they would head for Pasadena, California. Once they had completed their plans, Gamble and the Miller boys were ready by Saturday, 22 July 1922. Taking off with Zenos at the controls, the aircraft got into difficulties and Miller had to make a quick decision to get down. He spotted some open ground near Framingham, Massachusetts, as he lost height, but quickly observed that it would be unsuitable for a forced landing and tried to overshoot, but in doing so lost flying speed and stalled.

They crashed in a quagmire which hurled Gamble and Ralph out of the machine, both being seriously injured and initially trapped beneath the aircraft's wings. Zenos also became trapped in the wreckage, leaving just his head above a sea of mud, and in excruciating pain. Rescuers tried desperately to free him over a period of two hours, having to bring planks of wood, while the local fire brigade stretched ladders across the swamp in an attempt to have some solid platform over the muddy area. They were hampered by smoke from burning fuel and petrol fumes. Eventually Miller lapsed into unconsciousness and died. Later inspection found that Miller had suffered a fractured skull and a broken neck. One of the men trying to rescue him was Captain B. W. de B. Leyson, who had been with Miller in prison camp in 1918 having been shot down flying with 73 Squadron RAF, on 10 June 1918.

Miller was buried in Elvaston Cemetery, Hancock, Illinois. He was 25 years old.

*   *   *

Flight Lieutenant R. C. L. Holme MC, MiD, 4 October 1922

Born in Berkshire on 10 November 1896, Robert Charles Lyon Holme was the son of Mr & Mrs F. R. L. Holme. The family moved constantly, setting up various homes in Somerset, and Barnes in south-west London. Robert received his education at Repton between 1911 and 1914, and then went to Sandhurst Military College once war came, being commissioned into the Somerset Light Infantry the day after his eighteenth birthday, 11 November 1914.

Holme eventually requested a transfer to the RFC, gaining his RAC flying certificate, No. 1665, on 28 August 1915, but despite this achievement he was sent for observer training, which led to a posting to No. 16 Squadron in early September. With this experience in France he successfully moved to become a military pilot and was posted to a Home Defence Squadron, No. 39, in the spring of 1916. In the summer he moved to No. 33 Squadron. He flew several night sorties and was awarded the Military Cross (LG 24 January 1917) for consistent bravery during these night defence duties, received a mention in despatches, and was promoted to captain.

In 1918 he returned to France as a flight commander, posted to No. 29 Squadron, equipped with SE5A fighters. In July he shot down one Fokker DVII, two two-seater reconnaissance machines and a balloon, while on 1 August he and another pilot shot down a DFW two-seater.

Lieutenant R. C. L. Holme when an observer with 16 Squadron.

Holme remained in the Royal Air Force post war, and was posted out to Iraq joining No. 1 Squadron based at Hinaidi, ten miles from Baghdad, flying Sopwith Snipes. However he was killed as a passenger, not a pilot.

At around 12.30 pm on 4 October 1922 he took a flight in a 45 Squadron Vickers Vernon aircraft (J6865) from Baghdad, flown by 24-year-old Flight Lieutenant A. L. Messenger AFC. Holme was going along in order to be shown the way to Kirkuk. The Vernon crashed and burst into flames, Holme being killed instantly. Alfred Messenger was badly burned and died on the 16th, while his crew member,

A Vickers Vernon, the type in which Holme was killed.

Aircraftman First Class A. A. Milne, also badly burned, died six hours after the crash. The subsequent court of enquiry determined that the pilot had taken off with the control wheel strapped, therefore locking the aileron controls.

Holme was buried in Ma'asker Al Rischid RAF Cemetery, Baghdad. He was 25 years old.

*   *   *

Flying Officer J. W. Wallwork MC, 18 December 1922

Son of assistant workhouse manager James and his wife Marion Stuart Wallwork (née Wilson), John Wilson Wallwork was born on 6 May 1898, the family resident at 100 Cross Lane, Radcliffe, Lancashire. He received his education at the Stand Grammar School, following which he became employed as a bank clerk in London.

With the coming of war, he enlisted as a private soldier (No. 765096) in the 2/28 Battalion of the London Regiment (Artists Rifles), attending the unit's Officer Training Corps. Selected as officer material and deciding he would like to fly, he received a commission to the Royal Flying Corps on 20 April 1917 and completed his flight training as a pilot on 15 July. He had trained at Hare Hall Camp, Gidea Park, Romford, Wantage

Flying Officer J. W. Wallwork MC.

Hall, Reading, No. 49 Reserve Squadron at Spittlegate, and then No. 54 Training Squadron at Harlaxton.

Sent to France on 1 August 1917, he was posted to No. 40 Squadron, flying Nieuport Scouts and later SE5A machines. In early 1918 Wallwork was credited with five victories, all German fighters, during March and April, as well as participating in many ground attack sorties during the German offensive that was taking place, and was awarded the Military Cross. This appeared in the *London Gazette* dated 26 July:

> *For conspicuous gallantry and devotion to duty. During recent operations he participated in many offensive low-flying and bombing attacks, and carried them out with great courage and determination. From very low altitudes he bombed*

A Gloster Nightjar, the type in which John Wallwork was killed.

enemy troops and transport, inflicting heavy casualties. He caused while on offensive patrols more than one enemy machine to crash, and brought down others out of control. He set a magnificent example of courage and skill.

He remained in service after the war and by 1922 was employed within the aircraft industry at the Aircraft Experimental Establishment, Farnborough, which entailed testing and delivering aircraft. On 18 December 1922, he collected a Gloster Nightjar B.R.2 aircraft (J6930) for delivery to AEE, taking off at 12.15 pm. The aircraft suffered a massive engine failure at 200 feet and, in attempting to turn back to the airfield, stalled and crashed on the company's Brockworth aerodrome, resulting in him suffering serious injuries, not helped by his safety belt breaking. He was rushed to the Wooden Lodge Nursing Home in London Road, Gloucester, but died two hours later. He was 24 years of age.

The subsequent court of enquiry recorded:

1. *Loss of engine power, of the cause of which there is no evidence forthcoming, while taking off.*
2. *Owing to this, and the nature of the country, the pilot attempted to regain it but with very little height.*

3. *He stalled, probably owing to further loss of power, and spun into the ground.*

4. *If the belt had held it is very probable that the pilot would not have been thrown forward on to the instrument board.*

The air officer commanding added, 'Coastal Area concurs and considers that no blame whatever can be attached to him.'

* * *

Flying Officer E. E. Turner DFC, 28 December 1922

Edward Eric Turner, born 21 July 1896, came from Forest Hill, south-east London, son of Edward Turner, living then at 49 Carholme Road. He enlisted into the Territorial Army on 29 September 1914, going into the Artists Rifles as a private (2789). On 21 January 1915 he transferred from the 1st Reserve Regiment into the Light Infantry (1st Battalion) and on the following day proceeded to France where he remained on active service with a machine gun section until February 1917, remaining a private. A year earlier he had endeavoured to transfer to the RFC. Without a commission this was refused, but he was advised that as the Artists Rifles was now effectively an OTC, he should reapply when commissioned. His commission finally came through in May, although he had been attached to the RFC since his return from France.

Flying Officer E. E. Turner DFC.

Once trained as a pilot, Turner was posted to Home Defence duties and assigned to No. 61 Squadron based at Rochford in Essex, equipped with Sopwith Pups. Home Defence squadrons embraced a number of experienced pilots from France, who were either in England on 'rest', or between operational periods, occasionally 'war weary' and in urgent need of a break, or sometimes when increased German incursions over England forced RFC HQ to send whole squadrons back from France. As can be imagined, therefore, these Home Defence units had an amazing number of aces or would-be aces on strength, or at least several experienced flyers.

Experience was certainly a necessity, and above average piloting ability, for as well as day operations against German airships and bombing aircraft, increased night activity made it essential for these pilots to climb into the night skies to do battle with the raiders. That also took a high degree of courage, for there was very little assistance from the ground once the aeroplanes were airborne other than by searchlight cooperation or signal flares. No radio, no radar, and flying instruments that were themselves limited. Not every night was black, but generally they were dark enough to make it an extremely dangerous environment to be in, sitting in a fairly frail aircraft, in an open cockpit, no parachutes of course, and only their individual skill to aid them. Taking off was relatively simple. Landing back on some grass airstrip seemingly in the middle of nowhere was quite another. Occasionally searchlights might give an indication of direction, or the pilot may have some knowledge of where the lights were situated, always assuming they hadn't become totally lost in the gloomy and often cloudy sky. Finding the raiders was another far-from-simple task. If it was not so black a night that their darker bulk might be spotted by a keen-eyed observer, or perhaps their glowing exhausts might give their position away, it was fly, search and hope to luck.

Turner's first recorded sortie in fact came during the early evening of 12 August 1917, therefore in daylight. A force of German Gotha bombers attacked Southend and it is amazing how many aircraft took off to intercept them, not to mention the variety. Home Defence squadrons were not generally equipped with the best aircraft, many having been already well used in France. The RFC and RNAS shared the defence tasks and on any one operation the sky could be

A DH9A.

full of Pups, Camels, BE12s, AWFK8s, Spads, Vickers FB5s, Sopwith Triplanes, Nieuports, Bristol Scouts and Sopwith 1½ Strutters. In all 139 British aircraft became airborne on this night.

Chatham naval base was the main target and, although several air actions took place, only one Gotha was shot down, by the RNAS. Four others were damaged, three of these making crash-landings at their home bases. There is no record of Turner having been engaged.

Turner flew again on the 22nd, another day raid by Gothas on Kent coastal targets, his patrol timed at between 10.26 and 11.30 am. His next recorded HD sortie was not until the night of 29/30 January 1918, by which time he was serving with No. 78 HD Squadron at Sutton's Farm. His new squadron was flying BE12s, and his fruitless search was flown between 21.58 and 00.04 hours. The BE12 had been produced as a fighter back in 1916 but was no more than an antiquated BE2 with the observer's cockpit covered over and a machine gun mounted on the top wing, set to fire over the disc of the revolving propeller.

Then Turner changed squadrons again, for on the night of 16/17 February he was with No. 141 Squadron at Biggin Hill, Kent, but still slogging away on BE12s. His aircraft was equipped with a wireless tracking device. Without going into too much detail, a tracking aircraft trailed an aerial that could pick up signals from the ground giving the pilot an idea of where hostile aircraft were. But his 22.32 pm sortie only lasted twenty-five minutes before his W/T broke down. The following night Turner was among those who went aloft to try to find a single German bomber heading for London, his BE12 being in the air from 23.08 to 00.30.

By the night of 19/20 May (the 19th had been Whit Sunday), 141 Squadron were flying Bristol F2b fighters, which had two-man crews. A force of thirty-eight Gothas had set off to attack London, although only twenty-eight did so. They were supported by three Staaken R.IV Giants, with two Rumpler CVIIs flying weather reconnaissance missions. Defence sorties numbered eighty-eight, and with Turner was Lieutenant H. B. Barwise in the rear cockpit of C851 (23.02 to 01.25) from Detling. The raiders did not get off without injury and apart from another raid on the night of 5/6 August, this was Germany's last major raid of the war.

This May night the Germans lost four Gothas, all shot down by air defence aircraft, one falling to Turner and Henry Barwise. This bomber, Gotha G.IV No. 979/16 from BG3/17, was initially attacked by the CO of 143 Squadron, Major Frederick Sowrey DSO, MC, in an SE5A, but his guns jammed. The Gotha peeled away from its inbound track but was spotted near South Ash, today better known as the Brands Hatch racing circuit. Turner had little difficulty in closing in on the bomber, allowing Barwise to open fire with his Lewis gun, hitting the Gotha's port engine. The German pilot went into a dive to escape but Turner was able to follow, giving Barwise further opportunities to fire and see his bullets hitting the fuselage and starboard wings before his gun also jammed. Still diving, Turner said he saw the bomber's front gun firing vertically downwards which he thought might be a sign of surrender, but he was unable to continue his attack because, having throttled back, his engine refused to pick up for some time by which time sight of the Gotha had been lost.

This Gotha crashed between Frinsted and Harrietsham, the only survivor being Unteroffizier Hermann Tasche, the fuselage gunner. The pilot and observer, Vizefeldwebel Albrecht Sachtler, and Leutnant Joachim Flothow, were both killed. On the fuselage of the downed bomber were the letters FST, a letter for each of the three crew members. It was not certain if Turner and Barwise's attack had brought the Gotha down until Tasche was interrogated, and he confirmed that the attack by the Bristol Fighter had done the damage. Apparently he reported that Sachtler was trying to land, having one engine stopped as the fatal attack took place.

Both Turner and Barwise later received the DFC, gazetted on 12 June, Turner's citation reading:

> *While piloting his machine during a hostile air raid he displayed great determination and skill in manoeuvring at a height of 11,000 feet under heavy enemy fire, which enabled his Observer to bring effective fire on an enemy aeroplane, resulting in its being driven to the ground.*

Turner remained in the RAF post-war and by 1922 was serving as pilot and adjutant with No. 27 Squadron in India, which was equipped with DH9A day bombers, based at Ambala. At 10 am on the morning of 28 December he was taking part in a bomb raid against hostile tribesmen in their village at Palose, Waziristan, in E8468. In the observer's cockpit he had with him (246141) AC1 J. S. Sly. Over the target, as the bombers headed in at varying heights, Turner's machine was struck by a bomb released from another De Havilland above them, flown by Flying Officer J. W. J. Merer and AC1 Bell. It hit and smashed the port upper wing sending the bomber down to crash into the territory of the hostiles, so their bodies could not be recovered.

The court of enquiry deemed their deaths to be accidental and in no way due to carelessness on the part of the other crew, although the AOC India could not altogether agree with the finding, as the orders had been for the bombing to take place from 2,000 feet or the height of the leading aircraft. Evidence showed that the first bomb from John Merer's aircraft was dropped from 3-4,000 feet and although it was difficult to judge exact heights in mountainous country, and with a number of aircraft flying through a narrow valley, the AOC felt it incumbent on aircrew to pay meticulous attention to orders in future. However, this did not damage John Merer's career, for by 1939 he had risen to the rank of wing commander. A former RFC pilot, he served on the Indian Frontier until 1923, became adjutant at Cranwell between 1929 and 1931, saw active duty in the Middle East in the early war years, and by 1945 was with 5 Group of Bomber Command. He retired in 1955 as an Air Vice-Marshal, having been made a CB in 1949. Turner was 26.

* * *

Captain R. E. Keys DFC, 10 January 1923

Ralph Edmund Keys was a pilot in the Royal Naval Air Service in the First World War and in 1918 was with the RAF's No. 4 Group at Yarmouth Naval Air Station flying raids along the Belgian coast and also on Home Defence duties, along with such notable airmen as Egbert Cadbury and Robert Leckie.

On the night of 5/6 August, the German Zeppelin airships *L53*, captained by Kapitänleutnant E. Prölss, *L56*, Kapitänleutnant Walter Zaeschmar, *L63*, M. von Freudenreich, *L65*, W. Dose, and *L70*, Johann von Lossnitzer, headed towards Britain's Midland area. The former naval pilots were sent off in DH4 aircraft, Keys with 210675 Airman (Gunlayer) A. T. Harman in A8039. Cadbury was also aloft in A8032, with Leckie, and they found *L70* that also had aboard one of Germany's important airship captains, Peter Strasser.

Cadbury and Leckie found and attacked *L70* head-on, setting it on fire and seeing it head down into clouds. Keys, meantime, had reached 17,000 feet and attacked the same Zeppelin but his front gun then jammed so he flew in so that Harman could open up with his rear guns. Their fire also produced flames and they watched as the airship plunged down into the sea, eight miles off Wells-next-the-Sea. The time was 22.05 pm. Although reports did not support the Keys claim, it seems that both crews were obscured from each other by the bulk of the gas bag. In the event, the kill went to Cadbury and Leckie.

However, Cadbury, Leckie and Keys each received DFC awards, with a joint citation, recorded in the *London Gazette* for 21 September:

These officers attacked and destroyed a large enemy ship which recently attempted a raid on the north-east coast, and also succeeded in damaging a second airship.

The converted De Havilland 16 (G-EALM) in which Ralph Keys crashed on 10 January 1923. He and one of his four passengers were killed.

The services rendered on this occasion were of the greatest value, and the personal risk was very considerable for aeroplanes a long way out from the land.

Keys' observer, Arthur Tom Harman, was awarded the Distinguished Flying Medal: 'For Gallantry in the air in assisting in the destruction of an enemy airship which recently attempted a raid on the north-east coast of England. One airship was destroyed and another damaged.'

Ralph Keys resigned his commission on 8 November 1921 and became a pilot with the De Havilland Aeroplane Hire Service, operating with converted DH4s as four-seat commercial passenger aeroplanes. He was also involved with the Aircraft Transport and Travel Company Ltd, with converted DH4 machines and later the DH16. Flights were made between Heathrow and Paris or from Croydon to Amsterdam. One aircraft, G-EALM, had been used for newspaper deliveries but was withdrawn from this service.

On 10 January 1923, this aircraft, piloted by Keys, took off from Stanmore Common, Middlesex, on a test flight but suffered engine failure and crashed near Stagg Lane. Despite it being recorded as a test flight, Keys had four passengers on board. Keys and one passenger, Leslie Lihon Arnell, aged 20, were both killed, the other three men were all injured: Edward B. Bernett, Samuel Hawke and Harry Picken.

*   *   *

Major E. L. Foot MC, MiD (2), 23 June 1923

There are some names that became almost iconic during the First World War, and that of Ernest Leslie Foot was one of them.

Captain E. L. Foot MC.

He was the son of Doctor Ernest and Mrs Foot of Pulborough, Sussex, born on 19 May 1895 and educated at Epsom College, 1906-12. From January 1913 he got a job working in London, studying railway administration and control at offices by London Bridge Station, where he remained until the declaration of war in August 1914.

Volunteering immediately, he was gazetted Second Lieutenant to the 9th (Reserve) Battalion of the Oxford and Bucks Light Infantry. His brother Douglas joined the 8th Royal Berkshire Regiment but was killed in action on 13 October 1915. Tired of trench warfare, Foot effected a transfer to the Royal Flying Corps in early 1915, initially training as an observer, and was assigned to 4 Squadron with its BE2c observation aeroplanes. Flying with Lieutenant O. G. W. Lywood in BE No. 1800 on 15 July, he was attacked by a German aircraft while engaged on a reconnaissance between Cambrai and Péronne at 16.20 pm. The BE's aileron controls were damaged sending it earthwards in a spin but Oswyn Lywood, a pre-war airman, managed to get the machine under enough control to make a forced landing, although it ran into some wire and more or less crashed. Both Lywood and Foot escaped unhurt.

No doubt deciding that in future he would prefer to rely on his own expertise, Foot requested pilot training and, once accepted, returned to England. On 20 December he passed his flying tests and received Royal Aero Club Certificate No. 2257. Gazetted a flying officer on 10 February 1916, he was posted to No. 8 Squadron in France in March, flying BE2d machines.

Three months later he was posted to No. 11 Squadron, equipped with FE2b 'pusher' two-seaters, where he met and became firm friends with Albert Ball, one of Britain's earliest air heroes. By this time he had acquired the nickname of 'Feet'.

Flying with observer Second Lieutenant G. K. Welsford, this team was credited with three victories during September, and the day after his third claim he was sent to No. 60 Squadron (along with Ball) on 16 September, again as a flight commander; 60 flew single-seat Nieuport Scouts. However, Foot had been asked to fly a Spad (A253) to the squadron for operational trials, and on the 28th of this month, in the Spad, he shot down an Albatros two-seater over Avesnes les Bapaume, the first ever victory by a British pilot flying a French Spad; it was probably a machine of FA238(A). He had been chosen to fly the new Spad due to his experience. Both crewmen were wounded.

The squadron generally flew Nieuports, Foot driving down another two-seater on 20 October in company with a DH2 of another unit, and although not given credit for a victory, it was believed the observer had been wounded. The next day he was credited with a Roland two-seater shot down 'out of control'.

On 26 October, Foot was leading an afternoon patrol and spotted some Albatros Scouts attacking four BE2s near Ancre and went to their aid. They were in fact Jasta 2 machines, led by Oswald Boelcke. In the fight, one German pilot, Hans Imelmann (no relation to Max), got the better of Foot and a burst of gunfire set the Nieuport's petrol tank on fire. In a perilous position, Foot nevertheless managed to sideslip down, keeping the flames away from his body and, getting across the front lines, crashed. Remarkably he survived both the flames and the crash. He was Immelmann's third victory. He would achieve six before his death in combat on 23 January 1917. As for Boelcke, he survived for two more days but died in a crash following a collision with one of his pilots during a combat with 24 Squadron on the 28th.

Foot left the squadron on 3 November, returning to England on rest. The award of the Military Cross was gazetted on 14 November:

For conspicuous skill and gallantry. When flying a single-seater scout, he dived on to five hostile machines, which were flying at about 2,500 feet, and drove one down to the ground as a wreck. On many other occasions he has shown determination when fighting enemy machines.

He was also mentioned in despatches on two occasions.

After a period of giving flight instruction, he was posted, on 10 March 1917, to the newly formed No. 56 Squadron, Albert Ball being one of its flight commanders. They were less than a month from being sent to France with their new SE5 fighters but, unfortunately, Foot was injured in a motoring accident the evening before it was due to depart. He did not fly combat again.

Foot spent the rest of the war instructing at the School of Special Flying at Gosport, where only the best pilots were employed, under Major Robert Smith-Barry. He left the RAF at the end of hostilities to go into civil aviation.

Foot became a commercial pilot with the Handley Page Transport Company, flying on the London to Paris route until April 1923. He then took a position with the Bristol Aeroplane Company as a test pilot while also becoming an instructor on behalf of the RAF Reserve. From this he received a commission as a probationary flying officer (Class A) in the General Duties Branch of the RAFVR.

He also took part in a number of air races, popular at this time. In July 1921 he flew in the Sixth Aerial Derby organised by the Royal Aero Club, which entailed flying a 100-mile circuit twice around London, in a Martinsyde F.4. Unhappily, trouble with its 300-hp Hispano-Suiza engine forced his retirement on only the first lap.

In September of that year he led the 'White Team' during a relay race for the Air League Challenge Cup, being the opening event of the first Aviation Race Meeting organised by the RAC at Croydon Aerodrome, but again mechanical problems forced his team to withdraw. He flew the Martinsyde again in June 1922, during the third Croydon Race Meeting, coming in third in the First Sprint Handicap.

One year later he was entered into the first Grosvenor Challenge Cup, donated by Lord Edward Grosvenor, Foot being sponsored by Sir George Stanley White, the Managing Director of the Bristol Company, flying the Bristol M.1D monoplane (G-EAVP). The race took place in stages, starting at Lympne on the

The Bristol M.1D monoplane in which Ernest Foot was killed.

Kent coast, landing at Croydon, Birmingham and then Bristol, from where they flew back to Croydon. As he landed at Filton Aerodrome, Bristol, he reported that his machine had developed a petrol leak and he was being affected by fumes. After some repairs he took off again, but crashed on the Stonehill Road between Chertsey and Chobham, Surrey. The aircraft seemed to lose a wing and on hitting the ground burst into flames. Foot died instantly. He was 28 years of age and had only married a few months earlier.

*   *   *

Captain G. E. B. Lawson DFC, 19 November 1923

George Edgar Bruce Lawson was born in Cape Town, South Africa, of English parents, on 26 April 1899. His father part owned a dry cleaning facility in Cape Town, named 'Lawson & Kirk'. Lawson had one brother and one sister, and after the Union of South Africa was formed, the family moved to Johannesburg. After completing his education at King Edward School, where he was a cadet in the Officer Training Corps, he became a

George Lawson's grave stone.

laboratory assistant in the South African School of Mines and Technology, and when war came he was one of many young men recruited by Major A. M. Miller to join the Royal Flying Corps in England.

Once in England he learnt to be a pilot and was then sent to France where he was assigned to No. 32 Squadron, which flew SE5A fighters, in 1918. His first combat claim was over an Albatros Scout on 7 June, but he did not score again until September. In that month he shot down five Fokker DVIIs fighters, bringing his score to six. Two of these victories came on 27 September, one being the machine flown by German ace Oberleutnant Fritz Rumey of Jasta 5, a pilot with the *Pour le Mérite*, and forty-five victories. Lawson actually collided with Rumey's Fokker over Neuville-Saint-Rémy, and although the German took to his parachute, it failed to open and he fell to his death.

Lawson received the Distinguished Flying Cross, the citation appearing in the *London Gazette* of 8 February 1919:

Group picture of No. 32 Squadron, with Lawson marked Δ in the centre (9th from the right).

A pilot of courage and skill, bold in attack and gallant in action, who has accounted for five enemy aeroplanes. On 27th September he attacked fifteen Fokker biplanes that were harassing one of our bombing formations, driving down one in flames. He then engaged a second; in the combat the two machines collided and the enemy aeroplane fell down completely out of control. Although his machine was badly damaged, Lieutenant Lawson successfully regained our lines.

After the war Lawson returned to South Africa where in 1922 he joined the newly formed South African Air Force. Sadly, on 19 November the following year, he was seriously injured while flying as a passenger in an Avro 504K (H9701). His pilot, Lieutenant J. W. G. Shaw of the Special Reserve, died. Taken to Roberts Heights Military Hospital with head injuries Lawson did not recover. He was 23 years old.

Chapter Four

1924–28

Flight Lieutenant G. H. H. Scutt MC, 15 February 1924

George Howard Homer Scutt was the son of Brewer Master George Decimus Homer Scutt and Mrs Emmie Howard Scutt of Creywell, New Ross, County Wexford, born on 5 May 1898. He had one brother and one sister. George was educated at the John Ivory School in New Ross from 1908 to 1911, then at Cheltenham College, May 1912 to July 1915, where he became a member of the school's OTC. He also played rugby, being in the Cheltondale 3rd XV in 1915.

George Scutt aged 17.

Progressing to Sandhurst he was commissioned into the 1st Battalion of the King's Liverpool Regiment on 7 April 1916, having an uncle, Colonel Tripp, already with the KLR. Going to France, Scutt was wounded in the right arm by shrapnel during a trench raid at Serre, on the Somme, on 15 September and invalided back to England.

Once recovered he decided to move into aviation, becoming an observer, and, once trained, was posted to No. 48 Squadron, which was equipped with FE2 aircraft, which was changed to the Bristol F2b later. He flew with several pilots, including Captain L. A. Payne. With Len Payne, a South African, he was credited with shooting down at least four enemy fighters during February and March 1918. His Military Cross was gazetted on 22 June:

> *For conspicuous gallantry and devotion to duty. He has destroyed one hostile machine, and driven down three others out of control. He carried out an important single-machine reconnaissance, frequently descending to a height of 100 feet under heavy rifle and machine-gun fire. While returning, he attacked five enemy machines, and ably assisted his pilot in driving them back over their lines. He had carried out many successful photographic reconnaissances, and has at all times proved himself to be a keen and daring officer.*

A Sopwith Snipe, the type Scutt was flying when he was killed.

Leonard Payne was also awarded the Military Cross, gazetted 26 July 1918, and his death is recorded in Chapter One of this book.

Scutt remained in the RAF after the war and became a pilot, and promoted to flight lieutenant. On 15 February 1924, while piloting a Sopwith Snipe (E7601) with No. 25 Squadron, he hit the ground during a formation dive over their base at Hawkinge, and died in the subsequent crash. According to the court of enquiry:

> *The cause of the accident was in our opinion F/Lieut. Scutt found himself in the slip stream of the leading machine and in endeavouring to counteract the effect of this slip stream lost control of his aircraft and had insufficient height to regain control, and that F/Lieut. Scutt immediately prior to the accident had lost correct formation position as laid down in No. 1 Group letter on "Formation Flying" on 18.10.23.*

*   *   *

Flying Officer R. H. Daly DSC, DFC, MiD, 5 June 1924

Rowan Heywood Daly, son of Charles V. and Kate A. Daly, came from 'Ilma', Cliff Avenue, Leigh-on-Sea, Essex, although he was born in Trieste, then part of the Austrian Empire, on 30 March 1898. Before his death in 1924 he had a full and varied flying career.

In August 1914, despite only being 16½ years old, he enlisted as a private (No. 2288) in the 14th London Regiment, and then transferred to an electrical engineering unit the following February. Known as 'Bill' he joined the Royal Naval Air Service in August 1916 and obtained a RAeC Certificate (No. 4450) at the RNAS Station at Chingford on 8 February 1917. Daly went through the usual postings during his training – Crystal Palace, Chingford and Cranwell – and once passed out as a pilot, joined the Manston War Flight in April 1917, being engaged in Home Defence duties.

Flying Officer R. H. Daly DSC, DFC.

His first real war flights came on 25 May during a daylight raid by Gotha bombers on Folkestone, Daly taking up a Bristol Scout twice during the late afternoon. He was up again on 5 June, Gothas going for Sheerness. Despite the height flown by the bombers, Daly and others managed to climb to 16,000 feet. He also managed to fire at one Gotha as he came under return fire from others, but saw no results of his attack. Daly was up in a Sopwith Pup on the 13th, in fact twice during raids by Gothas on London, and although he found one off Southend, he lost it in cloud.

His persistence finally paid off on 7 July, the day Gothas again went for London. This time he was flying a Sopwith Triplane (N5382). Several RNAS and RFC aircraft were in this action, and initially Daly, along with his squadron commander, C. H. Butler DSO, circled in case bombers might be spotted nearby. After landing and being refuelled, Butler led Daly and others off again and this time found bombers returning from London over Kentish Knock. The naval pilots engaged the enemy, Butler and Flight Lieutenant J. E. Scott both shooting down one, while Daly set a third on fire off the Belgian coast. He followed another raider up the River Scheldt but his gun jammed as he closed in. Despite claiming three kills, it appears that only one was lost, this one falling in flames over Belgium. Butler, Scott and Daly were rewarded, Butler with a Bar to his DSO, while DSCs went to the others. Daly's citation read:

For skill and gallantry in attacking enemy aircraft returning from a raid on England. Giving chase he engaged and brought down one machine in flames. Afterwards he engaged another machine, but his gun jammed, and though he

continued the pursuit to the enemy coast he was unable to clear his jamb, and was
obliged to return to his aerodrome.

Daly was in action again on 12 August, during a daylight raid on Southend by
Gothas. This time he was flying a Sopwith Camel and again he attacked a bomber
heading towards the Belgian coast but finally had to break off the combat when at
1,000 feet near Zeebrugge. Other pilots also attacked the Gotha which eventually
crash-landed near Ostend, damaged but not destroyed.

Four days later Daly was posted to France, initially to join 12 Naval Squadron,
a holding unit, before being sent off to join 4 Naval, where he remained until 20
September. He was then posted to 10 Naval and before the month was out he
had claimed a two-seater reconnaissance machine shot down 'out of control' and
then an Albatros DIII Scout destroyed on 26 September. However, his Triplane
(N6359) was hit by ground fire and he was wounded.

In January 1918 he became an instructor at Eastchurch. In March he moved to
Redcar, but his instructional skills were not very good apparently and he was soon
transferred to testing duties at East Fortune. At the end of July he was with No. 1
Torpedo Training Squadron aboard HMS *Furious*. The war ended before he could
get back into action, but in 1919 he volunteered for duty with No. 47 Squadron
that was operating against the communist forces in Russia, in support of the White

A DH9A bomber.

(non-communist) Russians. Daly arrived in Russia on 10 July 1919, attached to C Flight, but moved to B Flight on 28 September. During the conflict, Daly and others of the fighter flight engaged numerous hostile aircraft, shooting down a number of them. Sammy Kinkead DSO, DSC, DFC, was the main inspiration in the flight, and he and others gained kills, and of these, Daly was credited with four combat victories, including two French Spads. For his work in Russia, which included a number of bombing and ground strafing sorties, Rowan Daly received the DFC, *London Gazette* 12 July 1920. He also received two awards from the Russians, the Order of St Vladimir, 4th Class, and the Cross of St George, 4th Class.

Back in England, Daly had decided to remain in the RAF, being sent to No. 100 Squadron, taking part in the RAF Aerial Pageant at Hendon in June 1922. In this show he won the Landing Competition, having to land in a 100 yard marked area after stopping the engine of his aeroplane at 1,000 feet. By May 1923 he was serving with No. 39 Squadron, based at RAF Grantham, equipped with DH9A bombers. He became part of a display team for an RAF pageant but on the afternoon of 5 June came disaster. Daly, with Sergeant William H. Brewer (244928) in the rear cockpit, took off in E8654, in company with another DH9 flown by Flying Officer L. G. Lucas (F7087) and his observer, Aircraftman First Class T. Coppleston. During their manoeuvring, Lucas apparently pulled up suddenly and the undercarriage of Daly's machine hit and became firmly embedded in the top wing of Lucas's bomber. Both aircraft began to descend, locked together, and just as Daly succeeded in wrenching his wheels from the other aircraft, they both hit the ground near Spittlegate. All four men died instantly. The court of enquiry reported:

> *The cause of the accident was in our opinion due to an error of judgement on the part of the pilots concerned.*
>
> *The Court would like to point out that had the machines involved been equipped with safety petrol tanks or parachutes, it is possible that two lives would have been saved.*

The AOC concurred. This suggests that one of the aircraft came down on fire, although there is no reference to this.

On this same date, another First World War airman recipient of the Military Cross lost his life in a flying accident. Flight Lieutenant R. H. C. Usher MC, AFC, was killed testing a De Havilland 42A 'Dingo' (J7006) at Northolt. The machine had been assigned to No. 41 Squadron for trials but broke up in the air above the aerodrome. Bill Daly was 26 years old.

*   *   *

Flight Lieutenant R. H. C. Usher MC, AFC, 5 June 1924

The pilot mentioned above, who died the same day as Rowan Daly, was the son of the Reverend Robert and his wife Alice Mabel Usher (née Edwards) of 2 Church Hill, East Knoyle, Wiltshire. He was Robert Howell Craster Usher, although he first saw the light of day in Wareham, Dorset, when he was born in 1896. Robert was educated at Shrewsbury between 1910 and 1914. Once war came he volunteered for the army, being made second lieutenant in the 3rd (Reserve) Battalion of the Wiltshire Regiment on 15 August. Looking to the air, he transferred to the RFC early in 1916, trained as a pilot and was gazetted a flying officer in May.

Soon after gaining his coveted 'wings' he was posted to France where he joined No. 27 Squadron, which flew Martinsyde G100 single-seater day bombers. On 31 July 1916, flying in Martinsyde 7282, he was part of a raid on Marcoing but became separated from the others. What happened next was recorded in his report:

The patrol seemed to break up just as we were crossing the Lines. As I didn't see any signals to return, and I had a Sopwith [a 70 Squadron Sopwith Strutter as escort] with me, I went on to Marcoing and dropped my bombs, both of which fell in the village. I turned quickly round and almost ran into an LVG. I gave him a drum of Lewis gun ammunition and he went down under me. I saw the Sopwith take him on and while I was changing drums I was attacked in front by a Roland. I gave him a drum and at the same time heard a machine gun behind me, looked round and saw three Rolands on my tail. I was hit in the leg almost immediately but managed to give him a drum of my side gun and they went away. My engine

A Martinsyde G.100 'Elephant', the type in which Usher won his MC.

started spluttering and I saw a hole in my petrol tank, my engine stopped so I started gliding down thinking I should have to land. Petrol was flowing all over my left leg so I put my left knee over the hole in the petrol tank. It struck me that by pumping I might be able to get up the pressure. By this time I was about 200 feet up, the engine started and I was 15 miles from our Lines.

I kept pumping hard all the time and managed to keep just enough engine going. I thought I would have to land, but my engine picked up in time three or four times. I came back to the Lines for about 15 miles at an average height of 50 feet. I had lost myself and was so low that I could see very little of the country. I then picked up a French biplane that was flying and followed him and eventually landed at Moreuil aerodrome, crashing the machine on landing. I was feeling very weak having lost a lot of blood and was exhausted by having to pump for so long.

After having engaged the first machine I did not see anything of the Sopwith. During the time that I was flying low I was subjected to a lot of rifle and machine-gun fire.

He was awarded the Military Cross, gazetted on 25 August 1916:

For conspicuous gallantry and devotion to duty in attacking three hostile machines and driving them off. On another occasion he fought five hostile machines, and although hit in the leg, continued to fight till his engine stopped. He succeeded under great difficulties in reaching an aerodrome, where he collapsed through loss of blood.

The De Havilland 42A in which Robert Usher was killed while it was being trialled by 41 Squadron.

Returning to England and once recovered from his injury he flew with No. 1 Aircraft Acceptance Park, with the rank of captain. On 1 October 1917 while flying a BE2c (A3148) the machine suffered engine failure and crashed on the outskirts of Radford aerodrome. Both he and his passenger, Captain W. E. Reason, suffered injuries. Returning to duty Usher became a flight instructor and test pilot, for which he received the Air Force Cross, gazetted on 2 November 1918. Remaining in the RAF, he was granted a permanent commission in 1922. In April 1923 he was posted to the RAF Depot at Uxbridge, and then to the HQ of the Superintendent of Reserves at RAF Northolt in May.

A keen rugby player, Usher represented England in Rugby Union matches post-war. He also played for London Scottish and Leicester teams and captained the RAF Rugby Team in 1924.

However, the 27-year-old Usher was killed while testing a De Havilland 42A 'Dingo' (J7006)[2] belonging to No. 41 Squadron on 5 June 1924. The squadron had the machine for trials, but it broke up in the air over Northolt. The court of enquiry report was short and sweet: 'The cause of the accident was in our opinion due to structural failure of the machine in flight.'

* * *

Captain H. A. Kullberg DFC, 5 August 1924

Howard Albert Kullberg was an American, born on 10 September 1896 in Somerville, Massachusetts. He attended Concord and Somerville Schools, and finally the Wentworth Institute in Boston, for engineering technology courses.

Like so many Americans, he felt it his duty to fight against Germany's aggression in Europe. Initially he applied to join the US Air Service, but was deemed too small to be a pilot; he therefore travelled to Canada, where he was able to join the British Royal Flying Corps, in Toronto, in August 1917. He received his flight training both in

Captain H. A. Kullberg DFC.

---

2. The RAF casualty card notes that the aircraft involved was a DH 42 'Doormouse' but as it was a DH 42A, it was known as the 'Dingo'. In any event, the life of the DH42 types was short.

Canada and Texas USA, and once this was completed he was shipped to England in January 1918.

Sent to France, he was assigned to No. 1 Squadron, which was equipped with SE5A fighters, and soon began to make a name for himself. His first victories were doubles, two C-type German two-seaters destroyed on 27 May, followed by another two two-seaters on the 28th. It has to be said, however, that 1 Squadron had a penchant for sharing victories with other members of a patrol, provided they all managed a shot at the target. This in its own way encouraged new pilots to engage the enemy. He scored a double again on 1 June, two Pfalz DIII Scouts, but one of them was a solo effort.

He brought his score to eight with yet two more kills on the 9th, a shared Fokker Triplane and a solo claim over a two-seater. A balloon followed on the 15th and, with two more two-seaters before the end of June, his score had risen to eleven.

Kullberg, promoted to captain and flight commander, continued to score regularly, with three victories in July, three more during August and two in September; all but one were solo efforts, and five of these were over the vaunted Fokker DVIIs. These brought his overall score to nineteen, and he received the DFC in August, gazetted on 2 November 1918:

One of the SE5s Kullberg flew with 1 Squadron in 1918 and in which he scored seven victories.

This officer has destroyed six enemy aeroplanes and has taken part in seven engagements when others have been destroyed by members of his patrol. A bold and keen Officer who possesses a fine fighting spirit.

A single DFC award seems scant reward for nineteen victories, but in all probability they were scored so quickly that his CO didn't have the time to forward a further recommendation, or if he did, Wing HQ may have thought a second recommendation was too close to the first.

In his last combat, on 16 September, he had been chased at low level by five Fokker biplanes and was hit in the leg in three places. He was taken off to hospital as soon as he got home, his injuries took several months to heal, and he did not see any further action.

Back in the USA, he was released from service in July 1919 and became involved in civil aviation. He became famous for being America's first citizen to make a citizen's arrest in flying circles, having become the President of the Akron Aeronautical Association of Ohio. In early November 1923 he became an aerial policeman. Two civilian airmen, Howard Culvert and his passenger Frank O'Neill, were spotted violating a city ordinance over Akron and Kullberg set off in pursuit, following them to Stow aviation field where they landed. Landing too, Kullberg confronted the two men and called for the police. Both men were later charged with stunt flying at low level above the city.

On Tuesday, 5 August 1924, Kullberg was instructing a Mr Henry Dunbar, aged 34, of Hudson, Ohio, and their aircraft suddenly went into a nosedive from 2,000 feet and crashed near Hudson, both men being killed. Kullberg was one month short of his twenty-eighth birthday. He was buried in Glendale Cemetery, Summit County, Akron, Ohio.

*   *   *

Flying Officer G. S. L. Hayward MC, 16 August 1924

George Searle Lomax Hayward had been a gunner/observer during the First World War and only became a pilot after an intensive period of air fighting in early 1918. He was born in Tunbridge Wells on 1 November 1894, one of three brothers and six sisters. The family moved to Catford, south-east London, where he and his brothers attended Brownhill Road School. At school George became the captain of the football team and also won a silver medal for swimming.

When war came George joined the 3rd Hussars and was a corporal in the 8th Battalion of the Royal West Kent Regiment before being commissioned into the same Regiment in September 1916. His brother John had been in Canada in 1914 and joined the Canadian Field Artillery. He was also commissioned but was killed in action near Passchendaele in October 1917.

Following service in France George responded to the call for men to transfer to the Royal Flying Corps, successfully becoming an observer in mid-1917. He proved to be an outstanding air gunner in the backseat of a Bristol Fighter with 22 Squadron and, flying with several different pilots, gained a total of twenty-four combat

Lieutenant G. S. L. Hayward MC.

victories. With this score he was the second highest scoring gunner of the war. The first two claims came before the end of 1917 and then, flying with Sergeant E. J. Elton in the front cockpit, knocked down six enemy fighters in early March 1918. His final pilot was Lieutenant F. G. C. Weare, the team accounting for a dozen enemy scouts between late March and 22 April. He was awarded the Military Cross, which was gazetted in July:

> *For conspicuous gallantry and devotion to duty. On three separate occasions when engaged with large hostile formations, he has attacked and sent crashing to earth two hostile machines on each occasion. He has displayed consistent skill, courage and determination in dealing with hostile aircraft.*

He and Captain Weare were both mentioned in the RAF's weekly *Communiqués*, firstly on 2 April:

> *Capt. F G C Weare and 2/Lt G S L Hayward, 22 Sqn, observed 10 EA scouts and led their formation round a cloud and then dived on one EA. Fire was opened at an Albatros Scout which went down out of control and was seen to crash. Two EA triplanes then got on the tail of Capt. Weare's machine; 30 or 40 rounds were fired at the nearest triplane which glided down with smoke coming from it and when at a height of about 3,000 feet burst into flames.*

And on 12 April:

> *Capt. F G Weare and 2/Lt G S L Hayward, 22 Sqn, brought down three Pfalz Scouts out of a formation of five. Two crashed in a field south-west of Sailly as the result of fire from the pilot's gun, and the third in a field north of this after the observer had engaged it.*

No. 22 Squadron is reputed to have been the first squadron of the newly formed RAF (1 April 1918) to fly operationally. The squadron's record book shows that two BF2bs took off at 08.30 am that morning for a patrol, followed ten minutes later by another six. The flight leader was Captain Weare, so he and Hayward would have taken off first. Upon their return on this historic day, a group photograph was taken, with the participants standing in front of a Bristol, along with the squadron CO, Major J. A. McKelvie, with Hayward indulging in a well-earned cigarette.

Crews of 22 Squadron, taken on the day the RAF was formed, 1 April 1918. George Hayward is standing fifth from the left, while Lieutenant S. H. Wallage is third from the left (see 26 April 1926).

Ending his period as a gunner he took flight training and post-war remained in the Royal Air Force serving for three years in India in the early 1920s. At the end of his tour he returned to England. By this time he had married Dorothy West and they had two sons and a daughter. Back in England he was with 'T' Depot Squadron and on 14 November 1922 was organising some games at Uxbridge when he injured his left knee.

Hayward became a flying instructor at RAF Duxford with No. 2 Flying Training School until this school moved to RAF Digby in Lincolnshire in July 1924. Five weeks later, on 15 August, he and a student pilot, Pilot Officer Charles Victor Brealey, flying an Avro 504 (H9863), crashed at Metheringham about three miles north-west of Digby and both were mortally injured. George Hayward was known as a very careful and expert pilot, and his untimely death came as a shock to his brother instructors and pilots. According to the court of enquiry: 'The cause of the accident was in our opinion due to an error of judgement on the part of the pilot in stalling the aeroplane at a height of about 150 feet.' While the A.O.C. agreed with the findings, one has to wonder if it might have been a case of the pupil making the error and Hayward having no time to correct it.

George Hayward's body was returned to Catford and interred at the Hither Green Cemetery with his family present. Military honours were given, including music by the Royal Air Force Band from RAF Henley, and three rifle volleys were fired at the graveside, while two buglers sounded the *Last Post*. He was 29 years of age. In the Second World War his son John was a rear gunner on Avro Lancasters.

*   *   *

Captain J. L. M. White DFC & Bar, CdG, 24 February 1925

Joseph Leonard Maries White, but known as John, was born in Halifax, Nova Scotia, Canada, on 6 January 1897, in the Town Clock room on Citadel Hill, where his father, William J. 'Gunner' White was caretaker. His father had been given his nickname following service with the Royal Artillery before joining the Halifax police force.

A student at Dalhousie University, on reaching his 18th birthday White enlisted in the Canadian Machine Gun Corps and saw active duty in France before being wounded on 17 April 1917. Transferring to the Royal Flying Corps in September he trained as a pilot, and once he achieved this goal, was posted to No. 65 Squadron in France in April 1918.

The squadron was equipped with Sopwith Camel fighters, John claiming his first combat victory on 9 May. By the end of May he had achieved five victories, four Albatros Scouts and one two-seater observation machine. Early June saw two more victories with two more in July. These achievements brought him the first of his DFCs, this one gazetted on 3 August:

Captain J. L. M. White DFC, CdG.

This officer is distinguished for his bravery and dash in action, never hesitating to attack, regardless of the enemy's numerical superiority. He has destroyed three enemy aircraft and driven down two out of control. In addition he has carried out most valuable reconnaissance service at low altitudes.

His victories mounted steadily with double claims on 8 August, two Fokker DVIIs down inside Allied lines, shared with his flight, and two more on the 9th, one of them in flames. The action on the 8th was recorded as follows.

White was leading a formation of 65 Squadron which was attacked by eight Fokkers. The Camels turned west and climbed but on meeting another flight of 65 Squadron, White led the combined force back against the enemy. He promptly shot down one Fokker and then began to chase another west. The whole formation got on the tail of the enemy machine and forced it to land behind British lines.

He was made a flight commander on 9 August and became famous for his double claims, for again, on 3 September, two more Fokker biplanes were shot down, then another double on 14 October, again against Fokkers, one of which fell in flames. The report of his action on this date said:

He got a burst at one E.A. from 20 feet range and the machine went down in a spin but came out of it and went gliding east. He then attacked another which was on the tail of a Camel and fired about 100 rounds into it as he approached, observing his tracers to be hitting the nose of the E.A. The enemy machine went down vertically and was burning. He then attacked another Fokker biplane from behind and, after having fired three bursts into it, the machine turned over on its back and a piece of the tailplane folded over. The E.A. righted itself and Capt. White put another burst into it, after which it went down completely out of control.

One more Fokker destroyed on 26 October brought his score to eighteen, but on 4 November he excelled himself by accounting for four DVIIs in a single fight, bringing his overall score to twenty-two. He received a Bar to his DFC, gazetted on 2 November:

In company with another pilot this officer recently attacked a hostile formation of fourteen scouts. One of these he shot down in flames, and a second out of control. Captain White not only displays courage and skill of a high order in attacking machines in the air and troops on the ground, but he has rendered excellent service on reconnaissance duty, obtaining most valuable information.

John White was also the recipient of the French *Croix de Guerre* with Bronze Star, gazetted on 10 April 1919. He was sent back to England on 22 November and after a break became an instructor at No. 3 Fighter School on 23 December. Finally he relinquished his commission on 7 July 1919 and left for Canada in August.

Back home in Canada, he joined the newly formed Royal Canadian Air Force in April 1924, but on 24 February 1925 his luck finally ran out. Based at Camp Borden, Ontario, he took off at 09.10 am in an Avro 504 (G-CYAM) with 24-year-old pupil pilot Flying Officer R. H. Cross from Toronto in the rear cockpit, practising gliding turns. Over the airfield ten minutes later, as they came through cloud, they collided with another machine being flown solo by Flying Officer A. L. Morfee (G-CYAU). Both machines started to go down. White's left a trail of flame and crashed, killing both occupants. Morfee had his lateral control lost by damage to his aileron, but with partial control he executed a side-slipping, spiral dive, flattened out into a partial flat spin at the moment of landing, and crashed without injury. Laurie Morfee lived until 1988 and at one time was National President of the RCAF Association and a Director of the Air Cadet League of Canada. He reached the rank of Air Vice-Marshal CBE.

White's body was transported back to his home town for burial. He was 28 years of age.

* * *

Flight Lieutenant J. A. Slater MC & Bar, DFC, 26 November 1925

James Anderson Slater was born in Worthing, Sussex, on 29 November 1896 although his parents John and Rose Slater later lived in Paignton, Devon. His mother wanted him to go into the church and it was while attending a seminary that the First World War began. He quickly absconded, enlisting as a private in the Royal Sussex Regiment, and within a month became a second lieutenant with the Royal Irish Rifles with the help of his father, who was a major in the 60th Rifles. However, Jimmy Slater quickly managed a move back to the Royal Sussex Regiment. It was not long before the lure of the air beckoned and he volunteered to become an observer with the Royal Flying Corps. Once trained he prepared for action.

2nd Lieutenant J. A. Slater soon after being awarded his 'wings'.

Going to France he served with No. 18 Squadron on Vickers FB5s – known as the 'Gunbus' – in late 1915 and it was not long before he requested pilot training and was sent back to England. By June he had received his 'wings' and was posted to No. 1 Squadron in France in August 1916 to fly Nieuport Scouts. He achieved two combat victories here before returning to England as an instructor in May 1917. Promoted to Captain, Slater was sent to the newly formed No. 64 Squadron, which was flying the DH5 fighter, in October. The DH5 was not a universally liked fighter due to the back-stagger configuration of the top wing. Nevertheless, he got on well enough with them and further victories came. For his work and prowess in air fighting he was awarded the Military Cross, the citation being gazetted on 4 February 1918:

Flight Lieutenant James Slater MC, DFC after the war.

For conspicuous gallantry and devotion to duty. When returning from a patrol he attacked enemy infantry, silenced a field gun and fired on transport. On another occasion he silenced a battery in very difficult weather conditions, fired on ammunition wagons and enemy infantry, and brought back his patrol safely. He also led a patrol of 12 machines in very bad weather to attack a wood held by the enemy. His patrol dropped over 30 bombs, fired 3,000 rounds and drove the enemy from the wood with heavy casualties. In the course of this flight six enemy scouts were engaged and driven off. Later, he led a similar patrol with great success. He showed great courage and determination.

By this time the squadron had changed its equipment to the SE5A fighter, and with this machine he began to score heavily against the German air force in March 1918. In fact that month he achieved ten victories, adding another three in April, finally bringing his score to 24 by the last day in May. This brought him a Bar to his MC, gazetted on 22 June, the citation reading:

For conspicuous gallantry and devotion to duty. On one occasion during the recent operations he attacked a large formation of hostile scouts, one of which he drove down in flames. Later, during the same flight, he took part in a general engagement, in which he drove down another enemy machine completely out of control. Two days later he attacked two enemy scouts, causing one of them to crash to earth. In 18 days he has engaged in 25 combats at close quarters, shooting down eight hostile machines. His great gallantry and fine offensive spirit have inspired all ranks to a very high degree.

This second award referred to his combats in March, and especially during the German offensive which began on the 20th. For his later successes, he was awarded the new Distinguished Flying Cross, gazetted on 2 July 1918:

This officer has led numerous offensive patrols with the utmost skill and determination, and it is entirely due to his fine leadership that many enemy aircraft have been destroyed with the minimum of casualties to his formation.

Slater returned to England in July and ended the war as an instructor.

By this time he was something of a master of aerobatics and one could say something of a daredevil in the air. On one occasion he gained fame for actually flying through an aircraft hangar at Sedgeford aerodrome. His piloting skill reached the ears of Queen Alexandra and, during a visit to Sedgeford from nearby

Sandringham, Slater was asked to put on a flying display. After watching his aerobatics for a few minutes, the Queen turned to the commanding officer and said, 'Order that young man down immediately, before he kills himself.'

Remaining in the service with the coming of peace, Slater continued in his role as an instructor until, like so many of his contemporaries, he was posted overseas, to Egypt, where he flew with No. 70 Squadron in Iraq in 1923, then DH10s with 216 Squadron for a while in 1923/4. Returning again to England he was eventually posted to No. 3 Squadron as a flight commander in April 1925, which was equipped with the Sopwith Snipe, a machine developed from the Sopwith Camel. The Snipe had seen late action towards the end of the First World War and still equipped a number of peacetime fighter squadrons. There was a smattering of two-seat Snipes in service, one or two attached to units as dual-instruction aeroplanes. Towards the end of 1925, Jimmy was attached to the Central Flying School at Upavon, probably for some display or other. On the evening of 25 November, Jimmy, who was married and 'lived out' came to the officers' mess for a guest night. Not being very tall, he was one who was grabbed by the others, thrown onto a carpet held by several pilots, and began to be tossed into the air much to the delight of everyone except Jimmy. After several attempts they finally got him high enough to touch the mess ceiling, Jimmy sticking out a hand to defend himself against the plaster and in doing so leaving a grubby handprint on the white emulsion, after which they let him go.

A Sopwith Snipe. Slater was killed flying a dual Snipe in 1925.

The following afternoon, the 26th, he took up a pupil pilot, Pilot Officer W. J. R. Early, for an instructional flight in a dual-Snipe. It seems that it was another case of an instructor not taking over control in time, and Jimmy very nearly retrieved the situation before hitting the ground, but they crashed and both were killed. For many years that grubby handprint remained on the ceiling of the mess to remind others of Jimmy's presence, for he had been a well-liked officer, and with his experience and splendid war record he was also a wonderful after-dinner speaker. Jimmy Slater was three days short of his twenty-ninth birthday, and his son became Wing Commander R. A. Slater DFC, AFC, flying Halifax bombers in the Second World War, and retiring in 1974.

*   *   *

Flight Lieutenant G. W. Hemming DSC, CdG(F), CdG(B), 26 February 1926

From Droitwich, Worcestershire, born on 3 April 1898, Geoffrey William Hemming joined the Royal Naval Air Service in 1916, with his initial training starting at HMS *President* on 5 July. By December he had become a pilot and been posted to No. 4 Squadron RNAS as it was forming at Ostend, flying Sopwith Pups.

His first victory, claimed on 12 May 1917, five miles off Zeebrugge, was a fighter, and he followed this by two more victories on 6 June, north-east of Dixmude. The squadron then converted to Sopwith Camels, and on 22 August, south-east of Ostend, 4 Naval engaged a formation of twenty Albatros Scouts, Hemming claiming to have shot down three within five minutes. He was awarded the Distinguished Service Cross:

Flight Lieutenant G. W. Hemming DSC, CdG.

In recognition of his services with a Wing of the RNAS at Dunkirk between March – September 1917, during which period he has been continuously employed on the Belgian coast, and on many occasions has been in charge of a flight. On the 22nd August, he led his flight against a formation of twenty enemy aircraft, and engaging three consecutively, brought them all down.

A Fairey DIII floatplane, the type in which Hemming lost his life.

Although he continued to serve with 4 Naval, and then 204 RAF after 1 April 1918, he did not add to his score of six by the time he left in June. He was promoted to flight commander on 1 January 1918 and on 22 February the Belgian government awarded him their *Croix de Guerre* and the Order of the Crown. He also received the French *Croix de Guerre.*

Surviving the war as an instructor, Hemming was granted a short service commission in September 1919. On 7 February 1923 he married Dorothy May Woods, daughter of Mr and Mrs R. J. Woods of Princetown Lodge, Bangor, County Down, at St. Comgall's Parish Church, Bangor.

In 1924 he was flying at Calshot, where, on 24 May, he suffered a flying accident in a Felixstowe F2A seaplane (N4499) damaging the tail housing, but he and his two crewmen, Aircraftmen G. Jones and W. Hawes were not hurt. The court of enquiry ruled the cause was that Hemming had attempted to land while still in a turn over the Solent. However, his commanding officer added that the main cause was his inexperience of handling a flying boat.

On 7 August 1924 he was posted to the Marine Aircraft Experimental Establishment at Felixstowe and on 16 February 1925 was sent to No. 480 Flight at Calshot, flying Supermarine Southampton II flying boats. Just over one year later, on 26 February 1926, he was flying a Fairey IIID floatplane with Flying Officer Robert Collins in the rear cockpit. Somewhere over Southampton Water, near Gosport, they crashed. Hemming was killed and Collins fatally injured. Hemming was 27 years old, Collins 28.

*   *   *

Flight Lieutenant S. H. Wallage MC, MiD, 17 April 1926

Stanley Harry Wallage came from Ipswich, Suffolk, where he was born on 24 July 1895. His father was a flour miller foreman. Young Stan was educated at Ipswich Municipal Secondary School and then at the Ipswich Technical School where he studied draughtsmanship, engineering and surveying. When the Great War started he enlisted into the 7th Battalion of the Suffolk Regiment as a private soldier and was almost immediately promoted to corporal.

Flight Lieutenant S. H. Wallage MC, MiD.

He went with his battalion to France at the end of May 1915, serving in the trenches until he was wounded on 16 October 1916. By this time he had married, in June 1916, but was to later desert his wife after she produced a child in 1917, Wallage saying that the child was not his.

When he was fully recovered from his wound, he was offered a commission and, deciding to become an airman, was gazetted a second lieutenant in the Royal Flying Corps on 3 May 1917. He was soon back in France having trained to be a pilot and was posted to No. 22 Squadron early in 1918, a unit equipped with Bristol F2b fighters.

The two-seat Bristol Fighter was more than a match for single-seat German fighter aircraft, for not only did the pilot have a forward-firing Vickers machine gun, but the observer in the rear cockpit had a single (sometimes double) Lewis gun mounted on a Scarfe ring. Many pilot and observer teams became adept at staying alive in deadly combat sorties, accounted for numerous enemy aircraft shot down, while also carrying out reconnaissance, photographic and bombing operations. Observers with whom he later flew were Lieutenant G. Thompson and Lieutenant A. P. Stoyle.

He and his first observer, Sergeant J. H. Jones, accounted for three German aircraft in February and March 1918, followed by a further six during May. He became a flight commander and was awarded the Military Cross. This was recorded in the *London Gazette* for 16 September 1918:

> *For conspicuous gallantry and devotion to duty during recent operations. He personally destroyed seven enemy machines. He showed a fine spirit of dash and*

tenacity, and his skill and success as a fighting pilot was a fine example to others in his Squadron.

Wallage was twice mentioned in the RAF *Communiqués*, on 8 May 1918:

2/Lt S H Wallage and Lt G. Thompson, 22 Sqn, engaged a formation of five EA scouts, one of which they shot down and observed to crash north of La Bassée.

And on 22 May:

A patrol of 22 Sqn attacked ten EA scouts near Cambrai. In the fight which ensued, 2/Lts S. H. Wallage and A. P. Stoyle crashed one machine and drove down another out of control.

Following a brief rest in England, he returned to his squadron late in the war and with Captain D. E. Waight in the back cockpit, downed a rare Pfalz DXII Scout on 4 November, bringing his overall score to ten.

Wallage remained in the RAF post-war and in the early 1920s found himself, like so many others, serving in the Middle East. He served with No. 14 Squadron

A DH9 in the Middle East.

from 1923, which was operating DH9A bombers at RAF Amman, Jordan. On 26 April 1926 he and the Acting Station Commander, Squadron Leader Harley Alec Tweedie, took off in DH9 No. J7108, a machine that had recently been repaired at Aboukir and had only just been assigned to 14 Squadron. Harley Tweedie, an ex-10th Hussar, had learnt to fly in April 1916 (RAC Certificate 2699) and until recently had been on staff work, firstly as a member of the British Delegation to Paris, and then while at the Air Ministry, working on arms control in post-war Germany. By this time Stan Wallage was an experienced DH9 pilot having been at Amman for three years while Tweedie may well have been out of practice. Whatever the reason for the crash (the accident record card is missing), Wallage and Tweedie were both killed. Wallage was 30 years old.

*   *   *

Flight Lieutenant R. C. B. Brading DFC, MiD, 26 July 1926

Reginald Carey Brenton Brading was the son of Francis and Rebecca Brading, born on 4 May 1899 in Croydon, Surrey. Living in nearby Addiscombe when the war started, he joined the Royal Naval Air Service when age permitted, which in his case was on 22 May 1917, a couple of weeks or so after his eighteenth birthday.

Once his flying training was completed he was sent to France and joined No. 201 Squadron RAF, the RFC and RNAS having just merged. Flying Sopwith Camels

The RAF's aerobatic team of 1921 at Hendon. Left to right: William E.G. 'Pedro' Mann DFC, Arthur Coningham DSO, MC, DFC, Thomas F.N. Gerrard DSC, CdG, Brading, and Christopher Draper DSC.

he scored his first victory on 2 May, a two-seater shared with other members of his flight, which was commanded by Captain S. M. Kinkead DSC. On the 15th he shared an Albatros DV Scout, again with Kinkead leading, but with the squadron CO, Major C. D. Booker DSO, DSC in on the action.

From then onwards he scored all his own victories, which in total numbered thirteen by mid-September, seven of them Fokker DVIIs and one reported as a Pfalz DXII. His final victory, on 16 September, saw the pilot of the Fokker attempt to take to his parachute, but it failed, taking its luckless owner to his death. Reg's first Distinguished Flying Cross was gazetted on 2 November 1918:

This officer has accounted for seven enemy machines – two shot down in flames and five out of control. In addition he has displayed marked skill and bravery in attacking troops and transport. Four times in one day he engaged troops, etc., on the roads with machine-gun fire, inflicting casualties and causing great confusion.

This was soon followed by a Bar, the citation appearing in the *London Gazette* of 3 December:

An exceptionally keen and daring patrol leader who has accounted for five enemy machines during the last month. On 2nd September while leading his flight, he observed twelve Fokker biplanes, which he at once engaged, driving down one out of control. Later, on the same day, he engaged a formation of Fokkers that were harassing our Corps machines, causing one to crash. This officer's skill and bravery have proved a great incentive to the other pilots of his squadron.

Immediately after the war Brading was sent to the Baltic, flying against the Russian Bolshevik forces, and for his work he received a mention in despatches. Remaining in the RAF, in 1921 his flying skills were recognised by being asked to join the service's aerobatic team, a team flying Sopwith Snipe fighters. The five-man team was led by another former Naval pilot, Major Christopher Draper DSC, the team putting on a spectacular show during the Air Pageant of July 1921 to an estimated crowd of 100,000 people at Hendon. All five participants were former First World War aces, W. E. G. 'Pedro' Mann DFC, Arthur Coningham DSO, MC, DFC, T. F. N. 'Teddy' Gerrard DSC, Brading and Chris Draper.

Serving at the Central Flying School at Upavon in 1922, he was flying a Snipe (F2386) on a test flight on 1 June. In doing so he accidently moved the main petrol cock with his foot while operating the rudder, causing the engine to fail. Luckily he got down safely.

In 1924 he was serving with No. 19 Squadron at Duxford. Again flying a Snipe (E8245) he was coming into land when he collided with an Avro 504 (3014) whose pilot was doing practise landings. Nobody was injured and the court of enquiry found:

The cause of the accident was in our opinion due to the difference of opinion on the part of the two pilots as to the direction of the very light wind, and that both pilots happened to be looking over the starboard side. The accident was not due to negligence.

Like so many other interwar airmen, Reg Brading received a posting to the Middle East, and by the end of 1925 was on the staff of Station Headquarters in Basrah. On 26 July, for reasons not totally clear, he hitched a ride in a 45 Squadron Vickers Vernon (J7143), a former Vimy Ambulance machine, rebuilt and converted into a Vernon III. The pilot was Flying Officer Oswald Kempson Stirling-Webb and, other than Brading, aboard was Squadron Leader Eric Miller Pollard, Flying Officer Percy Mee (the co-pilot), Leading Aircraftman Jock Henderson, Sergeant Edgar Kennedy, Aircraftman First Class Horace Leslie Davies and Mr Francis

The 45 Squadron Vickers Vernon in which Reggie Brading was killed at Hinaidi, Iraq.

Crawford Inglis from Works and Buildings. Pollard was commanding officer of No. 6 Armoured Car Company and a former First World War pilot. Upon take-off from Hinaidi, on what was a routine mail run to Kirkuk, the aeroplane suffered engine failure at 100 feet; it crashed into No. 1 Squadron's hangar and was so badly smashed it was written off. With the exception of Flying Officer Mee and LAC Henderson, who only suffered slight injuries, all were killed. Also killed was Aircraftman Second Class Edgar Whittle who had been working in the hangar. Brading was 26 years old.

*   *   *

Flight Lieutenant H. R. Junor DFC, 19 August 1926

Hugh Robert Junor was born in Gillingham, Kent, on 15 July 1895, the son of Robert Hugh Junor, a chief engine room artificer in the Royal Navy who came from Hebburn on Tyne originally. The family later moved to 4 Chelsea Road, Portsmouth, young Junor attending Milton School there. He became an apprentice fitter and worked a three-year apprenticeship with the Thorneycroft Company. While doing so he joined the Royal Horse Artillery (Territorial Force) in February 1913, becoming a bombardier. During this time he also attended the Duke of York's Royal Military School, then the Hibernian Military School, and the Queen Victoria School.

Lieutenant H. R. Junor by his BE12 in Palestine in 1918.

In 1916 he was told he would be going to the Middle East, and found himself bound for Egypt by ship from Devonport Naval Base in Plymouth on 19 February. Arriving at Port Said in March he began to think that aviation was the way forward, so enlisted into the Royal Flying Corps and was gazetted second lieutenant in October. On completing his training he became operational, often flying in support of Major T. E. Lawrence's (Lawrence of Arabia's) Arab forces. During September 1918 two aircraft had arrived from Aqaba, one piloted by Junor, the other by Lieutenant A. W. Murphy.

On 10 September, Lawrence and some of his men were in the process of blowing up the Turkish Yarmuck section of the Palestine railway line but an enemy aircraft started to snoop about, especially after one charge exploded, sending up black smoke. The enemy pilot spotted the Arab force

Colonel T. E. Lawrence with Captain T. Henderson MC, who, as part of the 'Arabian Detachment', assisted Lawrence in Palestine. Note the HP bombers to the right.

and headed for home with the news and not long afterwards two Turkish two-seaters and four scouts arrived. These proceeded to bomb and strafe the Arabs, but ground fire from those on the ground forced the hostile aircraft to climb to a higher altitude. Lawrence was hoping for support from Murphy in his Bristol Fighter (A7188) but his aircraft had been disabled in a fight on the 15th.

Junor had been advised about the enemy aircraft and decided to fly to Lawrence's support, in a BE12, arriving just as Lawrence was expecting more attacks from the air. Lawrence was to write in his book *The Seven Pillars of Wisdom*:

We watched with mixed feelings, for his [Junor's] hopelessly old-fashioned machine made him cold meat for any one of the enemy scouts or two-seaters: but at first he astonished them, as he rattled in with his two guns. They scattered for a careful look at this unexpected opponent. He flew westwards across the line, and they went after in pursuit, with that amiable weakness of aircraft for a hostile machine, however important the ground target. We were left in perfect peace.

With the lull, it gave Lawrence and his men time to disperse and get away from the area. He and his men had just set off towards Mezerib when:

*… again we heard the drone of engines, and to our astonishment, Junor reappeared,
still alive, though attended on three sides by enemy machines, spitting bullets. He
was twisting and slipping splendidly, firing back. Their very numbers hindered
them but of course the affair could have only one ending.*

*In the faint hope that he might get down intact we rushed towards the railway
where there was a strip of ground, not too boulder-strewn. Everyone helped to
clear it at speed, while Junor was being driven lower. He threw us a message to say
his petrol was [almost] finished. We worked feverishly for five minutes and then
put out a landing signal. He dived at it, but as he did so the wind flawed and blew
across at a sharp angle. The cleared strip was too little in any case. He took ground
beautifully, but the wind puffed across once more. His undercarriage went, and the
plane turned over in the rough.*

*We rushed to the rescue, but Junor was out, with no more hurt than a cut on
the chin. He took off his Lewis gun, and the Vickers, and the drums of tracer
ammunition for them. We threw everything into Young's Ford, and fled, as one of
the Turkish two-seaters dived viciously and dropped a bomb on the wreck. Junor,
five minutes later, was asking for another job. Joyce gave him a Ford for himself
and he ran boldly down the line till near Deraa, and blew a gap in the rails there
before the Turks saw him. They found such zeal excessive, and opened on him with
their guns, but he rattled away again in his Ford, unhurt for the third time.*

This action, witnessed by Lawrence, formed the basis of a recommendation
for Junor's Distinguished Flying Cross, which was approved and gazetted on 8
February 1919:

A Gloster Gamecock
of No. 43 Squadron,
similar to the one which
Junor was flying on 19
August 1926.

On 17th [sic] *September this officer performed an act of conspicuous merit and gallantry. Single-handed, he engaged five enemy machines, and so protected the Arab force from aerial attack at a most critical time when they were engaged in destroying an important railway. Lieutenant Junor continued the combat till he was driven down by force of numbers, his petrol supply being practically exhausted.*

After the war Junor saw service in Afghanistan, for which he received a mention in despatches in August 1920. In December 1919, Junor was granted a short service commission which became permanent three years later. By 1925 he was flying at the Royal Aircraft Establishment at Farnborough. He suffered an accident on 16 October in a BF2b (J6689) with Flight Lieutenant R. A. de H. Haig in the rear cockpit. They were testing landing lights during some night flying and crashed on Farnborough's airfield. Both men were slightly injured and were treated at Cambridge Hospital.

This year also saw Junor married to Elsie Tarrant, daughter of W. G. Tarrant whose company built 'Tarrant Huts' during the First World War and also the ill-fated Tabor Triplane. They set up home in Ash Vale, Hampshire.

A year later, on 19 August 1926, Junor was asked to test-fly a Gloster Gamecock of No. 43 Squadron (J7906) to investigate a reported wing flutter. He took off from Hucclecote but during the test one of the machine's ailerons became detached and the machine broke up. Junor baled out but was too low for his parachute to deploy properly and he was killed.

His funeral took place at St. Mary's Church, Byfleet, Surrey, where he and Elsie had married the year before. Junor was a month passed his thirty-first birthday.

* * *

Flight Lieutenant W. G. Meggitt MC, 28 January 1927

Losses and injuries in the Royal Air Force were recorded on Casualty Cards in the First World War and by post-war this card became known as the A.M. Form 470. Most officers suffering accidents, fatal or otherwise, might have one, but William Geoffrey Meggitt had at least four. Unfortunately the one recording his death on 28 January 1927 is missing.

Meggitt was born on 8 April 1894 and came from Newport in South Wales. In February 1913 he volunteered for the Hertfordshire Yeomanry as a private, but when war came, having left the Yeomanry in July 1914, he moved on once war began and was gazetted second lieutenant to the 3rd (Reserve) Battalion of the

Welsh Regiment, in March 1915. He was wounded in action on 9 July 1916, so he then decided to volunteer for the Royal Flying Corps as an observer. Back in France in September 1916, he was assigned to No. 25 Squadron that flew FE2b 'pusher' fighters. Seated in the wind-blasted open-front cockpit behind his Lewis gun, he achieved four combat successes with various pilots between October 1916 and February 1917. This brought him the award of the Military Cross, gazetted 17 April:

For conspicuous gallantry and devotion to duty while one of a patrol engaging five hostile machines. He drove down one enemy machine and then attacked another, which was seen to go down vertically. He had previously brought down three hostile machines.

This action was fought on 15 February 1917, his pilot on this occasion being Captain L. L. Richardson from Australia. Lance Richardson received the MC a month after Meggitt, but was killed in action on 13 April.

Flight Lieutenant W. G. Meggitt MC.

Posted home on rest Meggitt took pilot training, but during his period of instruction was injured while flying a BE12 (A4010) with 'A' Squadron at the Central Flying School on 1 June 1917, the cause being noted as an 'error of judgement'.

Once qualified, Meggitt returned to active duty in France, being posted to No. 22 Squadron flying BF2b machines, the famed Bristol Fighters. He joined the squadron in September but only achieved two victories, one each on 10 and 11 October, both Albatros Scouts. He was shot down in combat with Jasta 36 on 8 November, claimed by the German ace Leutnant Heinrich Bongartz, the twenty-first victory of the German's eventual thirty-three. Meggitt's observer, Captain F. A. Durrad, was killed.

Although wounded and a prisoner, he had at least survived, but he must have been in poor health as he was repatriated back to England on 2 June 1918, where he saw out the war. He decided to remain in the RAF after the war, gaining a permanent commission with effect from 28 June 1920. By 1921 he was living with his wife Lydia, in Stoke Newington, Middlesex. His next casualty record was filled out while he was serving with No. 14 Squadron at Ramleh, Palestine, a unit also

An Armstrong Whitworth
Siskin III of 41 Squadron.

equipped with Bristol Fighters. During an organised hockey game he received a hit from an opponent's stick on his right knee on 27 February 1923. His injury was described as synovitis – the inflammation of the membrane surrounding a joint. Nothing too serious, but painful.

By the end of that year, Meggitt was back in England and while playing rugger at the Portsmouth United Services Ground a tackle had him fall on his left shoulder causing a severe strain that again took him away from his flying duties.

His next posting was to No. 41 Squadron based at RAF Northolt. The squadron was equipped with Armstrong Whitworth Siskin IIIs, the first metal biplane fighter with the RAF. On 28 January 1927 he was involved in a crash at Norbury and succumbed to his injuries in Croydon General Hospital. He was 32 years of age.

* * *

Flight Lieutenant W. H. Longton DFC & 2 Bars, AFC, 6 June 1927

Known to everyone as 'Scruffy', Walter Hunt Longton was born at Whiston, just east of Liverpool, on 10 September 1892. Soon after he left school he became a motorcar test driver with the Sunbeam Motor Company and was well known locally as a motorcyclist. With his love of speed it was little wonder he joined the Royal Flying Corps when war came in August 1914 and he gained his Royal Aero Club Certificate (No. 2647) on 31 March 1916 and later his RFC 'wings'. However, he was retained as a test pilot, which would indicate that his instructors thought him an above average aviator. His work brought him the award of the Air Force Cross, promulgated in the *London Gazette* of 2 June 1918:

In recognition of distinguished service rendered during the War.

By this date he had finally been allowed to fly operationally, and joined No. 85 Squadron, commanded by the well-known Canadian, Major W. A. Bishop VC, DSO, MC, this unit being equipped with the SE5A fighter. His piloting skills helped him achieve six aerial victories between July and mid-August, which brought him the first of his Distinguished Flying Crosses. The citation for this award did not appear in the *London Gazette* until 2 November 1918, just a few days away from the Armistice, and it began with this account of his sixth and final victory with 85 Squadron:

Mr W. H. Longton in March 1916, having just completed his RAC flying tests.

> *On the 22nd August this officer led his formation of six machines to attack an equal number of enemy scouts. All the latter were accounted for, four being crashed and the remaining two driven down out of control. A brilliant performance, reflecting the greatest credit on this officer as leader, and all who took part in the engagement. During the last seven weeks, Lieutenant Longton has destroyed seven* [sic] *enemy aircraft.*

One action he was involved in occurred on 24 July. A patrol of 85 Squadron, flying in two layers, saw six enemy aircraft, which the lower section decoyed towards the British lines. In the meantime the higher flight, of which Scruffy was a part, then attacked from the east, which resulted in four of the enemy being shot down.

Captain W. H. Longton DFC, AFC.

Following a short rest leave, Scruffy was posted to No. 24 Squadron, another SE5A unit, serving as a flight commander. His next five victories were all achieved during October 1918, bringing his war total to eleven. All eleven were deemed as destroyed; many pilots were credited with 'out of control' victories in the First World War, which in the Second World War would be assessed as 'probables'. His victims included six enemy fighters, four two-seaters, and a kite observation balloon. A Bar to his DFC followed, the citation in the *Gazette* of 8 February 1919 relating:

Between 29th September and 9th October, this officer carried out twelve tactical reconnaissance missions, bringing back most valuable information; he also displayed great gallantry in attacking enemy troops on the ground. On 9th October, when on a low patrol, he observed a machine-gun nest which appeared to be the sole obstacle to our cavalry advance. Having informed the cavalry and field artillery of the situation, he co-operated with the former in their attack, and, after the enemy had been driven out, pursued them with machine-gun fire as they retreated.

His efforts on 9 October were written up in the RAF *Communiqués*:

Capt. W. H. Longton, 24 Sqn, landed near our cavalry and reported an enemy machine gun nest which was worrying them, enabling our guns to be turned on to it. Capt. Longton then took off and attacked the enemy with machine gun fire as they scattered.

During the last year of the war, fighter aircraft were increasingly used for ground attack and ground support operations. Longton and his fellow pilots were fully engaged in such missions as well as fighting in the air. It says much for his prowess in air combat that the second Bar to his DFC came in mid-1919, long after the war had ended, but was obviously for his success against the German Air Service.

By the time of this, his fourth award, Scruffy was no longer in the service, having resigned his commission, but he decided to re-enlist, receiving a permanent commission in August 1919. He now began a series of flying displays at various air pageants, such as one at Hendon on 3 July 1920, in a Sopwith Camel. He would also fly amazing aerobatics and, together with air exhibitions and air races, his name was almost constantly in newspapers, aviation magazines and journals. None of this hurt his RAF career, and on 1 January 1924 he was promoted to squadron leader.

He still continued with his exhibitions and air racing. However, his flying skill and experience did not help him during his final race meeting at Bournemouth between 4 and 6 June 1927. The racecourse at Ensbury Park served as the airfield and he was involved in a medium power handicap race, flying a Blackburn B1 'Bluebird' (G-EBKD). Among the contestants was Flight Lieutenant David D'Arcy Greig DFC, Lawrence Pratt Openshaw, the test pilot with Westland Aircraft, and Dudley Watts, a young pilot and private aircraft owner. Openshaw had been in the Navy and served in the Royal Naval Air Service and then the RAF during the war, having learnt to fly in March 1915. He was the son of Dr Thomas Openshaw CB, CMG, FRCS, LSA, TD, of Bury, Lancashire. In 1888 the doctor

The Westland Widgeon III (G-EBPW) flown by Openshaw on 6 June 1927, into which Longton collided.

and surgeon had gained a measure of fame for inspecting a liver from the Jack the Ripper murders.

The meeting did not get off to a good start, for on Saturday the 4th, Major Harold Hemming AFC, flying a DH37A (G-EBDO), hit the ground's scoreboard and crashed in front of the enclosures. Hemming was severely injured and his passenger, Mr. C. St. John Plevins, aged 24, died later in hospital.

There were twelve aircraft involved in the fateful race on Monday the 6th. It was the first race of the day, the 'Medium Power Handicap'. During the second lap, in the midst of one turn round the course, Greig heard some very close engine noise and, looking up, saw the wheels of Watts' aeroplane only two or three feet above him. Greig quickly pushed the stick of his DH Genet Moth forward to get out of the way. Moments later, as the aeroplanes began another turn, two aircraft collided ahead of him. Openshaw was flying a Westland Widgeon III (G-EBPW) and he and Scruffy Longton crunched into each other. The crumpled wreckage of both aircraft spun down and burst into flames upon impact. Both men died instantly. Greig later commented that in other races Scruffy had often made a practice of climbing slightly in all his turns and diving down again once the turn had been completed. This may have contributed to the collision on this occasion.

Scruffy Longton was buried at Upavon Cemetery, Wiltshire. He was 34 years old.

*   *   *

Colonel F. F. R. Minchin CBE, DSO, MC & Bar MiD (3), 31 August 1927
Flying Officer L. Hamilton MBE, DFC, 31 August 1927

In the mid-1920s, the aviation world was captivated by record-breaking flights. They could be endurance flights, races, long distance flights, pioneering flights – the world was the aviator's oyster. As more and more records, achievements or distances were conquered, those remaining necessarily became more and more dangerous. Crossing the vast oceans was among these.

Major F. F. R. Minchin CBE, DSO, MC.

Many had thought of flying the Atlantic as perhaps the biggest achievable goal for aeroplanes at this stage of aircraft development. John Alcock and Arthur Brown had crossed it from west to east in a Vickers Vimy in June 1919, taking just over sixteen hours, flying from Newfoundland to Ireland. Both had been knighted as a result. Then, as a number of aviators were seriously preparing for more transatlantic flights, Charles Lindbergh not only achieved success in a single-engined aeroplane but did it on his own, between 20 and 21 May 1927, flying a Ryan monoplane from Long Island, USA, to Paris, France.

The remaining goal was to fly in the opposite direction, east to west, without the benefit of prevailing westerly winds. Earlier in May 1927, two Frenchmen had

Dan Minchin and Leslie Hamilton prior to the Atlantic flight. Behind them is the Fokker FVIIA, *St. Raphael*, in which the Atlantic attempt was flown.

tried, the famous First World War fighter ace Charles Nungesser, with François Coli. They departed from France early on 8 May and were never seen again. In England, two other men were planning their attempt to fly from east to west: Colonel Minchin and Captain Hamilton.

Frederick Frank Reilly Minchin, born in Madras, India, on 16 June 1890, was the son of Major General Frederick Minchin from County Tipperary, Ireland. Coming to England he attended Eastbourne College and then Sandhurst in 1909, being commissioned into the Connaught Rangers in 1912. He also took great interest in early aviation and decided to learn to fly, achieving this in February 1913 by obtaining his Royal Aero Club Certificate No. 419 with the Eastbourne Aviation Company. He then went to Canada, but as war was declared the following year he volunteered to serve, being commissioned into the Princess Patricia's Canadian Light Infantry in September 1914. Sailing with his regiment, he was soon back in England where he decided on a secondment to the Royal Flying Corps in March 1915, his Aero Certificate making this an easy transition. Even so his first posting was as an observer with No. 1 Squadron.

By October he had completed his service in France, become a pilot, and was posted to No. 14 Squadron, going to the Middle East with this unit, as a founder member. For his work over the Eastern Desert, Minchin, known as 'Dan', was awarded the Military Cross in May 1916:

> *For conspicuous gallantry and skill on many occasions, notably when leading a successful bomb and machine-gun raid on a force of the enemy which he had located overnight. Next day he took part in two other raids. During these operations he flew for thirteen hours over enemy country.*

The Fokker taking off
for the ill-fated trip.

Promoted to flight commander, he continued supporting the British army into Palestine and in the Western Desert. This resulted in a Bar to his MC, gazetted 25 November:

For conspicuous gallantry in action. He flew 150 miles at night to bomb an enemy aerodrome, descending to 500 feet, and doing serious damage. On another occasion he landed 45 miles from our line to pick up a pilot of a damaged machine in hostile country.

On 2 November 1916, Minchin himself was rescued from behind the lines, having had his fuel tank shot through during a combat with a German aircraft. Minchin soon became a major and was given command of No. 47 Squadron in Salonika from 1 January 1917. His command of this unit brought him the Distinguished Service Order on 1 January 1918, which he added to three mentions in despatches for his war service. Returning to England he took up staff duties for the rest of the war. Continuing his RAF service he became a CBE in July 1920, although by this time he had become a senior pilot with Imperial Airways.

*   *   *

Leslie Hamilton was born on 26 October 1897 and when war came he was living in Crowborough, Sussex. He joined the colours as soon as age permitted, becoming a corporal in the 2nd Battalion of the Honourable Artillery Company in May 1915. He then moved to the Royal Engineers, attached to the IWT – Inland Waterways Transport Section. However, he decided his future was in the air and transferred to the Royal Flying Corps. Once he achieved his 'wings' he was posted out to the Middle East to join No. 17 Squadron in Salonika in early 1918, which was flying SE5A fighters.

Soon after gaining his first combat victory on 21 April, the fighters of 17 and Minchin's 47 Squadron merged to form 150 Squadron. Now Hamilton was among a fairly unique group of pilots, including Gerald Gibbs MC, A. G. Goulding MC, G. G. Bell and F. D. Travers. During the summer, Hamilton brought his score of kills to six, the last one being a Fokker DVII, the first of this type seen on this front. Along with Bell and Travers, he received the DFC for his prowess (*London Gazette* 8 February 1919):

A gallant and skilful scout pilot who never hesitates to attack enemy formations, however superior in numbers. During recent operations he has rendered exceptional service. He has himself brought down, or assisted in bringing down, six enemy machines.

Hamilton remained in the RAF post-war having been granted a short-service commission in October 1919 and by 1922 was serving with No. 24 Squadron, flying Bristol Fighters and DH9A aircraft at RAF Kenley, England. The squadron had been reformed in 1920 as a communications unit tasked with the responsibility of providing air transport for British government officials, visiting heads of state, and senior members of all three Military Services. In addition to the Bristols and DH9s it could also muster DH4As, Avro 504s and a Vickers Vimy.

He married Barbara Webber on 2 July 1921 and in June the following year took part in the third RAF Aerial Pageant at Hendon, coming second in a race between Avro 504s, while the rest of the squadron flew a demonstration of formation flying. That September, Hamilton took part in the first King's Cup Air Race, flying a DH9C belonging to Lady Anne Savile (Princess Loewenstein-Wertheim), who flew with him as a passenger. They came sixth.

In June 1923 he took part in the fifth RAF Pageant with a team representing Kenley, and Hamilton was in the winning team, flying a 504. Hamilton was made an MBE in June, and in September he received a permanent RAF commission. He continued to fly in various air displays but in September 1924 he was posted to the Inland Area Depot at RAF Henlow. That December he was placed on half pay until 15 September 1925, but he then decided to leave the service, resigning on 19 September.

It did not end his flying however. In a Martinsyde F6 he flew from London to St. Moritz, Switzerland, via Paris and Zurich, in eight hours, on 29 January 1925 and in August competed in events in the Royal Aero Club Meeting at Lympne, Kent. He then teamed up with Geoffrey de Havilland, Hubert Broad and others, becoming a founder member of the British Private Aircraft Owner's Club in early 1926. By this time, Dan Minchin and he had started talking about making a transatlantic attempt, the two men having, it will be remembered, known each other in Salonika during the war.

The idea was to fly from RAF Upavon to Ottawa, Canada, and they chose for the purpose a Fokker F.VIIA aeroplane, named the *St. Raphael* (H-NAEG). However, they needed a sponsor and this came in the form of Lady Anne Savile. Lady Anne was the daughter of John Savile, 4th Earl of Mexborough, born in May 1864, so aged 61 at this time. Her mother had been Agnes Raphael, hence the naming of the Fokker. Anne had married Prince Ludwig Loewenstein-Wertheim-Freudenberg in 1898, but strangely he had almost immediately gone to the Philippines during the Spanish-American War. In the Battle of Caloocan, between Emilio Aguinaldo's insurgents and elements of the US Army, he was killed on 16 March 1899. On his body was found a passport signed by the rebel leader. Anne had remained in Germany until 1918 before returning to England.

Lady Anne Savile,
also known as Princess
Loewenstein.

Having decided to fund the Atlantic flight, Anne took an immense interest in the project, being something of an aviator herself, as already mentioned. Shortly before the planned date of departure, in August 1927, Minchin and Hamilton arrived at Croydon, flying the Fokker in from Amsterdam. They then flew it to Bristol to get the machine's Bristol Jupiter 450 h.p. radial engine tuned up. Within days, the Fokker, the type used by K.L.M. but fitted with extra fuel tanks which allowed for an estimated forty hours of flying time, was ready. The plan was to fly to Baldonnel Airport near Dublin to top up the fuel load and leave for Ottawa.

The day of departure was set for 31 August, and as take-off time approached, Lady Anne arrived in her chauffeur-driven car and, to the consternation of the two flyers, insisted she be taken along, in order to be the first woman to make the trip. Against their better judgement, but conscious of the fact that it was her money that was funding everything, they reluctantly agreed.

Taking off from Upavon on 31 August they headed for Dublin for a final top up, and from there out across the Atlantic. Some 800 miles west of Galway a ship reported seeing a light in the sky, believed to be the Fokker, heading west. That was the last sighting of the aircraft. The fate of its three occupants still remains a mystery.

It was reported that Lady Anne had with her some £200,000 of jewellery in case extra money be needed in the US. A scheme thought up by Hamilton was to take with them 600 one-pound bank notes, which the three of them would autograph and sell for $25 to $30 each as souvenirs.

*   *   *

Wing Commander A. B. Gaskell DSC, 15 September 1927

A student at Lancing College, Sussex, in 1902/3, Arthur Bruce Gaskell was the only son of Charles Bruce and Mrs Evelyn Frances Gaskell of 6 Mortimer Road, Clifton, Gloucestershire, born 11 September 1888. From Lancing, with a Naval career in prospect, he went to the Royal Naval College Britannia in May 1903 as a cadet where he remained until July 1904. His first ship was HMS *London*, seeing service in the Mediterranean, while later ships were HMS *Africa* in 1908 and HMS *Gloucester* in 1910.

Squadron Commander A. B. Gaskell DSC, RN.

Becoming interested in aviation, he undertook flight training at the Central Flying School at Upavon, gaining his flying certificate (No. 503) on 2 June 1913. This led to a posting to the Isle of Grain Air Station and in July 1914 to the seaplane tender HMS *Engadine*, a converted cross-channel ferry. Therefore, when war began he was to see action as a pilot rather than a sailor.

The Navy mounted an air attack on the Zeppelin sheds at Cuxhaven on Christmas Day 1914, with two Short S81s that were called 'Folders' because the wings folded back for storage on board ship. There were only two assigned and Gaskell's engine became troublesome. He had to abort and the other eventually ditched close by a British submarine. However, Gaskell did fly on several bomb raids along the Belgian coast with targets such as Ostend, Zeebrugge and Bruges between February and March 1915. He was then sent to the Naval Flying School at Eastchurch.

In the meantime he married Dorothy Davies at Crickhowell, Breconshire, a marriage that produced two daughters, the family taking up residence at 201 Richmond Road, Kingston upon Thames.

Promoted to squadron commander on 1 January 1916, he commanded the RNAS at Gibraltar and later the station and aerodrome at Thermi-Mytilini on the island of Lesbos in the Aegean Sea. From here he led a number of air attacks on German and Turkish shipping and flew several anti-submarine patrols. In October 1917 Mytilini came under threat and Gaskell was ordered to evacuate all forces there, a job he completed successfully without a single casualty, bringing away all the stores as well. For this he received the Distinguished Service Cross, gazetted 26 April 1918:

In recognition of his services on the occasion of the evacuation of the Thermi aerodrome on the 9th – 15th October 1917 under continuous bombardment from the enemy.

With the formation of the RAF on 1 April 1918 he became a major, and on 30 June rose to lieutenant colonel. With the war over, he was given a permanent commission in the RAF in August 1919, and made wing commander on 1 January 1924.

He took the RAF Staff College course in 1924/5 and the next year he was on the staff of Air Vice-Marshal Sir Edward Ellington, AOC Iraq, being responsible for all training in the region. He kept his hand in by flying aircraft of local units and on 19 September 1927 borrowed a BF2b aircraft from No. 30 Squadron at Hinaidi. He took Leading Aircraftman William Ronald Kittow-Roberts (361810) up in the rear cockpit, but they crashed. Gaskell was killed instantly, Kittow-Roberts later dying of his injuries. Gaskell was 39 years of age.

*   *   *

Captain W. P. Erwin DSC, 18 October 1927

William Portwood Erwin was born in Ryan, Oklahoma, on 18 October 1927, son of a Baptist minister who also lived in Amarillo, Texas and Chicago, Illinois. Volunteering for service aviation, he was assigned, once trained as a pilot, to the 1st Observation Squadron, serving in France with the American Expeditionary Force.

Flying Salmson 2A2 machines, he and his various observers were often in action against German fighters and accounted for eight hostiles shot down. One of his observers, Lieutenant A. E. Easterbrook, was credited with five victories too, four of them with Erwin. Another, Byrne Baucom, with three, or possibly six (see later in this book). Erwin was awarded the Distinguished Service Cross and was also cited in French General Orders on 29 November 1918. His DSC citation read:

Captain W. P. Erwin DSC.

For extraordinary heroism in action in the Chateau Thierry and St. Mihiel salients, France. Lt. Erwin with Lieutenant Byrne V. Baucom, observer, by a long period of faithful and heroic operations, set an inspiring example of courage and devotion to duty to his entire Squadron. Throughout the Château Thierry actions in June and July 1918, he flew under the worst weather conditions and successfully carried out his missions in the face of heavy odds. In the St. Mihiel sector, 12 to 15 September 1918, he repeated his previous courageous work. He flew as low as 50 feet from the ground behind the enemy's lines, harassing German troops with machine gun fire and subjected himself to attack from the ground batteries, machine guns and rifles. He twice drove off enemy planes which were attempting to destroy an American observation balloon. On 12-13 September he flew at extremely low altitudes and carried out infantry contact patrols successfully. Again on 12 September he attacked a German battery, forced the crew to abandon it, shot off his horse a German officer who was trying to escape, drove the cannoneers to their dugouts and kept them there until the infantry could come up and capture them.

The French citation stated:

On 20 July 1918, he volunteered for an infantry liaison mission at night fall, executed this mission at 200 metres altitude. He brought back his observer who was mortally wounded, and his plane was full of bullet holes.

A Salmson 2A2 of the 1st Observation Squadron, USAS, being flown by Lieutenants W. P. Erwin and B. V. Baucom.

On 1 August, in two desperate attempts to take photographs of German batteries and machine gun positions at Fère-en-Tardenois, Erwin and his Spad escort battled through enemy fighter opposition with great determination. Unhappily, on the first sortie only a few plates were able to be exposed and on the second trip the plates were destroyed by enemy fire, while his observer, Lieutenant E. B. Spencer, was wounded. Erwin claimed a Fokker shot down with his front gun but this is not included in his final score.

Once back in the USA after the war, Erwin continued to fly, but also took time to marry a lady named Constance.

It was an age, just like in Europe, for the testing of the elements, especially in long distance flights and air races. At around the time of his 32nd birthday in October 1927, Erwin took part in the Dole Air Races, the objective of which was to fly between Oakland in California and Honolulu in Hawaii. Erwin flew in a Swallow Special Monoplane (NC1731), but, losing six feet of fabric from along the fuselage, was forced to abort.

On 18 October, together with Alvin H. Eichwaldt as navigator, Erwin decided to fly from Oakland to Auckland, New Zealand. In the meantime, two flyers had gone missing on the Dole Race over the Pacific, so Erwin was asked to try to locate them. The two men headed out towards Hawaii, then planned to cross to Manila and Hong Kong in a search pattern. Out of the blue, at 21.05 pm, an SOS was received from Eichwaldt saying that their airplane, the *Dallas Spirit*, was in a tailspin. Soon after came a second SOS, then all went quiet. As far as could be ascertained, they were around 600 miles out from San Francisco, having taken off at 14.15 that afternoon. They were never seen or heard from again.

* * *

Flight Lieutenant S. M. Kinkead DSO, DSC & Bar, DFC & Bar, MiD, 12 March 1928

Samuel Marcus Kinkead was born in Johannesburg on 25 February 1897, the son of Samuel and Helen Kinkead, he Irish from Ballykelly, she Scottish. The families of both parents had emigrated to South Africa in the late 1880s and Samuel had died in 1903 aged 55 leaving Helen to continue bringing up their four children, Tom, Samuel, Vilda and Nora. They lived at 69 Browning Street, Johannesburg. The two boys attended the Marist Brothers College there, with Samuel later going to Jepperson High School in January 1913 where he remained until the end of 1914. A keen athlete he represented his school in athletics, cricket and was in the football XI. By the end of 1913 he had joined the School Cadet Force and been made a sergeant. At this time his nickname was 'Babs' but that gradually changed to 'Kink' once in England.

Once he reached 18 he left for England to enlist into the Royal Naval Air Service and by the late summer of 1915 was learning to fly at the Naval Flying School, Eastbourne, Sussex. Once training was complete he was posted to the Dardanelles and to No. 2 Wing, and later to No. 3 Wing RNAS. He therefore took part in the Gallipoli Campaign, flying any number of flights in the area.

On 11 August 1916, flying a Bristol Scout, he escorted four bombers tasked with raiding an aerodrome at Maswakli, near to the Bulgarian city of Xanthi. The formation was attacked by a Fokker Eindecker which Kinkead engaged and was credited

Lieutenant S. M. Kinkead when with 201 Squadron in 1918.

with driving the enemy machine down. On the 28th, a more positive result occurred. Three enemy aircraft flew over Thasos aerodrome and were engaged by three RNAS machines. Kink was in a Nieuport two-seater (though some reports say a Bristol). They attacked two of them, chasing them off, and one was forced to land two miles north of Zinelli. Kinkead was credited with a third 'victory' before his tour ended, but details are not recorded, other than the date being 1 September.

With the Gallipoli Campaign ended and the RNAS withdrawn, Kinkead went into hospital on Malta with malaria, remaining there until repatriated to England. Unfit for duty until February 1917, he then went to the RNAS Central Training Establishment at Cranwell, spending three weeks on a refresher course. In September it was back to the war but this time to France and No. 1 Squadron RNAS, flying Sopwith Triplanes. In this same month his brother Tom was killed during flight training in England.

Kinkead wasted no time once back in action, downing two DFW two-seaters on 17 September, another on the 18th and a third on the 29th, this time an Albatros DIII Scout. One more victory in November brought his score overall to nine by the end of the year, although during those last weeks it is recorded he had indecisive combats with six enemy aircraft. He was also to the fore in attacking German troops on the ground, and forced down at least one balloon. By the end of the year, 1 Naval had swopped its Triplanes for Sopwith Camels.

The squadron had a period in England because of bombing raids on London but returned to France in February and based itself near Dunkirk. At this time Kinkead was awarded the Distinguished Service Cross, gazetted on 22 February 1918:

In recognition of the conspicuous gallantry and skill displayed by him in the face of the enemy in aerial combats, notably on the following occasions: On 14 October 1917, he brought down an enemy machine, and immediately afterwards encountered and drove off a group of seven hostile aeroplanes. On 4 December 1917, he brought down an enemy two-seater machine completely out of control. By his skill and determination in attacking enemy machines he has always shown a fine example to other pilots.

In March 1 Naval moved south to support the RFC, especially when the German March offensive began. During March he accounted for four aircraft shot down, then a Fokker Triplane on 6 April. In May he claimed seven more, all Albatros Scouts. His actions in March brought him a Bar to his DSC, gazetted on 26 April:

For the skill and courage displayed by him as a pilot. On 22 March 1918, he attacked and drove down out of control an Albatros Scout which was attacking a French machine. He has brought down many other enemy machines. He is an exceptionally good pilot, and a clever and plucky fighter, and has performed very fine work, on both Offensive Patrols and Low Flying missions.

It seems that Sammy Kinkead was always in the thick of any fighting, engaging the enemy both in the air and on the ground, harrying troops, guns and transport, something the RAF was becoming good at, and something that demoralised German soldiers to a great extent. By now of course, the RFC and RNAS had merged to become the Royal Air Force, so rather than being a Naval flight commander, he was now officially a captain.

His final six claims were all over Fokker DVIIs, during July and August, which brought his overall score to thirty-two, although an unofficial score might be as high as forty. Kinkead was awarded the Distinguished Flying Cross, the citation appearing in the *London Gazette* for 3 August:

A skilful and gallant leader, who has attacked enemy formations superior in numbers with marked success. In a recent engagement, his patrol flew to the assistance of some of our machines which were greatly outnumbered by the enemy, and succeeded in accounting for three enemy machines and scattered the remainder.

On 13 August, 201's commanding officer, Major C. D. Booker, was shot down in combat, leaving Kinkead as acting CO. However, when a new CO was appointed it seemed a good time for Kinkead to be rested. On the 26th he was posted back to England where he had been recommended for a fourth decoration, which turned out to be a Bar to his DFC. Gazetted on 2 November, the citation read:

On a recent date, this officer engaged a large party of troops in a wood. The engagement lasted for an hour, but so persistent was his attack that the enemy broke and dispersed. During this attack he was harassed by six hostile Scouts. Later on he shot down an enemy two-seater in our lines. A bold and daring airman.

Back in England, Kinkead took two weeks leave before being posted to the Grand Fleet School of Aerial Fighting and Gunnery at East Fortune on 14 September. He remained there as a fighting instructor until November. Wishing to remain in the RAF he was offered a short service commission in 1919 but was then recruited by another former RNAS and RAF ace, Raymond Collishaw DSO, DSC, DFC.

Sammy Kinkead in a Sopwith Camel, 47 Squadron, 1919.

Collishaw was recruiting people to help form a group of airmen to fly in Russia, where a war was taking place between the Bolshevik Red and the Provisional All-Russian Government's White Army – in other words, a Russian revolution that had followed the 1917 anti-government revolution which overthrew the Czar.

Kinkead became part of the fighter element of No. 47 Squadron RAF, flying Camels, which also had a bomber section with De Havilland 9 bombers. Without dealing with the intricacies of this war, suffice to say that Kinkead and his fellow volunteers saw a lot of action against aircraft of the Red Army as well as attacking their forces on the ground. Kinkead himself claimed a number of aerial victories, although only three appear to be positively recorded, all three being Nieuports, during September and October 1919. For his work in Russia, Kink received the Distinguished Service Order, although it was not promulgated in the *Gazette* until April 1920 – after the withdrawal of British forces from Russia:

On 12 October 1919, near Kotluban, this officer led a formation of Camel machines and attacked the Cavalry Division of Dumenko. By skilful tactics in low flying he dispersed this force, which had turned the left flank of the Caucasian Army, and threatened to jeopardise the whole defence of Tsaritsyn. Flying Officer Kinkead has carried out similar attacks on enemy troops, batteries, camps and transport with great success and at considerable personal risk.

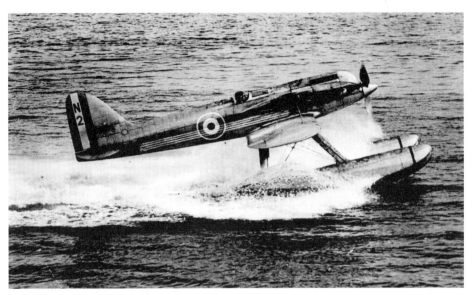

A Supermarine S5 about to take off. It was in this type of aircraft that Kink was killed on 12 March 1928.

Leaving Constantinople in the spring of 1920 he sailed to Egypt where he joined No. 70 Squadron briefly, before heading for England and a post on the staff at the Central Flying School. He was also mentioned in despatches on 20 July. Kink was to remain at the CFS until October 1921. His permanent commission had been confirmed in August 1919 and on 1 January 1921 he made flight lieutenant rank. In preparation for a posting to the Middle East he was attached to No. 24 Squadron for a refresher course. At the end of January 1922 he was posted to No. 30 Squadron in Iraq, whose CO happened to be Ray Collishaw. The squadron was involved in all the usual activities of the RAF's policing role and when a new CO arrived, James Robb DFC, Kink was recommended for an RAF Staff College Course. Kinkead was also given the opportunity to join the RAF's High Speed Flight, whose target was the Schneider Trophy contests.

In the meantime, Kinkead and his squadron were involved in actions over Kurdistan and Mesopotamia, flying DH9A bombers. Following leave in England Kinkead was posted to Cairo on staff duties in March 1925, and soon afterwards came a chance of some long-range flying. Flights were being planned from Cairo to The Cape, helping to establish landing grounds on the way. Kinkead was part of the team.

The next team he was involved with was the RAF's High Speed Flight which, after some wrangling, he joined in 1927, flying in the Venice race that year. The following year he took command of the flight. Preparing for the 1928 race, Kinkead was flying the Supermarine S5 (N221) over Southampton Water on 12 March, but somehow the machine stalled and crashed into the sea. Kink's body was terribly mutilated in the crash, a flying wire decapitating him while the rest of his body was pushed back down the fuselage and had to be cut free. There was no satisfactory explanation as to how the crash had occurred, probably a misjudgement of his height over a glassy sea, but whatever happened, the RAF had lost a brilliant and brave pilot.

He was buried at All Saints' Church, Fawley, Hampshire. He was 31 years of age.

* * *

Captain W. G. R. Hinchliffe DFC, 13 March 1928

The world of flying lost two of its great men in March 1928, Sammy Kinkead on the 12th and Walter George Raymond Hinchliffe on the 13th. Hinchliffe was born in Liverpool on 10 June 1894 to Richard George and Florence (née Williams) Hinchliffe. He was educated at Liverpool College where he became a member of the Officer Training Corps, and then attended medical school, intent on training to become a dentist. He spoke four languages.

However, he then decided to join the army, being commissioned into the North Lancashire Brigade Company (TF) of the Army Service Corps on 20 March 1912, becoming a full lieutenant on 17 September 1914. Moving to the Royal Artillery in 1914, he served with them until deciding to transfer to the Royal Naval Air Service, having gained his Royal Aero Club Certificate (No. 3595) on 21 September 1916.

Once trained he was kept back as an instructor at Cranwell and clocked up an amazing 1,250 flying hours in the next thirteen months, so had gained much valuable experience. Finally

Captain W. G. R. Hinchliffe DFC.

released for more active duty, he was sent to France where he joined No. 10 Naval Squadron, flying Sopwith Camels, in early 1918, claiming his first two victories before the merger of the RFC and RNAS became the Royal Air Force on 1 April.

By mid-May he had accounted for six German aircraft, although his log book indicates he shot down an Albatros two-seater on 17 February, killing its observer, and shared in forcing down three kite balloons on 21 May. His CO noted in the records his claims were nine destroyed, three out of control plus two balloons, making his score fourteen. He also participated in two raids on German airfields, one at night. On 3 June, in Camel C62, he flew a night patrol but had to make a forced landing. Taking off again, the port tyre came off, the Camel swerved to one side, overturned and was badly smashed. Hinchliffe suffered severe facial injuries and lost his left eye. For the rest of his life he wore a patch to cover his disfigurement. He was awarded the Distinguished Flying Cross, although it was not gazetted until the 1919 New Year Honours List.

Hinchliffe spent several weeks in hospitals and eventually was released from the RAF in September 1919. The loss of an eye did not put paid to his flying career, and in 1920 he joined Imperial Airways and then KLM – Royal Dutch Airlines – and flew some of the first air mail flights from Holland to the UK. In 1921 he also flew some of the first civilian passenger night flights from Lympne to Amsterdam, and then Amsterdam to Berlin as well as opening up other routes. From 1922 to 1923 he was KLM's Chief Pilot.

In 1923 he joined Instone Airlines, covering Denmark, Belgium and Paris, and when they merged with Imperial Airways he flew De Havilland Hercules aircraft to Cairo, opening up other eastern routes. His fame spread, and in 1927, when millionaire Charles A. Levine became the first man to cross the Atlantic from America as a flying passenger, it was Hinchliffe who got the job of flying him back to the States.

By this time he had married, to Emilie Gallizien, whom he had met while with KLM, she being the assistant to the company's general manager.

*   *   *

It was now that Elsie Mackay entered his life. The Atlantic Ocean was still a great attraction in the late 1920s, especially after Lindberg's solo flight in 1927, and she wanted to be the first woman to fly the Atlantic. To this end she purchased a Stinson Detroiter aeroplane.

Elsie Mackay, born in 1893, was the daughter of a well-known businessman, James Mackay. Chairman of the Peninsular and Oriental Steam Navigation Company, at one time President of the Bengal Chamber of Commerce, and a member of the Legislative Council of the Viceroy of India, he was also a member of the Council of the Secretary of State for India. It was while in India that his daughter had been born, in Simla. He became the 1st Earl of Inchcape.

Elsie had also been an actress, her stage name being Poppy Wyndham. This name came from her marriage to an actor named Dennis Wyndham in May 1917. Her father disinherited her in response, but the marriage was annulled in 1922. Elsie took

Elsie Mackay, daughter of James Mackay (Earl of Inchcape), who was lost over the Atlantic with Captain Hinchcliffe.

up flying seriously in 1923 and gained her pilot's licence at the De Havilland Flying School. She was often seen flying her Avro biplane and driving her Rolls Royce car – so her father must have taken her back after her divorce. She was also elected to the advisory committee of pilots to the British Empire Air League.

With her Atlantic ambitions uppermost in her mind she approached Hinchliffe with the idea. How keen he was is uncertain but he evidently agreed and she shipped over her Stinson aeroplane, which she named *Endeavour*, to Brooklands. The Detroiter (N4183) was a monoplane with gold-coloured wing tips and a black fuselage, powered by a single Wright Whirlwind 300 h.p. engine that gave a cruising speed of 84 mph.

Having heard of the scheme, her father forbade her to proceed and she promised to comply. However, when he was away on business, she completed the arrangements, but kept everything very secret, even putting the name 'Gordon Sinclair' on the flight manifest to disguise the fact she was going. Even Mrs Hinchliffe was telling people her husband and Elsie were off somewhere else.

Finally at 08.35 am on the morning of 13 March 1928, they boarded the *Endeavour*, lifted off from RAF Cranwell, and headed west. At 13.30 pm the chief lighthouse keeper at Mizen Head on the south-west coast of Cork saw a monoplane over the village of Crookstown. A French steamer later reported seeing them on course for Newfoundland but that was the last sighting. In December that year a single piece of undercarriage, a recognisable tyre included, washed ashore on the coast of north-west Ireland. Hinchliffe was 33 years old, Elsie Mackay, 35.

* * *

Captain B. V. Baucom DSC & Oak Leaf, CdG, 30 May 1928

Byrne Virchow Baucom began flying as an observer but once the war was over trained to become a pilot. The son of Dr. James B. and Mrs Edith E. Baucom (née) Hamill, Byrne was born in Milford, Ellis County, Texas, on 19 June 1892. After graduating from Milford High School, he worked as a linotype machine operator and a reporter for various newspapers in Central Texas, before enrolling into the University of Texas in Austin to study Arts and Sciences in August 1915.

Once America came into the war he joined the US Army in May 1917, becoming a second lieutenant with the 343rd Field Artillery Battalion, but soon afterwards transferred into the Aviation Section of the Army Signals Corps. Trained as an observer he was sent to France in April 1918, the third Baucom brother serving 'over there'. Initially he was attached to a French observation escadrille before being posted to the 1st Observation Group, USAS, where he teamed up with Lieutenant W. P. Erwin (see earlier). His unit flew Spad XIs and later Salmson 2A2 machines.

He and Erwin had any number of experiences during the summer of 1918 and both received the Distinguished Service Cross. Baucom also received an Oak Leaf Cluster and the French *Croix de Guerre*. In air actions he did well in defending their two-seater machine, and in varying accounts is sometimes credited with six combat victories and sometimes three, with others as possibles. In any event, the team survived and so did Baucom on the occasions he flew with other pilots. The citation recorded above in Erwin's story could also relate to Baucom's actions.

Baucom left the service as a captain in 1920, returning to the University of Texas to study law and became involved in politics. In fact he became the 26th Governor of Texas for a while, but then returned to the Air Service and trained to become a pilot in 1921. In July of that year he was at Langley under General Billy Mitchell, flying Martin MC2 bombers. Mitchell and his crews were involved in Mitchell's contention that air power would overshadow sea power, demonstrating this by bombing and sinking four warships set up as targets,

On the left is Lieutenant Byrne V. Baucom with Lieutenants William P. Erwin (centre) and Arthur E. Easterbrook, two of Erwin's observers with the 1st Observation Squadron in 1918.

including the obsolete battleship USS *Alabama*. They were not popular with the Navy in proving how vulnerable they could be to aeroplanes.

Also in 1921 he married Connie Conner of Lexington, Texas, and the following year was serving with the 94th Pursuit Squadron. Later he became director of pursuit training at Kelly Field. Baucom followed this with staff jobs in Washington and then California, before commanding the 47th Training School Squadron.

On 30 May 1928, he was leading a three-plane element flying from Kelly Field to March Field but crashed and was killed near Douglas, Arizona. He was buried in his home town of Milford on 3 June, several thousand people turning out to say farewell to their local hero. As the coffin arrived by train, a lone aeroplane flew over to drop flowers, which was followed by four more aircraft in a five-plane formation with a 'missing-man' slot in honour of Captain Baucom. He was just short of his thirty-sixth birthday.

*   *   *

Flight Lieutenant L. H. Browning MC, DFC, 2 August 1928

The son of a schoolmaster, Lancelot Harold Browning came from Bournemouth, where he was born on 25 September 1897. He received his education at Rosehill School, Banstead, Surrey and then at Wellington 1911-14. Joining the colours upon the outbreak of war, he was gazetted a second lieutenant in the Royal Field Artillery in July 1915. Deciding the air was the way forward, he had himself seconded to the Royal Flying Corps in May 1916 as an observer. Once trained, he was posted out to the Middle East to join No. 30 Squadron in Mesopotamia a month later. Observers usually had to serve a period of apprenticeship before being awarded their observer half-wing, and Browning achieved this by August.

Fight Lieutenant L. H. Browning MC, DFC.

He flew operations as an observer until August 1917 and, requesting pilot training, was sent to Egypt. Once qualified as a pilot he returned to 30 Squadron on 7 December. Once again he accomplished a long tour of flying operations, with a variety of aircraft including RE8s, BE2s Martinsyde Elephants and Bristol Scouts, which resulted in the award of the Military Cross. The citation for this award was not made until October 1918, an unusually long time, for with the formation of the RAF in April 1918, the MC was superseded by the new DFC for RAF aircrew. His citation read:

For conspicuous gallantry and daring while carrying out independent bombing behind the enemy's lines. He was attacked by a fast enemy scout machine, which by skilful piloting and accurate shooting he drove down to its aerodrome. No sooner had the enemy aeroplane landed than Lt Browning dropped a bomb, completely obliterating the pilot who had begun to run away, and damaged his machine. He then continued bombing and while doing so was attacked by two more enemy scouts, both of which he drove off. He showed fine skill and courage throughout.

Promoted to captain, he returned, after a brief leave in England, to Egypt in July 1918, and was then posted to No. 111 Squadron in September, but by November,

A Hawker Woodcock, the type in which Browning was killed in 1928.

with the war at an end, he returned to England. He managed to remain in the service and in 1919 he once again flew back to Mesopotamia, to join No. 63 Squadron and saw active duty during the Kurdistan campaign, flying from Samara and Baghdad on RE8 machines. His efforts were again rewarded, this time with the award of the Distinguished Flying Cross, gazetted on 12 July 1920 (no citation published).

At the end of his tour in the Middle East, he came home to England once again, and by 1928 was a pilot with No. 3 Squadron at RAF Upavon, Wiltshire, flying the Hawker Woodcock fighter aircraft. The Woodcock was not a well-liked aeroplane, displaying a tendency to wing flutter at high speed and a reputation for weakness to the main spar. It was considered unsuitable for aerobatics, while spinning was certainly discouraged.

On 2 August 1928, Browning was approaching Holbeach Range, Lincolnshire, and began lining up on No. 2 target. Completing his firing pass he pulled up and flattened out, starting to turn and climb for another circuit. At this point, people on the ground clearly heard a sudden crackling sound, followed by the sight of the Woodcock's starboard upper wing folding back. It then broke off completely and the machine rolled in an inverted spiral dive into the ground. He died instantly. He was 30 years old.

As a matter of interest, his was the fifty-second serious accident sustained thus far by the RAF in 1928. Comparing this to 1921's fifty-seven, of which twenty-two had been fatal, and 1927 when there had been fifty-five serious accidents, the RAF were keeping up a good average.

Chapter Five

1929–40

Squadron Leader A. G. Jones-Williams MC & Bar, CdG, 17 December 1929
Flight Lieutenant N. H. Jenkins OBE, DFC, DSM, 17 December 1929

The son of Mr and Mrs A.H. Jones-Williams of Cwy Park, Talybont-on-Usk, Breconshire, South Wales, Arthur Gordon Jones-Williams was born on 6 October 1898. He attended Haileybury School (1912-15) and then Sandhurst in 1916. He was commissioned into a Regular Army battalion of the Welsh Regiment on 16 August 1916, and immediately seconded to the Royal Flying Corps.

On completing his training, he was sent to France where he was assigned to No. 29 Squadron, equipped with Nieuport XVII Scouts, arriving at the front on 22 March 1917. He was just in time to participate in Bloody April, the worst month for RFC casualties since the war began, but he survived and even managed to achieve three victories.

During May he became a flight commander and was awarded the Military Cross, the citation being recorded in the *London Gazette* dated 18 July:

Captain A. G. Jones-Williams (right) with Captain D'Arcy Hilton MC, of 29 Squadron (from Michigan), eight victories, in 1917.

For conspicuous gallantry and devotion to duty. He has continuously shown the utmost dash and gallantry in attacking superior numbers of hostile machines. On one occasion he attacked twelve hostile scouts and succeeded in destroying one and driving down another.

His score standing at six, he was hospitalised for a short period in July. Then, back with the squadron, he claimed two more in September. All his victories had been over Albatros Scouts. The award of a Bar to his MC was gazetted on 17 September:

For conspicuous gallantry and devotion to duty when engaged in combat with hostile aircraft. On several occasions he attacked enemy formations although they were in superior numbers, fighting them in more than one instance single-handed, and showing the finest offensive spirit. He drove several machines down completely out of control, fighting until his ammunition was expended.

Sent back to England on rest, he returned for another tour of duty in the late summer of 1918 as a flight commander with No. 65 Squadron which flew Sopwith Camels. In September and October he downed three Fokker DVIIs to bring his score to eleven by the war's end. He was awarded the French *Croix de Guerre avec Palme*, promulgated in the *Gazette* on 5 April 1919.

Remaining in the Royal Air Force after the war he was with the Flying Wing at Cranwell when he injured his right knee playing rugby on 12 December, but then saw active service during the Kurdistan campaign of 1923, flying DH9A bombers. He served with No. 100 Squadron in 1926-28 and was promoted to squadron leader. In 1927 he flew Sir Philip Sassoon GBE, CMG, MP, Under-Secretary of State for Air, on a tour of the USA. It was a year or so afterwards that Jones-Williams got into long distance flying. On 24 April he and fellow pilot Flight Lieutenant N. H. Jenkins came together to fly the Fairey Long Range Monoplane (J9479) from Cranwell to India.

* * *

Squadron Leader Jones-Williams and Flight Lieutenant Norman Jenkins OBE, DFC, DSM.

Flight Lieutenant Norman Hugh Jenkins was born in Liphook, Hampshire on 24 May 1895, lived in Southampton, and was educated in Cardiff. In 1915 he enlisted into the Royal Naval Air Service as a mechanic and later volunteered to train as an observer. For his early work with the RNAS he was awarded the Distinguished Service Medal gazetted in October 1917, and promoted to commissioned rank. He served with 2 Naval Squadron, which became 202 Squadron RAF on 1 April 1918. He was wounded in combat on 27 June flying in a DH4 (A7868), his pilot on this occasion being Lieutenant L. A. Ashfield who would be killed in action a month later.

Once recovered he trained to be a pilot and returned to active duty. At the end of the war he received the DFC, gazetted 3 June 1919, for his work in Flanders and when flying on anti-submarine patrols over the North Sea. In 1920 he served in the Army of Occupation's Rhine forces. In 1922 he was posted out to Iraq and later served with No. 84 Squadron there. He was made an OBE on 3 June 1925. Returning to England he was posted to No. 22 Squadron at Martlesham Heath. Meeting up with Jones-Williams, he became second pilot and navigator for their trip to India, an estimated 4,130 miles. They accomplished this in a flight time of fifty hours, thirty-seven minutes of non-stop flying, which began on 24 April 1929. There was a bed on board the aircraft. They landed at Karachi as it began to get dark.

The Fairey Long Range monoplane (J9479) in which they flew to India in April 1929 and in which they were killed in December in Tunisia.

Due to headwinds encountered on the flight it was short of breaking the record, so the two men decided on another record attempt, this time flying to Cape Town in South Africa. They took off from Cranwell but their aircraft crashed at 21.40 pm into mountains at Djebel Lit, Zaghouan, some thirty miles south of Tunis on 16 December. Both were killed. Jones-Williams was 31 and Jenkins 35.

*   *   *

Colonel W. G. Barker VC, DSO & Bar, MC & 2 Bars, CdG, 12 March 1930

Canada's top Camel ace was William George Barker, born in the Dauphin Valley, Winnipeg, Manitoba, on 3 November 1894, to George William John Barker and his wife Jane Victoria Alguire. George senior was a farmer and blacksmith, and George Junior was the first of ten children, seven boys and three girls. George was educated at Dauphin College, Manitoba, and volunteered for the army as soon as he left, going into the Canadian Mounted Rifles.

Becoming part of the Machine-Gun Company, he left for England with his regiment in early summer 1915 where on arrival he sought a transfer to the RFC, firstly as a mechanic, then an observer, and finally a pilot. His first flying unit was No. 9 Squadron, with BE2c machines, in December. He had several encounters with enemy aircraft, even claiming a couple, but they were never credited to him. His main

Lieutenant W. G. Barker MC, while flying RE8s with No. 15 Squadron in 1917.

job was one of reconnaissance and contact patrol work, and it was in doing this that he received his first decoration, the Military Cross, gazetted on 10 January 1917:

For conspicuous gallantry in action. He flew at a height of 500 feet over the enemy's lines, and brought back most valuable information. On another occasion, after driving off two hostile machines, he carried out an excellent reconnaissance.

Volunteering to train as a pilot he returned to England in November 1916 and once he had won his 'wings' he returned to France to join No. 15 Squadron on 24 February 1917. Again his job was Corps work, reconnaissance and artillery observation and directing, flying RE8 aircraft. He obviously carried out these important tasks with courage and fortitude, for he was awarded a Bar to his MC, gazetted on 24 February:

> *For conspicuous gallantry and devotion to duty. He has done continuous good work in co-operating with the artillery, and has carried out successful reconnaissances under most difficult and dangerous situations.*

He was slightly wounded by anti-aircraft fire on 7 August and returned again to England where, once recovered, he became an instructor for the next six months. He quickly tired of this and began to agitate for a return to France, his frustration boiling over at one point resulting in a beat-up of the Air Ministry building in London. Fortunately his admonishment was a posting to No. 28 Squadron that was about to leave for France, a unit that flew Camel fighters. He was no sooner in action than he downed three German aircraft. Then his squadron was assigned to

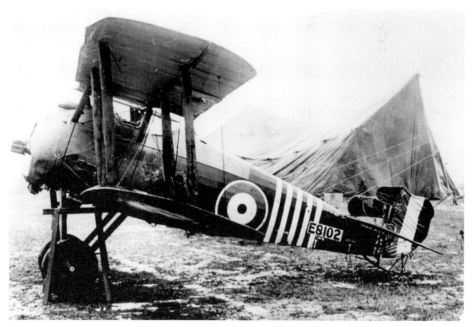

The Sopwith Snipe (E8102) in which he won his VC on 27 October 1918, having been retrieved from its forced landing.

the Italian Front, where it arrived in mid-November. Before the end of the month he had scored his fourth victory. A Distinguished Service Order resulted, gazetted on 5 January 1918:

> *For conspicuous gallantry and devotion to duty. When on scouting and patrol work he has on five different occasions brought down and destroyed five enemy aeroplanes and two balloons, though on two occasions he was attacked by superior numbers. On each occasion the hostile machines were observed to crash to earth, the wreckage bursting into flames. His splendid example of fearlessness and magnificent leadership have been inestimable to his squadron.*

There followed an amazing run of combat successes with 28 Squadron lasting until March, during which he was credited with a further eighteen victories. Some of his victories were kite balloons; in fact on 12 February, he and another pilot claimed five destroyed. By the end of April he had downed twenty-three aircraft and balloons in total and the award of a second Bar to his MC followed:

> *For conspicuous gallantry and devotion to duty. When leading patrols he on one occasion attacked eight hostile machines, himself shooting down two, and on another occasion seven one of which he shot down. In two months he himself destroyed four enemy machines and drove down one, and burned two balloons.*

In April, Barker moved to another Camel unit, No. 66, and rather uniquely took his personal Camel with him. This was B6313 which he had been flying since joining 28 back in October. In fact he would fly this machine in every combat, not only with 66, but later with 139 Squadron that he would command in mid-July, even though it was a Bristol Fighter outfit. At this time the French awarded him their *Croix de Guerre*.

Being with 66 Squadron he continued his phenomenal run of successes, so that by July when he took over 139, his victory score stood at thirty-eight. Finally, in his Camel, he added a further eight victories to his score, to bring his overall score to forty-six. He also flew a Savoia-Pomilio SP4 bomber across the lines in order to drop a spy. For this he was awarded the *Medaglia d'Argento* – the Silver Medal for Military Valour by the Italians.

He was posted back to England and had to leave his Camel behind. According to the aircraft's log book, he had flown in it for 379 hours and 25 minutes for his forty-six victories, a record for any First World War aeroplane. He was also awarded a Bar to his DSO, gazetted on 2 November:

Major William George Barker, DSO, MC, a highly distinguished patrol leader whose courage, resource and determination have set a fine example to those around him. Up to the 20th July, 1918, he had destroyed thirty-three enemy aircraft – twenty-one of these since the date of his last award (second Bar to the Military Cross) was conferred on him. Major Barker has frequently led formations against greatly superior numbers of the enemy with conspicuous success.

Post-war portrait of Barker with his medal ribbons, VC, DSO and Bar, MC and two Bars, French *Croix de Guerre*, Italian *Medaglia d'Argento* and Bar.

Although the date and victory tally is inaccurate, and not all his claims resulted in the total destruction of enemy machines, the sentiment is there.

Back in England he became commander of an air fighting school at Hounslow, but keen to get back into the action, argued that as it had been a year since being in France, he needed to bring himself up to date with the latest thinking if he was to do his job properly. He was therefore allowed to attach himself to No. 201 Squadron that was now flying Sopwith Snipe fighters. He had no luck in getting into combat until the day he was returning home. Edging close to the front line while heading north, he spotted a Rumpler two-seater which he attacked and shot down in flames. This attracted several Fokker DVIIs and he was soon involved in a desperate dogfight with them. In this scrap he was wounded several times but later claimed to have shot down at least three of the Fokkers. He eventually crash-landed to earth. All this was in plain view of front line troops and a report from their commander eventually led to the award of the Victoria Cross, promulgated in the *London Gazette* on 30 November:

On the morning of the 27th October, 1918, this officer observed an enemy two-seater over the Forêt de Mormal. He attacked this machine and after a short burst it broke up in the air. At the same time a Fokker biplane attacked him and he was wounded in the right thigh, but managed, despite this, to shoot down the enemy aircraft in flames.

He then found himself in the middle of a large formation of Fokkers, who attacked him from all directions, and was again severely wounded in the left thigh, but succeeded in driving down two of the enemy in a spin.

He lost consciousness after this, and his machine fell out of control. On recovery he found himself being again attacked heavily by a large formation, and singling out one machine, he deliberately charged and drove it down in flames.

During this fight his left elbow was shattered and he again fainted, and on regaining consciousness he found himself still being attacked, but, notwithstanding that he was now severely wounded in both legs and his left arm shattered, he dived on the nearest machine and shot it down in flames.

Being greatly exhausted, he dived out of the fight to regain our lines, but was met by another formation which attacked and endeavoured to cut him off, but after a hard fight, he succeeded in breaking up this formation and reached our lines, where he crashed on landing.

This combat, in which Major Barker destroyed four enemy machines (three of them in flames) brought his total successes up to fifty enemy machines destroyed, and is a notable example of the exceptional bravery and disregard for danger which this very gallant officer has always displayed throughout his distinguished career.

Major Barker was awarded the Military Cross on 10th January, 1917; first Bar on 18th July 1917; the Distinguished Service Order on 18th February 1918; second Bar to Military Cross on 16th September 1918, and Bar to Distinguished Service Order on 2nd November 1918.

After a long recovery period, Barker left the RAF in April 1919 and, back in Canada, went into partnership with fellow Canadian, W. A. Bishop VC, DSO, MC, DFC, in a civil aviation concern but this failed. However, he had met Jean Kilbourn Smith, a cousin of Major Bishop, and they were married on 1 June 1921 in Toronto, with Bishop as best man. They would have a daughter.

Barker then served in the new Canadian Air Force during 1920-24, before starting a tobacco business, but it was not a happy time for Barker. Alcohol caused problems and his marriage suffered.

Still keen on aviation, he became Vice President of the Fairchild Aviation Company of Canada. The company was keen on publicising their new aeroplane, the Fairchild KR-21 light trainer, and Barker was trying to sell it to the RCAF. It was demonstrated at Rockcliffe aerodrome on 12 March 1930, the home of the RCAF's Ottawa Air Station, by D. C. Shaw, a company pilot, which went off satisfactorily but Barker thought he could show it off more spectacularly. It seemed he had seen a pilot at the Detroit Air Show land his aeroplane off the back of a loop, and thought he could do the same. Although warned not to try – indeed there was no reason for him to demonstrate the aeroplane at all – he did.

The crashed Fairchild
KR-21 in which
Barker was killed on
12 March 1930.

Barker had logged very few flying hours since joining Fairchild, mostly on the KR-34, but was confident that the KR-21, being lighter, would not give him any problems. Instead of gaining some height and flying across the Ottawa River where he might practise some turns and loops, he simply took off and banked the machine as soon as he got airborne then headed low over some spectators. He then made two diving passes towards two hangars before pulling up into a steep climb, followed by an equally steep wingover. As he came down for a final pass on the south side of the River, aiming the KR-21 (CF-AKR) at the slipway, he increased speed as he did so, and then started what was thought to be a loop. Was he going to attempt that landing off the back of it?

Watchers on the ground saw the manoeuvre but also saw what was obviously going to be a stall. At around 250 feet the stall seemed to take the aeroplane backwards on its tail, then it flopped inverted onto its back. With the engine screaming the aircraft rolled and went down behind some trees. The first on the scene of the crash found the machine upright on the ice-covered river. Its wings and undercarriage had collapsed, and the engine, torn from its housing, had gone skidding across the ice.

Cutting through the fabric, two RCAF airmen found Barker dead, still sitting upright in his seat. His head had been smashed on impact, thrown forward on the instrument panel. His left arm and right ankle were broken and his left leg was broken and twisted. The subsequent enquiry concluded the crash was due to pilot error of judgement and loss of control due to too steep a climb with insufficient height to recover. Barker was 35 years old.

* * *

Captain A. W. Saunders DFC, 22 May 1930

It is difficult to piece together Alfred William Saunders' background. He was born on 16 January 1888 in Ireland, his mother being Amelia Adelaide Saunders, née White, who came from London. In the 1900 census, father Matthew Johnston Saunders, also possibly from London, was not living in the family home at 14 Leinster Street, Dublin, but Saunders' four brothers and sister were. Also at this address was Amelia's mother.

Captain A. W. Saunders DFC.

When war came, Pat Saunders, as he was known at the time, joined the Royal Field Artillery and saw service at Gallipoli in 1915, holding a commission in the Special Reserve. Following that ill-starred campaign he moved to transfer to the Royal Flying Corps in late 1916. A bad crash while training early in 1917 disfigured his face, but after hospitalisation he returned to complete his training, gaining his Royal Aero Club Certificate on 20 July.

That October he was sent to France, and posted to No. 60 Squadron, which flew SE5A fighters. It took a while for him to find his feet, for his first victory was not claimed until 10 May 1918, a Pfalz DIII Scout destroyed, but he gained two more before the month was out, shot down two Hannover CL two-seaters on 9 June, then three Pfalz Scouts on 2 July, two of which collided in their haste to avoid his attack. In August he scored four times, three Fokker biplanes and a two-seater which brought his victory tally to twelve. He was awarded the Distinguished Flying Cross, gazetted on 3 August:

> *A gallant and determined officer whose fighting spirit and enthusiasm has been a splendid example to his squadron. On one occasion while leading a formation of six machines, he attacked six enemy aeroplanes. Diving from 11,000 to 3,000 feet, he singled out a group of three, and shot down one. He then engaged the other two, which in their endeavour to get away collided and crashed.*

Taking command of one of 60's flights in June his tour of duty ended in mid-August and he returned to England to work as an instructor, but then became a King's Courier, and in September 1918 arrived in New York while in transit to Canada. It is also recorded that he visited his father who was living in London, at

Kelfield Gardens, Kensington. He remained in the RAF until October 1919 leaving the service for an unusual appointment. On 12 November 1919, he and a handful of other pilots were somehow sent to join the Air Force of the Lithuanian Army, engaged in fighting the Bolsheviks, as flight instructors, until released in January 1920. It seems that after that he rejoined the RAF, for his records show he saw active service on India's famous north-west frontier. In May 1923, now a flying officer, he journeyed to Freemantle, Australia, with the intention of living there. Just how this transpired is unclear, for he did not relinquish his RAF commission until 25 May 1927. Perhaps more work as a King's Courier was how he managed to travel about.

He does seem to have started a new life in Australia, indeed, his mother, one brother and a sister had moved to Perth. Perhaps a clue to his mother's move was through her second name, Adelaide? Pat Saunders became well known in Perth. His flying took him into pioneer flying on the Perth-Derby air route, and he became chief pilot on the Sydney-Adelaide mail route, flying with Australian Aerial Services.

Later he turns up flying in New Zealand, and it was here that he met his end. On 21 May 1930, he was flying a De Havilland Moth, having with him a passenger, Mr Alfred Trench Minchin, aged 24. It was in the afternoon and he had said that they were going to 'do some stunting'. People on the ground saw the Moth, flying at 1,000 feet, go into a spin and attempt to flatten out. It ran out of height and at fifty feet stalled and nosedived into the ground. The Moth crashed at Te Awamutu in the Waikato at 4.25 pm; both occupants were killed.

Saunders was buried in the local cemetery close to the crash site. He was 42 years of age.

*   *   *

Lieutenant Colonel G. L. P. Henderson MC, AFC, BA, MiD (4), 21 July 1930

Known to his friends as 'Budgie', George Lockhart Percy Henderson was born around 1887, the son of Lieutenant General Sir Edward KCB and Lady Henderson, residing at 42 Leinster Gardens, Bayswater, in West London, circa 1888. He was educated at Eton (1902-7) and Trinity College, Oxford, where he gained a BA in 1910. Upon the declaration of war, Henderson volunteered to serve as a motorbike despatch rider in France, enlisting into the Royal Engineers, earning the 1914 Star. He decided to move to the Royal Flying Corps and achieved his RAC Certificate, No. 1143, at the London and Provincial School at Hendon on 31 March 1915.

Once his training finished he was posted to No. 3 Squadron in France to fly Morane N-types. In a fight with two German aircraft on 2 December he received a bullet to his face, and despite pain and blinded by blood, still managed to get his machine down safely. He was awarded the MC, gazetted 22 January 1916:

Lieutenant Colonel G. L. P. Henderson MC, AFC, post-First World War.

For conspicuous gallantry and skill. On 28 November 1915, over La Bassée and Lille, after he had driven down one Albatros, he attacked two other hostile machines and in spite of heavy fire, put them both to flight. Then under anti-aircraft fire he chased two more machines and drove them off. On 2 December, near Don, when on escort to a bombing expedition, he was hit by a bullet in the head in a fight with a German machine. Though partially stunned and half-blinded, he succeeded in bringing his own machine back to his aerodrome.

After his recovery, which left his facial features a little altered, he was given command of No. 49 Squadron, February to May 1917, then 66 Squadron in England during June 1917, taking it to France where he led it until 15 November. His command ended due to a crash in his Sopwith Camel; he was thrown from the plane, broke his nose, and the aircraft burst into flames. After this experience he did not wear safety belts again, for had he worn one he would have burnt to death. After this he held various training posts for which he received the Air Force Cross at the end of the war. During the war he was mentioned in despatches on four occasions.

Remaining in aviation post-war he became one of the first pilots with Imperial Airways, while also designing and building aeroplanes. He also ran his own small airline, Walcot Air Line, at Croydon. He also joined forces with Captain K. N. Pearson MC, who worked at Brooklands, as well as J. A. G. Glenny, of Glenny & Henderson in Byfleet, Surrey.

Henderson had a German Junkers F.13ge (G-AAZK) with Walcot and, in addition to taking passengers on various journeys, flew joy-rides for anyone willing to pay. On 20 July 1930 he was hired to fly a party of socialites to Le Touquet for a party and some gambling at the casino. The weather was not very good when they took off at 11.30 pm on the return flight on the 21st, but it calmed a little upon reaching Kent. However, it is believed that the engine cowling came adrift

The crashed Junkers F.B.ge in which Henderson was killed at Meopham, Kent, 21 July 1930.

and with this and the buffeting of the wind the port horizontal stabilizer became detached, which in turn caused the whole tail to disintegrate. Then the port wing snapped off and, with the engine also separating, the Junkers literally fell apart, throwing all but the co-pilot into space, including Henderson, who had continued to fly without a seat belt. People on the ground heard the Junkers break up and saw several bodies tumbling earthwards, falling into Leylands Orchard near Meopham. It was 2.35 pm. What remained of the aircraft crashed inverted, narrowly missing a house, with the co-pilot still in his seat. Although he was pulled out alive he died shortly afterwards. Wreckage was well spread, with one wing narrowly missing a bungalow, the other found a mile away. The engine landed in a driveway and what was left of the tail fell 300 yards from the crash site.

The passenger list was impressive:

- Lt-Colonel G. L. P. Henderson MC, AFC, BA, aged 43.
- Charles D'Urban Shearing, co-pilot aged 27, ex-RAF.
- Frederick Hamilton-Temple-Blackwood DSO, 3rd Marquess of Dufferin and Ava, aged 55, Speaker of the Northern Ireland Parliament.
- Rosemary Millicent Ward Leveson-Gower, Viscountess Ednam, aged 36, daughter of the 3rd Earl of Dudley.
- Captain Sir Edward Simons Ward GBE, KCB, KCVO, 2nd Baronet Ward, aged 48, who was a Permanent Secretary at the War Office.
- Mrs Sigrid Loeffler, aged 45, wife of Henrik Loeffler, mining Engineer and businessman in South Africa.

* * *

Captain J. O. Donaldson DSC, DFC, CdG, 7 September 1930

From Fort Yates, North Dakota, John Owen
Donaldson was the son of Major General Thomas
Quinton Donaldson and Mary Elizabeth (née
Willson) Donaldson, born 14 May 1897. He was
also known as Jack. With his parents often away,
his father serving with the US 7th Cavalry (at one
time in the Philippines) John went to live with his
aunt Nannie Donaldson Furman in Greenville,
South Carolina. He went to Greenville High
School 1915-16 then to Sibley College of civil
engineering as well as Furman University. After
his freshman year he moved to Cornell University
in Ithaca, New York, to major in civil engineering.
However, with America likely to enter into the war
he halted his studies and he went to Canada where
he joined the Royal Flying Corps in March 1917.

Captain J. O. Donaldson DSC,
DFC.

Following his final flight training in England, he was sent to join No. 32
Squadron in France to gain experience, as he had volunteered to transfer to the
United States Air Service. He served with this unit during the summer of 1918,
claiming seven Fokker DVIIs shot down in little over a month during July and
August. He received the British DFC and the American DSC.

He was shot down himself on 1 September, by the German ace Theodor Quandt
of Jasta 36 over Pronville, his eleventh victory of an eventual fifteen. Before being
sent to a prisoner of war camp, Donaldson managed to escape his guards. While in
Conde, he found his way to a German airfield and was in the process of trying to
steal a two-seater with fellow prisoner Oscar Mandel of the 148th Aero. However,
they were caught, and in the initial struggle with guards, Donaldson received
a bayonet wound to his back. They still managed to get away, a French farmer
tending his wound, but on 9 September they were apprehended while swimming
a stream in no man's land.

Three days later, Donaldson, Mandel and three others escaped again, this time
by cutting a hole in the roof of their hut with a broken saw they had found. This
time Donaldson made it to the Netherlands in October but Mandel was recaptured.
Donaldson returned to the US and, still in uniform, entered a transcontinental air
race in October 1919, which he won, receiving the Mackay Gold Medal. Resigning
his commission in 1920, he continued his engineering studies at Cornell University,
where he graduated in 1921.

He received the DFC, the citation being as follows:

For gallantry. On July 22, Lt. Donaldson, when on a patrol, attacked a formation of 20 Fokker biplanes over Mont-Notre-Dame. He singled out one of the hostile machines and engaged it from behind, firing a short burst at close range. The EA side-slipped to the right and then to the left, finally bursting into flames and crashing. On August 8, he engaged five enemy scouts over Licourt. He singled out one and diving on it from behind, opened fire at very close range. The EA immediately went into a straight dive and crashed into the ground between Licourt and Morchain, becoming a total wreck. On August 9, he observed a British machine being attacked by three hostile scouts over Licourt. He immediately flew to the scene of the encounter and engaged one of the EA, firing a long burst at very close range. Almost at once a white stream of escaping petrol was observed and a little later the EA burst into flames. On August 25, he attacked, single handed, four Fokker biplanes over Hancourt, diving into their midst and firing a short burst into one machine at close range. The EA went down in a slide-slip dive and having fallen about 2,000 feet the left wing broke off. The pilot descended by parachute and shortly after leaving the machine the other wing was observed to crumple up. In addition to the above this officer has driven down out of control three enemy machines as follows: July 25 1918, one Fokker biplane over Fismes; August 10, one Fokker biplane over Péronne; August 29, one Fokker biplane over Cambrai. 2nd Lt. Donaldson also did magnificent work attacking ground targets with machine gun fire and bombs during the recent retreat on the Somme in August. He invariably showed the greatest devotion to duty and gallantry in the face of the enemy.

His Distinguished Service Cross, noted in General Orders, No. 13, W.D., 1924, is virtually a repeat of this citation. He also received the Belgian *Croix de Guerre*.

After the war he continued flying, entering air races and becoming President of Newark Air Services in New Jersey. He married Harriot McCullough of Atlanta, Georgia in 1922, and they lived in Newark.

On Sunday, 7 September 1930, came tragedy. That day, 35-year-old Mrs Opal Kunz (aka Opal Logan Giberson or Opal van Zandt Giberson Kunz, whose husband was Dr. George F. Kunz) had flown in a Travel Air Whirlwind aircraft and won the twenty-five miles 'free for all' in the American Legion Air Race meet in Philadelphia, having also come third in the National Air Races in Chicago ten days previously. She was a friend of Donaldson, who had helped with her flying training. Also on the 7th, Donaldson had flown and won the fifteen-mile race in a Curtiss aeroplane. Afterwards Donaldson persuaded Opal to let him fly her machine. She had no objection, so off he went in her Whirlwind, a much heavier aeroplane than his Curtiss.

He crashed while stunting over the airfield, in full view of some 40,000 spectators. He dived into the ground from 1,800 feet. The tremendous force of the crash telescoped the aircraft's fuselage and the tail was snapped off. Donaldson was alive when Captain Brehan rushed over in his police car, followed by another policeman, Captain Dunn. Mrs Kunz also arrived on the scene and helped with the extrication of Donaldson's broken body, along with Donaldson's mechanic, Vernie E. Moon.

He was taken to the nearest hospital, where an examination revealed a fractured skull and internal injuries. He had in fact died soon after being pulled out of the smashed machine. He was 33 years of age. The *Syracuse Herald* had this to say on 8 September:

Capt. John O. Donaldson, 32, World War ace, army instructor and commercial aviation executive, crashed to his death yesterday while doing aerobatics flying at the conclusion of the American Legion air race at the Municipal Stadium.

Flying the plane of Mrs. Opal Kunz, New York aviatrix, Donaldson, whose home was in Newark, N.J., and several other aviators, were entertaining the crowd with fancy flying and stunts. Suddenly the captain's plane went into a tail spin and plunged to earth. Donaldson suffered a fractured skull and internal injuries and died soon after being extricated from the wreckage of his plane.

Said to be the fourth ranking American World War ace, Captain Donaldson was credited with eight victories over German airplanes. He received a number of decorations for valour, among them the Distinguished Service Cross and the British Distinguished Flying Cross. The latter was presented personally by the Prince of Wales.

* * *

Captain P. F. Baer DSC & Oak Leaf, Ld'H, CdG, 9 December 1930

Paul Frank Baer, from Fort Wayne, Indiana, born 5 January 1896, his mother is named as Mrs Emma Baer Dyer. After leaving school he became a car mechanic and salesman for the Cadillac Motor Car Company, but like many Americans felt compelled to support France in her hour of need, so volunteered to join the Lafayette Flying Corps in February 1917.

After training to be a pilot, he was assigned to Escadrille N80 on 14 August where he honed his skills until 10 January 1918. Following America's entry into the war, and the arrival of US forces in France, the famed Escadrille Lafayette Squadron, officially Escadrille N124, became the 103rd Pursuit Squadron of the USAS, flying Spads. Baer and others of the Flying Corps also became members of the US 103rd Aero.

Captain P. F. Baer DSC.

Although he had not achieved any aerial victories during his time with the French, he downed his first German on 11 March, his second five days later. Number three fell to him on 6 April. He was awarded the Distinguished Service Cross on 12 April:

> *On 11 March 1918, alone attacked a group of seven enemy pursuit machines, destroying one which crashed to the ground near the French lines northeast of Reims. On 16 March, he attacked two enemy two-seaters, one of which fell in flames, striking the ground in approximately the same region.*

On this same date he downed another enemy scout and on the 23rd a two-seater, shared with another pilot. This brought him ace status but in May, now with his eye in, he shot down a two-seater and two scouts, bringing his score to eight. On 22 May he was shot down and wounded by pilots of Jasta 18, crashed and became a prisoner of war. He was, nevertheless, awarded an Oak Leaf to his DSC:

> *For the following repeated acts of extraordinary heroism in action on 5, 12 and 21 May 1918, Lt. Baer is awarded a Bronze Oak Leaf to be worn on the Distinguished Service Cross awarded him 12 April 1918. Lt. Baer brought down enemy planes on 6 April, 12 April and 23 April 1918. On 8 May he destroyed two German machines and on 21 May he destroyed his eighth enemy plane.*

The French also awarded him their *Croix de Guerre*. He was also credited with bringing down one German aircraft during the action which resulted in his loss, reported by other members of the squadron upon their return. Recovering from his wounds, he attempted to escape captivity, and when this failed he was treated poorly by his captors.

A Loening C-2, the
type in which Baer
was killed.

Released from prison camp at the end of the war, the French made him a
Chevalier de la Legion d'Honneur, on 9 April 1919. This same year, upon his return
to America, he was made a member of the American Flying Club. He also flew as a
test pilot for an aeronautical laboratory in Detroit. For the next several years Baer
was associated with flying and by 1927 was a Department of Commerce aeronautics
inspector in San Antonio, Texas. This was followed by a year as a commercial pilot
in South America while also flying with the air mail service. Often these flights
took him to various places around the world.

In 1925 the airfield at Fort Wayne was named after him, and the French ace,
Charles Nungesser, came over to dedicate it. Nungesser was to go missing on a
trans-Atlantic attempt in May 1927 (as mentioned above). The airport became
more substantial in the Second World War as Baer Field, and was renamed Fort
Wayne International Airport in 1991, but one of the terminals retains Baer's
name.

In early December, Baer found himself in China, flying mail and passengers for
Chinese Airways Federal Inc., and the Chinese National Aviation Corporation. On
the 9th of that month, he flew a Loening C-2-H floatplane from Shanghai harbour
with mail from Nanking to Shanghai, and a Russian lady as one of the passengers.
There was a co-pilot and two other passengers, including General Hsiung Shih-
Hui,[3] commander of Shanghai garrison. On becoming airborne the aircraft hit
the mast of a junk on the Yangtze River and crashed. Paul, the co-pilot and the

---

3. The general (1892-1974) later served under Chiang Kai-shek in a number of military and
   civilian posts.

lady were killed, the others injured. It was a tragic accident, Baer being such an experienced flyer, having, it is said, some 3,500 flying hours in his log book.

His body was taken home and buried in Lindenwood Cemetery, Fort Wayne. He was 33 years old.

* * *

Flight Lieutenant H. M. Moody MC, 23 April 1931
Air Vice-Marshal F. V. Holt CMG, DSO, MiD (2), 23 April 1931

Born in Welshampton, Shropshire, on 2 September 1898, Henry Michael Moody was one of twin boys to Evelyn and the Reverend Henry Moody, vicar of Welshampton, and Rural Dean of Ellesmere. The other twin, Charles Angelo Moody, flew with No. 1 Squadron in the First World War but was shot down and killed over Belgium on 21 August 1917 by Fritz Loerzer of Jasta 26 and buried at Tyne Cot Cemetery. It was the German's fourth victory of a total of eleven. Loerzer's brother Bruno was also a First World War ace with forty-four victories, a close friend to Hermann Göring and a future Luftwaffe general.

Flight Lieutenant H. M. Moody MC.

Educated at King William's College on the Isle of Man between 1912 and 1916, Henry joined the colours to become a mechanic with the Royal Flying Corps, making corporal in December 1916. Selected for a commission on 13 April 1917, he was gazetted a flying officer on 21 June. Posted to No. 45 Squadron, equipped with Sopwith Camels, he achieved four victories between 4 September and 13 November, and his squadron was then posted to Italy. Promoted to captain, he gained a further four victories and returned to England in June 1918. He was awarded the Military Cross, although the citation was not published in the *London Gazette* until 16 September:

Air Vice-Marshal Vesey Holt CMG, DSO.

For conspicuous gallantry and devotion to duty in leading patrols. He has destroyed four enemy aircraft and shot down three out of control. He has further carried out very successfully a number of low-flying patrols, photographic reconnaissances and escorts, and has on all occasions shown a very fine spirit of dash and determination.

Ending the war as an instructor, he remained in the RAF and, with the rank of flight lieutenant, served with No. 31 Squadron at Dardoni on the North West Frontier. Returning home, he was posted to Winchester and then took up an instructing role at Cranwell.

In 1922 he married Austin Robina 'Bobby' Horn of Canterbury, daughter of Mr and Mrs C. A. Horn of Beaumont, Jersey and Adelaide, South Australia. They married at St. Aubin's Church, Jersey, and their marriage produced a son and a daughter.

In August 1923 he went to No. 28 Squadron in India. Returning again to England, he was sent to the Depot at RAF Uxbridge and then to the Electrical and Wireless School at RAF Flowerdown in May 1927. On 30 March 1931 he transferred to the HQ of the Fighting Area at Uxbridge.

*   *   *

Felton Vesey Holt was born on 23 February 1886, the third son of the late Sir Vesey Holt of Holt & Co, army bankers. He was educated at Eton and deciding on an army career, went to Sandhurst in 1903, and in August 1905 joined the Oxford Light Infantry. He was commissioned into the Ox and Bucks Light Infantry in 1910, but in 1912 decided to learn to fly, which he did, receiving his RAeC pilot licence (No. 312) on 1 October 1912.

Promoted to captain in July 1914, he served with No. 4 Squadron early in the war and became OC No. 16 Squadron in February 1915 as a major, and then OC No. 25 Squadron in September 1915. He took command of No. 16 Home Defence Wing in June 1916, then commanded No. 22 Wing in February 1917. He had earlier been awarded the Distinguished Service Order, gazetted 18 February 1915:

For gallantry on 22nd January 1915, in engaging, single-handed, a group of twelve German aeroplanes which were attacking the town of Dunkirk. He was subsequently joined by two of our own biplanes, which resulted in one of the German machines being brought down, and its pilot and observer being captured.

This was an Albatros B1 of BOA, a bombing unit based at Ostend, which came down at Bray Dunes.

Once the war was over, Holt was made CMG in the 1919 New Year Honours, and soon afterwards was seconded for special duties with the Chinese Government between 1920 and 1922, after which he commanded the RAF's Central Flying School. In July 1925 he was made air commodore and sent to HQ Air Defence of Great Britain. In December 1928 he became Director of Technical Development at the Air Ministry. By this time he and his wife had been blessed with two children.

In January 1931 he was made air officer commanding of the Fighting Area of the Air Defence Great Britain organisation at Uxbridge.

*   *   *

On 23 April 1931, Holt and his P.A. planned a visit to RAF Tangmere, taking off in two De Havilland Gipsy Moths of No. 24 Squadron based at Northolt. Holt was in one, with Henry Moody piloting (K1838), while Flight Lieutenant E. H. Bellairs piloted the second one.

They arrived safely, had lunch, proceeded with the flag-waving inspection and, having seen the two resident fighter squadrons flying across the sky, said their goodbyes, then went out to the airfield for the flight back to Northolt. Bellairs took off first, and then Moody. In the air was 43 Squadron's formation of Armstrong-Whitworth Siskin IIIA fighters preparing to land, No. 1 Squadron at Tangmere having already done so. The leader of 43 Squadron, L. H. Slatter OBE, DSC, DFC, saw one of the Moths below and, thinking this was the AOC, signalled his pilots to dive past in salute. However, it was Bellair's machine.

As the Siskins dived from 3,000 feet to 500 feet in formation, the pilot on the extreme left, Sergeant Charles George Wareham, in J8893, was concentrating on his right-hand side, watching closely his flight commander, when he suddenly felt his left wingtip touch something. It had hit Moody's Moth, which none of the Siskin pilots had seen climbing up from below.

Moody's Moth went into a spin followed by a steep dive and was too close to the ground to recover. Holt, seeing the danger, attempted to bale out but he was too low for his parachute to deploy fully, and the Moth and Moody smashed into the ground at Seahurst Park, Sussex. Both men died instantly. Moody was 32, Holt 45. Sergeant Wareham got down safely.

*   *   *

Flying Officer G. F. M. Apps DFC, 24 October 1931

Lieutenant G. F. M. Apps DFC.

The second oldest boy of four sons and one daughter, Gordon Frank Mason Apps was born to sanitary inspector Henry Mason Apps and his wife Kate Helena, in Lenham, near Maidstone, Kent, on 3 May 1899. Before the war began the family relocated to nearby Sutton Valence, Kent, where Gordon went to school at the famous local school (1911-16). The family home was named 'The Nest'. His first job after leaving school was as an engineering apprentice at the Tilling-Stevens Motor and Munitions factory in Maidstone.

Once Gordon reached military age in 1917, he joined the Artists' Rifles but was commissioned into the Royal Flying Corps in May. In November came the sad news that his elder brother, Jack Henry Mason Apps, aged 19, serving with the 1/5th Northumberland Fusiliers, had been killed in action on the 20th.

Once trained as a pilot he was posted to No. 66 Squadron in Italy, which flew Sopwith Camels. He quickly established himself as a successful fighter pilot and between 11 March and 16 July 1918 claimed a total of nine victories against German and Austrian aeroplanes and flew over one hundred sorties. He was wounded in the leg during his last combat and, having spent several months at the front, was shipped back to England. He received the Distinguished Flying Cross, gazetted on 21 September:

> *A bold and skilful airman who in recent operations has destroyed six enemy aeroplanes, accounting for two in one fight. He displays marked determination and devotion to duty.*

Once released from hospital he was posted to No. 50 Squadron as a flight commander in September, a Camel squadron on Home Defence duties. There then followed a two months' wireless course at No. 2 Wireless School at Penshurst.

At the war's end he left the RAF on 19 March 1919 and his first civilian occupation was with the Imperial Radio Chain, a project to erect a chain of radio stations aimed at spanning the Empire. He was employed for some two and a half years, during which time he had approximately one hundred men under his direction, building stations, plant rooms, erecting masts, while also installing engines, dynamos and wiring.

He then travelled to Ontario, Canada, where he took a position with the H.E.P.C. (Hydro-Electric Power Commission) Ontario, for about six months although it was only going to be a short term employment. In the meantime, in touch with his old flight commander in 66 Squadron, Major William Barker VC, who had become involved in the creation of the Canadian Air Force, Apps was encouraged to join. Apps applied, becoming accepted on 19 March 1924, no doubt helped by Barker's influence. His position was confirmed on 1 April of that year, serving at Camp Borden.

During his time with what was now the Royal Canadian Air Force, he served at Winnipeg's Victoria Beach, so dealing with flying boats, on the shores of Lake Winnipeg and Barrie, by Lake Simcoe, Ontario. In April 1925 he was appointed to Norway House on Fort Island, Manitoba, as air pilotage officer.

The following year Apps became part of the aerial photographic mapping scheme of the Red Lake district, using two Viking flying boats. This was a fairly long-term job, as can be imagined, and a further four flying boats were later supplied. Apps also needed to visit a number of RCAF stations around the areas to be surveyed.

A Fairchild 71, the type in which Gordon Apps was killed.

On 10 December 1927 he married Norma Kennedy at the Winnipeg Air Station. In December 1930 Apps was seconded to RAF Calshot in England and he took his wife with him. During this trip his father passed away.

Back in Canada after an air pilotage course, he went back to Camp Borden, posted to No. 1 School of Aeronautics at the end of May 1931. On 26 October 1931, Gordon Apps was flying a Fairchild 71 (No. 114) with Sergeant John Hand but, attempting to land at Peterborough (Ontario) Airport, crashed. Both men were killed and three passengers on board were injured. It is possible that Apps did not die immediately, for his wife, when told of the crash, rushed from Toronto to be with him but was told of his passing when she arrived. Apps was 32 years old and is buried in St. Johns. The RCAF provided a military escort. A court of enquiry ruled the crash was due to pilot error.

* * *

Captain F. G. Gibbons DFC, 21 May 1932

Frank George Gibbons was born in Peterborough, Northamptonshire, on 13 June 1899, the son of Peter and Fanny Gibbons. When war came he was still at school, living at 'Rathgar', Lincoln Road, Peterborough, but as soon as he was able he joined the army, enlisting into the Northumberland Regiment. Then he transferred to the Royal Flying Corps as a mechanic. Requesting pilot training, he was commissioned on 25 November 1917. He completed his flight training and gained his 'wings' on 2 February 1918, and his RAeC licence, (No. 7860), on the 28th. Posted to France, he was sent to No. 22 Squadron, which flew two-seater BF2b fighters. In general, Bristol Fighter two-man crews fought as a team, the pilot with his

Fight Lieutenant F. G. Gibbons DFC.

front Vickers gun, the observer with one, sometimes two, Lewis guns from his rear cockpit. In air combat they were not liked by the opposition as they were deadly efficient and highly manoeuvrable in an air fight.

Gibbons' first five victories were all Pfalz DIII Scouts, from 31 May to 5 June. He and his observer, Lieutenant V. St. B. Collins, downed two Fokker Dr.I

Triplanes on 28 June and 10 July. Collins was credited with ten victories with both 48 and 22 Squadrons before his own death in September.

In one month, 27 August to 27 September, Gibbons accounted for seven Fokker DVII biplanes, bringing his overall score to fourteen. He received the DFC, gazetted 3 June 1919.

Back in England, he was an instructor at No. 10 Training School and then went to the Middle East in July 1919 but resigned his commission in 1920. However, he appears to have remained in the service for, following a period flying with No. 111 Squadron in Palestine, he returned to the UK to take an Instructor's Course at the Central Flying School. Two years later he was back in the Middle East, serving in Constantinople with RAF HQ and in 1923 was posted to No. 25 Squadron in England.

Later in the same year he was off again, this time to Aden and from there to No. 208 Squadron at Heliopolis, Cairo. His yo-yo like service had him back in England later and to No. 19 Squadron at Duxford on 16 March 1927. Almost four years later, on 5 January 1931, he went to Calshot and then to No. 204 Squadron, which flew flying boats at Mount Batten. He excelled in fencing, representing the RAF against the Navy, and also played hockey.

In his spare time he took part in the King's Cup Air Races in both 1930 and 1931. In the first race he was forced to retire, but in the next year he came second.

A line-up of Sparton 3-seaters, the type Gibbons crashed on 21 May 1932.

He also acted as navigator to Mr H. T. Andrews in a Sparton Arrow in the summer of 1930, flying in the Circuit of Europe Race.

On 21 May 1932 he took part in an air race at Stanton, Norfolk, organised by the *Morning Post* newspaper, flying a Sparton three-seater (G-ABTT) of the Sparton Aircraft Company. His luck ran out when he hit a tree and crashed. It was believed he was looking at a map and failed to notice the tree. He was not married and aged 33.

* * *

Captain L. H. Holden MC, AFC, 18 September 1932

Leslie Hubert Holden was born in East Adelaide, South Australia, on 6 March 1895, son of Mr and Mrs Hubert William Holden who later resided at 'The Chalet', Winton Street, Warrawee, New South Wales. After his schooling he worked as an assistant business manager in Turramurra, NSW.

Once of age, he enlisted into the Australian Imperial Forces as an infantry private in May 1915, before transferring to the ever-popular Australian Light Horse as a trooper in June. He saw active service during the Gallipoli campaign after which he decided to transfer to the Australian Flying Corps in Egypt in December 1916. Once trained as a pilot he was sent to No. 68 Squadron at Heliopolis, a unit that would later become No.

Captain L. H. Holden MC, AFC.

2 Squadron, AFC. Coming to England, he was posted to France to join No. 57 Squadron, RFC, a unit flying DH4 bombers. This was May 1917 and he remained with the unit until July, at which time he moved to No. 71 (Australian) Squadron, which became No. 4 Squadron AFC.

He was only with 71 for a short period before being posted back to 68 Squadron that had now come to England. This unit flew DH5 fighters and went to France in September 1917. 64 Squadron were heavily engaged during the Battle of Cambrai, especially in ground attack missions, in fact Holden was initially reported missing on the first day of the battle, 20 November, brought down by ground fire. Three days later he was forced to land by a German fighter but again survived. He continued with the squadron, even when it changed its identity to No. 2 AFC.

In the spring of 1918 he was credited with four combat victories and received the Military Cross, gazetted on 4 February, with details in the 5 July 1918 edition:

For conspicuous gallantry and devotion to duty. While on a special mission he dropped a bomb direct on a support trench full of enemy [troops], causing them to scatter, and another bomb upon a strong point which was holding up our advance. He also bombed a large group of enemy infantry, and turned his machine gun on them from a height of 100 feet. He rendered very valuable service throughout the operation.

He returned to England in April and posted as an instructor at the Central Flying School, and then to the School of Special Flying. Holden's expertise at instructing was ultimately recognised with the award of the Air Force Cross, *London Gazette* 3 June 1919.

With the war won, Holden returned to his native Australia on 6 May 1919, where he continued to serve, this time with the Citizen's Air Force, which later became the Royal Australian Air Force. In the 1920s he began commercial flying. In 1929 he made headlines by rescuing the famous Australian pioneer duo Charles Kingsford-Smith MC and Charles Ulm. These two, together with a radio operator and a navigator, had become famous the previous year by making the first trans-Pacific flight from the USA to Australia. They flew a Fokker F.VII tri-motor monoplane which they named *Southern Cross*. Later that year they made the first

The DH.80 Puss Moth in which Holden was killed flying as a passenger.

non-stop flight across Australia. On another trip, in March 1929, Kingsford-Smith had to make a forced landing near the mouth of the Glenelg River in Western Australia. Several searches were made and they were eventually found by Leslie Holden.

On Sunday, 18 September 1932, Holden was a passenger aboard a DH.80 Puss Moth (VH-UPM) owned by New England Airways, flown by Ralph Virtue and accompanied by one of Holden's old school chums, Dr George Hamilton. They crashed due to a wing failure caused by aileron flutter and all three men were killed. It appears that, heading over the Burringbar Range at about 100 feet, just below cloud, the aircraft was caught in a sudden down-draught and turned a somersault. The pilot tried to correct but the left wing and rudder snapped off and the machine crashed in a sideways dive at Myocum, near Byron Bay, New South Wales. Holden was 37 years old.

*   *   *

Squadron Leader O. A. P. Heron DFC, CdG, 5 August 1933

Oscar Aloysius Patrick Heron was born at Banbrook Hill, Co. Armagh, Ireland, the son of a school teacher, on 17 September 1896. In fact his father Charles was principal of St. Patrick's Boys School, Armagh, and his mother principal of the girl's section of the school. He had a brother, C. B. Heron, who later became superintendent in Donegal. Oscar had been a member of the Inns of Court OTC prior to joining the Connaught Rangers but then transferred to the Royal Flying Corps. He was trained as a pilot, and once having done so was sent to France where he joined No. 70 Squadron, equipped with Sopwith Camels.

He arrived in May 1918, and succeeded in downing his first German aeroplane on 30 June, in fact he scored twice this day, both Albatros

Squadron Leader O. A. P. Heron DFC, CdG.

DV Scouts. His next victory did not come until 19 August, a Fokker biplane, and then number four, another Fokker DVII, was achieved on 28 September. During October he excelled in air fights. On the 1st he shot down an LVG two-seater, and by the 28th he had claimed eight Fokkers, bringing his score to thirteen, including one that he and other pilots managed to force down inside British lines on the 9th. He was promoted to captain and received the Belgian *Croix de Guerre* in 1919. By this time he had also been rewarded with the Distinguished Flying Cross, although not promulgated in the *London Gazette* until 8 February 1919:

> *An officer conspicuous for his skill and daring in aerial combats. He has accounted for eight enemy aeroplanes. On 28th September he attacked, single-handed, three Fokkers, one of which he shot down. On another occasion he, in company with five other machines, engaged six Fokkers, all six being destroyed, 2nd Lieutenant Heron accounting for two.*

Towards the end of the war, Heron gained some fame for being the first member of the Allied forces to enter the French city of Lille. Flying over the city, he noticed that it appeared to have been abandoned by the Germans. He decided to take the risk of landing to check and luckily he found he had been correct.

Following the end of the war, Heron joined the Irish Air Corps following its establishment in 1922 as the National Air Service. His main task was in training pilots at Baldonnel near Dublin. Heron was married, to a French lady, and they lived in married quarters at Baldonnel.

In August 1933, the first Irish Air Corps Pageant was held at Phoenix Park, Dublin, but sadly it resulted in more than one tragedy. On Thursday the 3rd, Lieutenant J. P. Twohig, flying an Avro Cadet, crashed and was killed. His funeral took place on the morning of the 5th, Oscar Heron being one of the pall bearers.

That same afternoon, Heron was back at the flying field as part of a mock air battle over the host of spectators who had come to watch the display. Watching too was Heron's wife along with the wife of Lieutenant Sheeran who was also flying in this display. At about 4.40 pm, four Air Corps machines were above the airfield, Heron in a Vickers Vespa V6, along with a soldier, Private Robert Tobin. Their machine, acting as the 'bombing plane', was being 'attacked' by the other three. Two of the attackers had been forced to break off and head down while the third flew away. Heron had amazed the onlookers with a marvellous aerobatic show, and then, when he was about a mile away, but still in full view, he turned and began to descend gracefully, either to land or to swoop suddenly upwards. There was no sign of the impending disaster.

The crowd were about to applaud Heron's display when the aircraft, now at low level, went into a nosedive and crashed in front of the whole crowd. There was silence for a moment until a white-overalled mechanic was seen running across the field towards the upturned tail of the Vespa. With the sudden realisation of the

A Vickers Vespa, the type in which Heron crashed to his death on 5 August 1933.

disaster, people began running towards the spot too, but most were stopped by police and stewards. Those at the crash site got the two airmen from the wreckage. Heron and Tobin were both badly injured and Tobin died on the Sunday morning.

Heron's wife, along with Mrs Sheeran, had no idea in which aeroplane their husbands had been flying, and at first Mrs Heron was told her husband had been injured. It was not until some time later that she was informed he had died and was being removed from the wreckage. Heron was 37 years old and was buried in Glasnevin Cemetery, Dublin.

*   *   *

Captain A. J. G. Styran MC, AFC, 1 October 1933

From Londonderry, Arthur John Graham Styran was born on 28 July 1890. He joined the army as a boy soldier with the Royal Field Artillery in 1904 aged 14 and two months. He then served as a gunner in India from January 1911 until war began in August 1914. Returning home, he was almost immediately sent to France as part of the British Army contingent, and in so doing he became eligible for the 1914 Star medal.

Becoming a sergeant, he was selected for a commission and gazetted second lieutenant to the Royal Artillery on 27 August 1915, but seconded to the Royal Flying Corps soon afterwards. Trained as an observer he was soon back in France, joining No. 9 Squadron, that flew BE2c observation machines, as a founder member.

Much of his unit's work was directing artillery fire against hostile targets across the German lines, a dangerous occupation at any time. He was awarded the Military Cross in 1916, which was promulgated in the *London Gazette* dated 14 November 1916:

> *For conspicuous gallantry and devotion to duty. He has done fine work with artillery for a long time, often in bad weather and under heavy fire. On one occasion he directed the fire of nine batteries on the enemy's trenches, and obtained a large number of direct hits.*

Ending his 'tour' with 9 Squadron, he requested pilot training and back in England was given this opportunity. Once he had completed his training he was posted out to the Middle East where he joined No. 63 Squadron in Mesopotamia, flying DH4 bombers.

Captain A. J. G. Styran MC, AFC at a flying rally in 1933.

Returning to England he took up several instructional training jobs, and for this work he received the Air Force Cross, announced in October 1919. In 1922 he was living in Rushall, Marlborough, Wiltshire, and although he was gazetted to the Unemployed List in January 1923, he retained a reserve commission in the Reserve of Air Force Officers (RAFO).

He was employed by the British Air Navigation Company for some time and in July 1933 took part in the King's Cup Air Race in a Leopard Moth, finishing in third place. On 1 October 1933 he was killed while piloting a Percival D.2 Gull Four (G-ACAL), which crashed at Sandhurst, near Hawkhurst, Kent. On board were two passengers, Ian Charles McGilchrist (27) and Bertram Wilson (38), both of whom also died. Styran was 43 years old.

* * *

Captain Sir C. E. Kingsford-Smith KBE, MC, AFC, 7 November 1935

This famous aviator was born in Hamilton, Brisbane, Australia, on 9 February 1897, the fifth son and seventh child of banker William Charles and Catherine Mary (née Kingsford) Smith. He was educated at Sydney Technical High School but later in Canada at a school in Vancouver, then, upon his return, went to St. Andrew's Cathedral School, Sydney, and finally to Sydney Technical High School. In 1903 he worked in the real estate business and later as a clerk with the Canadian Pacific Railway. The family came back to Sydney in 1907. When war began 'Smithy' was living in Neutral Bay, Sydney training to be an electrical engineer, and he enlisted into the 4th Signals Troop of the Australian Engineers. He served at Gallipoli and later as a despatch rider in Egypt. Successfully becoming a flying cadet towards the end of 1916, he was commissioned into the RFC (SR) on 17 March 1917.

Captain C. E Kingsford-Smith MC.

Once trained as a pilot in England, he was posted to France, assigned to the Spad VII-equipped No. 23 Squadron. He saw considerable action during the Third Battle of Ypres, both in air combats and ground attack missions. He claimed an Albatros Scout 'out of control' on 13 July and crashed a DFW two-seater on 10 August. However, four days later, in a fight with Jasta 11, he was shot up by Oberleutnant Wilhelm Reinhard and wounded in the foot. Smithy was awarded the Military Cross, gazetted on 26 September, with details published on 9 January:

> *For conspicuous gallantry and devotion to duty. He has himself brought down four machines during his first month at the front, and has done most valuable work in attacking ground targets and hostile balloons. Of the latter he forced at least nine to be hauled down by his persistent attacks, during which he was repeatedly attacked himself by large hostile formations, and by his efforts undoubtedly stopped all hostile balloon observation during a critical period. His efforts and fine offensive spirit and disregard of danger have set a fine example.*

Kingsford-Smith returned to England for medical attention and for the rest of the war was an instructor. After the war he gained fame as one of aviation's great aerial pioneers. Included in his CV was the first trans-Pacific flight from USA to Australia in June 1928, for which he received the Air Force Cross. In September 1928 he made the first return flight from Australia to New Zealand and in 1929 flew record-breaking trips from Australia to England. In 1930 he flew from Ireland to the USA followed by a flight across the US, following this by a record-breaking flight from England to Australia in October 1930. The next year he flew mail from

Australia to England and back. He married Mary Powell in 1930, which produced a son. In June 1932 he was knighted (KBE) for his aerial achievements. In 1935 he and his wife were living at 27 Greenoaks Avenue, Darling Point, Sydney.

On 8 November 1935, he and co-pilot John Thompson 'Tommy' Pethybridge were flying from Allahabad to Singapore as part of their attempt to break the England to Australia speed record but disappeared over the Andaman Sea. Despite a number of searches nothing was ever found. Some eighteen months later a Burmese fisherman discovered the wheel of their aircraft in the Gulf of Martaban. Smithy was 38 years old.

*   *   *

Squadron Leader C. R. Davidson MC, MiD, 21 May 1936

Charles Robert Davidson was the son of Lieutenant Colonel C. F. H. Davidson of the 93rd Highlanders and Mrs Davidson of Folkestone, Kent. He was born in Poona, India, on 2 November 1886, where his father was serving. He received his education at Dover College, and later at Oundle and finally at the University of London, having been a member of the Officer Training Corps during these periods.

Soon after war was declared, Davidson enlisted as a private soldier into the 10th Battalion of the Royal Fusiliers (known as the Stockbrokers Battalion), City

A Flying Flee, a self-build aeroplane in which Davidson crashed on 21 May 1936.

of London Regiment. This had been raised when the war began with volunteers from the city's businessmen, more than 1,600 having come forward within days. He then contrived a transfer to his father's old regiment and accompanied the 11th Battalion of the Argyll and Sutherland Highlanders to France on 9 July 1915. He saw action during the Battle of Loos, distinguishing himself on the first day, 15 September, for which he received a mention in despatches, *London Gazette*, 1 January 1916.

With the Royal Flying Corps asking for volunteers to become observers, he applied to transfer and was immediately sent out to Aboukir, Egypt, for training. He received a commission into the Highland Light Infantry on 31 May 1916 and was seconded to the RFC. Completing his observer training in September he was given the chance of pilot training, and once he achieved this goal, was posted to No. 14 Squadron early in 1917. Later that year, No. 111 Squadron was formed as a fighter unit for Middle East Forces and he was chosen to join it.

Flying the Vickers FB19, he accounted for two enemy aircraft, and once 111 re-equipped with the BF2b two-seat fighter, scored, with his observers, four more victories in December. On 9 January 1918, he and his observer, Captain J. J. Lloyd-Williams, were involved in a combat (flying Bristol Fighter A7192), Davidson receiving a painful wound in the ankle. Nevertheless he managed to get back to base and land safely. For his actions he was awarded the Military Cross, gazetted on 14 January 1918, with the graphic details appearing in the *Gazette* on 22 April:

For conspicuous gallantry and devotion to duty. He forced a hostile aeroplane to land, and, descending to a low altitude despite heavy rifle fire, shot down one of the occupants as he was escaping from the machine. On two later occasions he forced an enemy machine to land, and drove down another, which was last seen diving into country where it was impossible to land. Finally, though his ankle was fractured by a bullet during an air combat, he landed without injury either to his Observer or his machine.

John Lloyd-Williams also received the Military Cross and later took pilot training. Post-war 'L-W' rose to police inspector with the Metropolitan Police Force. Davidson was admitted to hospital and from there invalided back to England in March, where he saw out the war as an instructor at No. 2 Flying Training School.

Davidson was granted a permanent commission after the war and became a flight lieutenant in the January 1923 New Year Honours. Later that year he was posted out to India where he served with No. 20 Squadron, again on Bristol Fighters, on the North West Frontier. In 1927 he was given a post at Headquarters, RAF India,

Oundle School's OTC members, c.1911.

before returning to England in December 1928. In June 1929 he served with No. 4 Squadron at South Farnborough, and was then sent to the RAF's Staff College the following year. He was promoted to squadron leader on 11 March 1931. A keen and useful golf player, Davidson became part of the RAF's gold team in these years.

On 5 June 1931 he was sent out to the Middle East again, with a post at RAF Headquarters, in Transjordan and in Jerusalem. Returning to the UK once more, he found himself back at No. 2 FTS at RAF Digby.

Davidson built himself a Mignet HM14 'Flying Flea' aeroplane from a 'do it yourself' kit and, once assembled and tested, it received the civil registration of G-AEBS in February 1936. Sadly in flying it there was a problem and the machine dived into the ground at Digby killing the 39-year-old squadron leader. He was the third British pilot within a month to die while flying this type of aeroplane which resulted in it being banned. It was discovered that the Flea had a fatal flaw in its design which caused the machine to go into an uncontrollable dive should the pilot put the nose down to prevent a stall.

Davidson was buried in the grounds of the Church of the Holy Cross, Scopwick, Lincolnshire.

*   *   *

Captain M. H. Findlay DSC, DFC, 1 October 1936

Born in Aberdeen, Scotland, on 17 February 1898, Findlay's final education was at Aberdeen University, where he obtained a first class diploma in agriculture. Maxwell Hutcheson Findlay was living in Canada in 1914, later returning to the UK and living in Stonehaven, Scotland. He enlisted into the Black Watch (Royal Highland Regiment) but eventually, with an urge to fly, transferred to the Royal Naval Air Service in June 1916.

Captain M. H. Findlay DSC, DFC.

Once trained as a pilot he was sent to France where he joined No. 6 Naval Squadron RNAS, a unit which was equipped with the Sopwith Camel. He was credited with two 'out of control' victories in July and August, before his squadron became a bomber unit and he was moved to No. 1 Naval, another Camel squadron.

With this squadron he continued to add to his score with two more victories by the end of the year and another four during March 1918. He was awarded the Distinguished Service Cross, gazetted on 16 April:

> *For the courage and daring displayed by him as a pilot. On 8 March 1918, while on patrol, he engaged an Albatros Scout, firing effectively from very close range. The enemy aircraft went down completely out of control. He has destroyed or driven down out of control many other machines.*

Maxwell Findlay in front of a Camel in the First World War.

The squadron became No. 201 Squadron on 1 April 1918 with the merger of the RFC and RNAS, but it made little difference to front line squadrons in France. During May he accounted for a further five hostile aircraft, all but one being Albatros Scouts, the other a two-seater observation machine. One of the

Scouts, downed on 15 May, was shared with other pilots in the patrol, including Sammy Kinkead and Reg Brading, both of whom are featured in this book. With a total of fourteen victories to his name, he was sent home for a rest and awarded the Distinguished Flying Cross, which appeared in two editions of the *London Gazette*, 2 July and 3 August 1918:

> *A skilful and courageous patrol leader. During the past few months this officer has destroyed seven enemy machines and brought down seven more out of control. On one occasion he fought an enemy machine from 18,000 feet down to an altitude of 10,000 feet, at which point he gained an advantage and destroyed his antagonist.*

Findlay chose to remain in the RAF after the war, taking his Royal Aero Club test at the Military School at Freiston on 6 December, and was awarded a permanent commission with effect from 1 August 1919. During the next year he saw active duty abroad in the Third Anglo–Afghan War and in the Waziristan Campaign. On 1 October 1920 he resigned his commission and returned to his home country of Scotland where he took up farming.

Five years later, on 13 January 1925, he applied to become an RAF Class 'A' Reservist and was successful. He held the position for three years, although he was able to remain on the Reserve List after May 1929. He also took an interest in gliding, while also becoming an examiner for instructors to the Guild of Air Pilots. The following year he joined National Flying Services Limited as their chief flying instructor, a post he held until 1933. From there he became an instructor and sales manager at the Brooklands School of Flying in Surrey.

At this stage of his flying career he got into air racing. He competed in the King's Cup Air Race in July 1930 (753 miles from Newcastle upon Tyne and back, via London and Bristol), flying a De Havilland Puss Moth. Among the entrants were many notable flyers of the time, many being former First World War pilots, including Francis Symondson MC, Richard Atcherley, George Vlasto, Louis Strange DSO, MC, DFC, Harold Balfour MC, Tommy Rose DFC, Hubert Broad, Leonard Slatter OBE, DSC, DFC, Frank Gibbons MC, Herbert Rowley, Charles Pickthorn MC, Sydney Pope MC, Harold Whistler DSO, DFC, Geoffrey de Havilland and Henry Orlebar AFC. Slatter, Gibbons and Whistler are mentioned elsewhere in this book. There were 101 entrants but only 88 starters, of which only 61 finished.

In 1936 the industrialist and financier I. W. Schlesinger put up a prize of £10,000 for a race between Portsmouth (England) to Johannesburg, called the Schlesinger African Air Race. Isidore Schlesinger wanted to promote the Johannesburg Empire

Exhibition. Several pilots were involved, including Findlay, who chose an Airspeed Envoy aircraft (G-AENA) in which to compete. He had with him a radio operator/navigator, A. H. Morgan, plus Kenneth Waller and C. Derek Peachey as passengers.

Findlay got as far as Abercorn in Northern Rhodesia (now known as Mbala, Zambia). After refuelling, and despite bad weather and a warning to wait a while for it to clear, he took off so as not to delay. The airfield was at 6,000 feet above sea level where the air would be thinner than normal. In addition the wind direction had changed forcing the decision to take off uphill and towards some trees. Findlay failed to clear the trees at the edge of the field, hit them and crashed. He and Morgan were killed, the other two injured. On the tail fin of the Envoy was the number '13'. Findlay was 38 years old.

* * *

Major F. W. Stent MC, MiD, 28 June 1938

Another former First World War pilot involved in races in the King's Cup Air Races was Frederick William Stent, who was born on the island of Cyprus in 1891. After completing his education at King's College and the Imperial College of Science and Technology, he worked with the civil service in Egypt until war came, at which time he decided to join the Royal Flying Corps, in May 1915. He achieved his RAeC flying certificate (No. 2748) on 31 August 1915 and was sent to No. 77 Home Defence Squadron at Turnhouse. His next posting was to No. 17 Squadron in the Middle East.

When HQ discovered he spoke fluent Arabic, he was sent to be second in command of the Arabian Detachment of No. 14 Squadron, spending some nine months with it, often in inhospitable country, finally rejoining the main 14 Squadron in August 1917. No sooner was he back than he and three other pilots flew one hundred miles south of Gaza to a roughly prepared landing ground at El Quntilla from where, two days later, they attacked a railway station and troops sixty-five miles east, at Ma'an. Colonel

Wing Commander F. W. Stent MC, MiD.

T. E. Lawrence confirmed the success of this raid in his book *Seven Pillars of Wisdom.* Thirty-five soldiers were killed, fifty more wounded, the engine shed hit, damaging plant and stock. One bomb hit the Turkish general's kitchen which 'finished his cook and his breakfast.' The following day another raid on the Turks at Abu el Lissan stampeded horses through the camp area.

Following this, Stent was made CO of 'X' Flight at Aqaba, detached to Prince Feisal's forces there. This flight gave tremendous support in the Arab advances along the Hejaz railway. Stent's MC was gazetted on 22 June 1918, oddly enough for air combat rather than bombing:

> *For conspicuous gallantry and devotion to duty. He attacked and brought down a hostile two-seater, the observer of which was in a position to give the enemy valuable information of our movements. On another occasion he encountered and brought down an enemy two-seater, wounding both pilot and observer, who were made prisoners. On both occasions he showed great gallantry and ability.*

He then took command of No. 111 Squadron from November 1917 to July 1918 and received two mentions in despatches. Post-war he was the recipient of the Japanese Order of the Rising Sun, 4th Class, gazetted on 4 January 1921, and the Hejaz Order of Al Nahda, 4th Class, gazetted on 25 January 1921. Another award was the Khedive's Sudan Medal for services in Darfur and Salonika. In 1922 he returned to Imperial College and passed a post-graduate course in Aeronautical Engineering.

Remaining in the RAF he became a wing commander and from 1932 was engaged in Engineering Staff Duties, Wessex Bombing Area, before retiring in 1936. He then took up a position as test pilot for Phillips and Powis Aircraft Ltd at Woodley Aerodrome, Berkshire, close to where he lived at Sonning, near Reading, with his wife Gladys Emily. During one test flight he was forced to bale out of the prototype Miles M.7 Nighthawk (G-ADXA) during spinning trials in January 1937, which made him one of the first men to bale out of an aircraft fitted with an enclosed cockpit, and for that he received the Caterpillar Club badge from the Irvine Parachute Company.

Later in 1937 he took part in the King's Cup Air Race in a Sparrow Hawk and was placed seventh. The following year he prepared again to enter the race, this time flying a Miles M.11c (G-AEYI). On 28 June he was flying from Woodley to Martlesham, probably fairly low, as was usual for the race, but near Uxbridge he seems to have been caught by a gust of wind which put his aircraft into the ground before he could recover. The machine came down at Harefield, Buckinghamshire, with fatal consequences. He was 47 years old.

*   *   *

Captain L. C. Holden Jr. DSC, Ld'H, CdG, 13 November 1938

Born in Brooklyn, New York, on 8 October 1896, Lancing Colton Holden Jr., whose father was a prominent American architect, began his education at the Collegiate School, New York City, where he was an excellent swimmer. 'Denny' as he was known, then went to Princeton University where he joined the flying group, but dropped out when war came and wound up in France. Volunteering for flight training with the French Air Force, he trained at Orly from March 1917.

Captain L. C. Holden Jr. DSC, LdH, CdG on the left, with Zenos Miller, in France, 1918 (Miller's story is in Chapter Three).

Having gained his flying brevet he was assigned to Escadrille N.471 on 4 April 1918 where he remained until he transferred to the USAS on 23 July, and was sent to the 95th Pursuit Squadron. He did not get off to a great start, being shot down on 10 August by a Fokker DVII but he managed to force land in Allied territory by the French balloon lines. He scored all of his seven victories in the last two months of the war, starting with a kite balloon he flamed on 29 September. On 23 October he downed a second balloon and a Fokker DVII, and then a Hannover CL two-seater on 27 October. He downed another balloon on the 30th, followed by two more he burned on 3 and 4 November, and received the DSC and Oak Leaf:

> For extraordinary heroism in action near Montigny, France, 23 October 1918. Lt. Holden was ordered to attack several German balloons, reported to be regulating artillery fire on our troops. After driving off an enemy plane, encountered before reaching the balloons, he soon came upon five balloons in ascension, one kilometre apart. At attacking the first, which proved to be a decoy without a basket, his guns jammed; after clearing them he attacked the second balloon, forcing the observer to jump. His guns jammed again before he could set fire to this balloon. Moving on to the third balloon at a height of only fifty metres, he set fire to it and compelled the observer to jump. He was prevented from attacking the two remaining balloons by the further jamming of machine-guns.
>
> For extraordinary heroism in action near St. Jean lès Buzy, France, 4 November 1918. Flying at a low altitude to evade hostile pursuit patrols, Lt. Holden attacked a German observation balloon in the face of anti-aircraft and

machine-gun fire. Although the balloon was being rapidly pulled down, he set fire
to it in its nest and also caused much damage to adjacent buildings.

After the war Holden returned to his studies and delayed graduation at Princeton. Following his father's occupation, he became an architect. However, in 1924 he returned to France, going to the Beaux Arts School, in Paris. He became well known for his etching and painting, actually exhibiting in a salon in the French capital. That year he was married to Edith S. Rogers from Massachusetts, his son Lancing C. Holden III being born in 1927.

He became involved in Spain's Riffian War in 1925, taking part in several raids with the Moroccan Air Service, operating from a Spanish aerodrome near Tétouan. Another American taking part in operations with him was Paul Rockwell, brother of Kiffin Rockwell. Both Rockwell boys had flown with the Lafayette Escadrille in the First World War. In 1931 they both received medals – the Medal of Moroccan Peace – from the Spanish Government. The French, in the meantime, awarded Holden the *Légion d'Honneur* and the *Croix de Guerre*.

Back in the United States, Holden joined the New York National Guard on 24 June 1929, commissioned as a second lieutenant in the 102nd Observation Squadron, and was promoted to first lieutenant in July 1930, transferring to the Reserve in 1933.

In the early 1930s Holden illustrated fellow US ace Harold Buckley's book *Squadron 95*, and flew in a few Hollywood movies becoming a co-director with Merion C. Cooper. Cooper came from Florida, three years older than Holden. He too had been in the USAS and post-First World War had seen action with the *Kościuszko* Squadron, manned by American volunteers to support the Polish Air Force in conflict with the Russians. He was shot down and taken prisoner at one point, and spent nine months in captivity before he managed an escape. Cooper's most famous film was *King Kong* in 1933.

Then in 1937 Holden became production director of films in colour, the first being *The Garden of Allah* starring Marlene Dietrich and Charles Boyer and produced by David O. Selznick.

On 1 August 1938 Holden transferred back to the NY National Guard. On 13 November 1938 Holden and another former First World War American flyer, Raymond W. Krout, also in the New York State National Guard, who had flown with the 135th US Squadron, as well as being at Princeton with Holden, took a trip to Tennessee. They were going to attend the annual duck hunting event at Reelfoot Lake. They would make the trip by aeroplane, and once in Nashville they would meet up with Hunter McDonald who had been Ray Krout's observer

A Douglas O-46A, the type in which Holden lost his life in November 1938.

in France. Krout was aged 43 and lived with his wife Dorothy, daughter of the late State Senator Wood McKee, in Patterson, NY, along with their two young daughters.

They flew in an army Douglas O-46A machine but five miles north of Sparta, Tennessee, they not only ran into fog but, amazingly, a heavy rainstorm, the two seldom occurring together. The aircraft hit a fog-enshrouded hillside at 1830 hours local time, killing Holden and Krout outright. Holden was 42. In the *Princeton Alumni Weekly*, 9 December 1938, was written:

> *At Miller Field, Staten Island, on November 20, after a salute had been fired and taps had been sounded, Denny's ashes and those of Captain Krout were scattered over the sea, just beyond New York City's lower bay, from one of the planes of his squadron flying in full formation.*

* * *

Wing Commander B. Ankers DSO, DCM, MiD (2), 6 August 1939

Burton Ankers was born in Dudden, Cheshire, on 20 March 1893, to David and Alice Ankers. In the 1901 census the family shows also a daughter Agnes, aged 10, Burton, then 8, brothers George, aged 4, and 1-year-old John.

Soon after the war began, Burton joined the Royal Flying Corps and volunteered as an observer/gunner, became a sergeant (No. 3464), and posted to No. 18 Squadron in France, which was equipped with the two-seat 'pusher' type FE2b. The crew of pilot and gunner sat in a gondola with the engine situated behind the pilot, pushing the machine through the air, while two large lattice-like booms went back from the mid-wing area to a tail-plane at the rear. It looked an ungainly warplane but it could see off even the most determined enemy fighter pilot, especially if in a formation of several FEs. The gunner was situated right out in the front, in full blast of the airstream, and expected to handle the two Lewis machine guns at his disposal. Both had free range, one fixed to the forward edge of his cockpit, the other on a pole mounted behind him, facing back. If attacked from the rear, he was expected to undo his safety harness and stand on his seat to operate the rear gun, firing back over the top wing, all the while his pilot manoeuvring the aircraft to avoid enemy fire.

Burton Ankers DCM in 1918.

Burton soon teamed up with a fiery Irishman, Joseph Creuss 'Casey' Callaghan from County Dublin, one of three brothers in the RFC all destined to die in that terrible war. No. 18 Squadron had a variety of tasks to perform, including fighting patrols, day and night bombing, reconnaissance and aerial photography, with both Callaghan and Ankers soon in the thick of these daily actions. They were particularly successful in night bombing raids, something very new in 1916 and it took brave men to operate in a black sky at night with no aids such as radio or radar, and only a compass and the 'Mark 1 eyeball' to help guide them to and from a target, and to locate their home airfield in the darkness.

Some of their achievements are recorded in the RFC *Communiqués*, such as on the night of 9/10 October, during a raid, they were being annoyed by two searchlights, so Callaghan dived towards them while Ankers opened up with his Lewis gun, extinguishing one of them. Exactly a month later they successfully bombed a German airfield and the next night they bombed a railway station and again attacked searchlights that probed for them.

Another entry in the *Communiqués* covered their efforts on 11/12 November:

Capt J. C. Callaghan and Sgt B. Ankers, 18 Sqn, crossed the lines at 10.40 pm with the intention of bombing aerodromes. When over Achiet-le-Grand they saw a machine flying at about 1,000 feet and attempted to follow. Finding no aerodromes lit up they decided to go to Cambrai. They were subjected to heavy, but inaccurate anti-aircraft fire over Havrincourt and Cambrai. Seeing no activity at Cambrai they went over to Valenciènnes. All lights in Denain were extinguished on their approach. The station at Valenciènnes was lit up and Mons which could be seen in the distance was well illuminated. There appeared to be about four trains in Valenciènnes station and 6 bombs were dropped there. The bombs burst on the station and a fire broke out and burned brightly for several minutes. On their way home 2 searchlights attempted to pick them up, so they dived at them and fired 2 drums and 1 of the lights was extinguished.

For his work Ankers was awarded the Distinguished Conduct Medal, gazetted on 11 December, while Callaghan received the Military Cross, gazetted on 13 February 1917. Callaghan's citation read:

For conspicuous gallantry in action. He displayed marked courage and skill on several occasions in carrying out bombing operations. On one occasion he extinguished a hostile searchlight.

The pair finished their tour with 18 Squadron in the new year of 1917, and while Callaghan became an instructor, Ankers applied for pilot training. Achieving this ambition, his former pilot Callaghan had in the meantime been given command of the newly-formed No. 87 Squadron, and he managed to get Ankers posted to it. 87 Squadron was working-up on the new Sopwith Dolphin fighter and, once ready, Callaghan took it to France in April 1918, Ankers being placed in B Flight. In one of the first combat actions, the squadron claimed three German fighters shot

Blenheim I's in formation.

down on 16 May, Burton claiming one of them. While not altogether successful in combat, his drive, enthusiasm and aggressiveness marked him for leadership and on 2 August he was sent to another Dolphin squadron, No. 23, as a flight commander. Unhappily he only lasted six days, being wounded in one leg during a low-bombing and ground attack sortie. This effectively knocked him out of the war and, sadly too, his old CO Callaghan had been killed in action on 2 July 1918.

Captain Ankers received a permanent commission on 1 August 1919 and served in the RAF in the immediate post-war years. Seeing operations on the North West Frontier of India and in Waziristan in the late 1930s, he rose to wing commander rank with effect from 1 January 1937, commanding No. 3 (Indian) Wing. He received a mention in despatches and the Distinguished Service Order for operations during the Waziristan Campaign. The recommendation, made by Group Captain N. H. Bottomley, OC No. 1 (Indian) Group, RAF, dated 23 December 1937, read:

> *Throughout these Waziristan operations this officer has commanded all the Army Co-operation squadrons engaged. His high standard of command and inspiring example both on the ground and in the air has been reflected in the outstanding achievements of these units.*
>
> *His co-operation with Army formations has been most effective and amicable. The splendid spirit of co-operation and good fellowship which has characterised inter-service relations in Waziristan during these operations is largely due to his high example. He has applied initiative, courage and imagination to the development of the tactics of the air support of troops. The success of this form of operation is due in a great measure to him.*
>
> *I consider his devotion to duty, his enthusiasm, his outstanding leadership, and his inspiring example in the air to be deserving of reward. I recommend him for the Distinguished Service Order, failing which the Distinguished Flying Cross.*

This recommendation weaved its way through to General J. D. Coleridge, Commander in Waziristan, who recommended the DSO on 22 December, and this was finally approved by Air Marshal P. B. Joubert, OC RAF India, dated 14 February 1938. For his services on the Frontier he received another mention in despatches later in February 1938.

Ankers then took command of the 2nd Indian Wing Station. By this time, war in Europe with Germany seemed a distinct possibility and the UK government felt that certain bases in the Far East needed boosting. Therefore, in early 1939 the RAF was ordered to fly units to bases further east. The first to go was 60 Squadron with their Wapitis to Ambala in March, followed by 39 Squadron in August to Singapore. 39 Squadron was working up with its new equipment of the Bristol Blenheim Mk I at Risalpur. On the morning of the 6th, nine Blenheims took off on the first leg of the journey, led by Wing Commander Ankers. Each aircraft, in addition to its three-man crew, also carried two ground crewmen plus spares and personal luggage, so were somewhat over-loaded.

The first leg to Ambala took just two hours, but one Blenheim pilot unwittingly raised his undercarriage after landing, so a local reserve aircraft took its place. There had been some build-up of cloud, threatening the start of a monsoon, but this was not thought imminent so the aircraft continued on, bound for Allahabad, three hours right across the centre of India. Landing here, the airfield was fairly well flooded, and while eight Blenheims got down, the ninth swung off the runway and tipped over onto its back.

Weather conditions made it necessary to stay on the ground for the next three days but on the 9th it was decided to start the next leg to Calcutta. They soon met heavy rain and low cloud. They had been flying for less than two hours when disaster struck. Bolts of lightning hit at least three of the Blenheims, one (L1546) flown by Ankers being set on fire. Ankers must have ordered the occupants to bale out but at such a low altitude only three managed to escape; he and the other man were killed as the aircraft hit the ground. One of the parachutists hit the ground before his 'chute had opened. No doubt too, the overloaded aircraft made it impossible for everyone to get out even if they had more height, and it seems probable that some of the equipment being carried had shaken loose and this in such a small cabin area impeded the men's movements.

The machine came down at Kutumba, and the two others who died were Corporal Robert Samuel Gilbert and AC1 Arthur Reginald Harris. A second aircraft went into a spin and although the pilot recovered the machine was badly strained and was left at Calcutta. In a third aircraft the radio burst into flames which the crew managed to extinguish with coffee and 'bodily fluid'; the aircraft became unserviceable. The remaining six aircraft reached Calcutta, from where they headed out again on the next leg to Rangoon, but again monsoon conditions cost the flight two more Blenheims, one crash-landed after its crew had become lost, the other force-landed on a beach short of fuel and the crew unsure of their position. The flight finally ended at Singapore (Tengah) on the 19th. It had taken 13 days to cross an area that should have taken 20 hours, with six aircraft lost and three men killed. Burton Ankers was 46 years old.

*   *   *

Group Captain A. H. Whistler DSO DFC & 2 Bars, 1 March 1940

Alfred Harold 'Willy' Whistler came from Theddlethorpe, Lincolnshire, where he was born on 30 December 1896, son of clergyman Alfred James and Mrs Mary Maud Whistler, living at the Rectory, Little Carlton, Lincs. Determined to follow a military career, on leaving Oundle School and London University, he was accepted into the Royal Military College at Sandhurst and commissioned into the Dorsetshire Regiment. From here he transferred to the Royal Flying Corps in 1916 and in France flew Morane Parasols with No. 3 Squadron until he was wounded on 29 January 1917. He and his observer, Corporal E. J. Hare, were engaged on a photographic reconnaissance mission when they were attacked and shot up, being forced to put down near Memetz Wood. Whistler had been wounded in the air and Hare injured in the crash landing (Parasol No. A239).

Recovering from his wound and following a period as an instructor, he was posted to No. 80 Squadron later that year as a flight commander, going back to France with this new squadron in January 1918, equipped with Sopwith Camels. Although using these fighter aeroplanes, the squadron was heavily engaged in ground attack missions and became so adept at this type of operation that it was used in this role almost continually for the rest of the war, being sent from sector to sector wherever its skill was needed. It even cooperated with the Tank Corps'

Captain A. H. Whistler DSO, DFC and Two Bars, in front of a Sopwith Camel.

attacks along the whole front. It moved airfields constantly and rarely stayed in one place for more than 12 days; in fact it flew from around 17 different aerodromes during 1918.

With its definitive role, opportunities for air fighting were limited; nevertheless the squadron claimed some sixty victories. Whistler's share was 23, with 13 destroyed, 9 out of control, plus one observation balloon. His first four victories were during the days just before and just after the massive German 'Michael' offensive in March, and he continued to add to his total until the war's end. All except two were fighter types, Albatros Scouts, Pfalz Scouts, Fokker Triplanes and Fokker DVIIs. On 1 June 1918 the plywood behind his seat was set on fire by a tracer bullet during a combat with Pfalz DIIIs, but he managed to put out the flames, shoot down two of the enemy and fly home.

His first Distinguished Flying Cross appeared twice in the *London Gazette*, for 2 July and 3 August:

A very courageous and enterprising patrol leader, who had rendered valuable services. He has done exceptionally good work in attacking ground targets, which he engaged at very low altitudes. During the past month his patrol attacked eight enemy scouts who were flying above him. He attacked a triplane and brought it down in a crash, and while thus himself engaged, another of his pilots destroyed a second enemy machine. The remainder of the enemy formation were driven off.

His score continued to rise, with four victories in each month, July, August and September. His final two, a Halberstadt CL two-seater and a Fokker DVII, were downed on 2 October. The award of the DSO was gazetted on 2 November 1918:

During recent operations this officer has rendered exceptionally brilliant service in attacking enemy aircraft and troops on the ground. On August 9 he dropped four bombs on a hostile battery, engaged and threw into confusion a body of troops, and drove down a hostile balloon, returning to his aerodrome after a patrol of one and a half hours duration with a most valuable report. He has in all destroyed ten aircraft and driven down five others out of control.

This was followed by a Bar to his DFC, gazetted on 8 February 1919:

This officer has twenty-two enemy machines and one balloon to his credit. He distinguished himself greatly on 29th September, when he destroyed two machines in one combat, and on 15th September, when following two balloons to within twenty feet of the ground, he destroyed one and caused the observer of the second to jump out and crash. He has, in addition, done arduous and valuable service in bombing enemy objectives and obtaining information. Captain Whistler is a gallant officer of fine judgement and power of leadership.

Whistler remained in the RAF after the war and was given a permanent commission, and at one time was an instructor at No. 2 FTS. He then served in Iraq in 1926-28 for which he received a second Bar to his DFC while commanding No. 55 Squadron, based at Hinaidi, operating against Najd Bedouin tribesmen. This citation appeared in the *London Gazette* of 15 March 1929:

In recognition of gallant and distinguished service rendered in connection with operations against the Akhwan in the Southern Desert, Iraq, during the period November 1927 to May 1928.

He became Chief Flying Instructor at No. 5 FTS until 1930, and from 1930 to 1932 was an instructor at the prestigious Central Flying School at Upavon, rising to the rank of wing commander. Whistler went to the Imperial Defence College in 1937 and later, back in India, attended the Staff College at Quetta. By the late

The HP42 *Hannibal*, lost en route to Sharjah, 1 March 1940.

1930s he was Chief of Staff with RAF India as a group captain. Soon after the Second World War was declared he left India, posted home to England, to become an air commodore. His trip home was in a HP42, formerly of Imperial Airways, but taken over by the RAF when the Second World War began. This was G–AAGX named *Hannibal*.

There were eight men aboard when it lifted off from Drigh Road, Karachi on 1 March 1940 bound for Egypt. The crew consisted of Captain N. Townsend, First Officer C. J. Walsh, Radio Officer A. H. H. Tidbury and Steward C. A. F. Steventon. The four passengers were Whistler, Captain Alf Bryn, a Norwegian Marine superintendent of an American Oil Company, Sir A. T. Pannirselvam, a 51-year-old attorney, politician and leader of the Indian Justice Party going to London to join the Secretary of State's Indian Council, and Warrant Officer H. Hutchinson of the Royal Indian Ordnance Corps, carrying important documents.

After a refuelling stop the *Hannibal* took off on the next stage of the journey, to Sharjah. Somewhere over the Gulf of Oman the huge biplane airline simply disappeared and, although searches were made, no survivors and no wreckage was ever found. Like many similar disappearances some mystery has surrounded the aeroplane's loss. Group Captain Whistler is officially listed as missing on 1 March 1940. He was 43 years old.

Index